The IIA Research Foundation
Handbook Series

IMPLEMENTING THE INTERNATIONAL PROFESSIONAL PRACTICES FRAMEWORK
UPDATED 3RD EDITION

By
Urton Anderson, PhD, CIA, CCSA, CGAP, CFSA, CCEP, and
Andrew J. Dahle, CIA, CPA, CISA, CFE

Disclosure

The IIARF publishes this document for informational and educational purposes. This document is intended to provide information, but is not a substitute for legal or accounting advice. The IIARF does not provide such advice and makes no warranty as to any legal or accounting results through its publication of this document. When legal or accounting issues arise, professional assistance should be sought and retained.

The Institute of Internal Auditors' (IIA's) International Professional Practices Framework (IPPF) comprises the full range of existing and developing practice guidance for the profession. The IPPF provides guidance to internal auditors globally and paves the way to world-class internal auditing.

The mission of The IIARF is to expand knowledge and understanding of internal auditing by providing relevant research and educational products to advance the profession globally.

The IIA and The IIARF work in partnership with researchers from around the globe who conduct valuable studies on critical issues affecting today's business world. Much of the content presented in their final reports is a result of IIARF-funded research and prepared as a service to The Foundation and the internal audit profession. Expressed opinions, interpretations, or points of view represent a consensus of the researchers and do not necessarily reflect or represent the official position or policies of The IIA or The IIARF.

ISBN 978-0-89413-676-4
09/09
First Printing
03/10
Second Printing
03/11
Third Printing
09/11
Fourth Printing

In memory of Bill Bishop
and his lifelong dedication
to the profession of internal auditing.

CONTENTS

EXHIBITS

APPENDICES

ABOUT THE AUTHORS

Urton Anderson, PhD, CIA, CCSA, CGAP, is Clark W. Thompson, Jr. Professor in Accounting Education and Chair of the Department of Accounting at the McCombs School of Business, The University of Texas at Austin. His research has addressed various issues in internal and external auditing — particularly corporate governance, compliance, enterprise risk management, and internal control. He is a published author and is a co-author of the internal audit textbook *Internal Auditing: Assurance and Consulting Services, 2nd Edition*. Some of his books have been translated into various languages. He is actively involved in The Institute of Internal Auditors Research Foundation and has twice served as chair of the Internal Auditing Standards Board (2002-2003 and 2007-2010). In 1997, Urton received The IIA's Leon R. Radde Educator of the Year Award and in 2006 The IIA's Bradford Cadmus Memorial Award for outstanding contributions to the field of internal auditing. He serves on the board of directors for the Health Care Compliance Association and the advisory board of the Society Corporate Compliance and Ethics. He is also active in the Auditing Section of the American Accounting Association, where he served as a past president (2009-2010).

Andrew J. Dahle, CIA, CPA, CISA, CFE, is a partner at PricewaterhouseCoopers (PwC) LLP. He serves as a Risk Assurance partner, specializing in Internal Audit Services. He provides internal audit performance enhancement and quality services and internal audit sourcing solutions to major clients. He also is a frequent speaker and author on internal audit and risk-related topics. Andrew received Bachelor of Science in Accountancy and Master of Accounting Science degrees from the University of Illinois at Urbana-Champaign. He is a past president of The IIA's Chicago Chapter and a global award winner on the Certified Internal Auditor (CIA) exam. As the PwC representative on the Internal Audit Standards Board, he currently serves as the board's chairman.

ACKNOWLEDGMENTS

The authors would like to thank the following individuals and their organizations for donating their insights, experiences, and time to this project. They are true representatives of The Institute of Internal Auditors' commitment to *Progress Through Sharing*.

Bruce A. Adamec, CIA

Dick Anderson, *Center for Strategy, Execution and Valuation and Strategic Risk Management, DePaul University*

Shannon L. Bieberdorf, *Solutions Training Group*

Richard F. Chambers, CIA, CGAP, *The Institute of Internal Auditors*

Angelina K.Y. Chin, CIA, *General Motors*

Giovanni Grossi, CIA, CCSA

Wayne G. Moore, CIA, *DuPont* (retired)

Heriot Prentice, MIIA, FIIA, QiCA, *The Institute of Internal Auditors*

Larry E. Rittenberg, CIA, *University of Wisconsin-Madison*

James P. Roth, CIA, CCSA, *AuditTrends*

Paul J. Sobel, CIA, CAE, *Georgia-Pacific LLC*

Dan M. Swanson, CIA, *Dan Swanson & Associates*

Colleen G. Waring, CIA, CGAP, *Office of the City Auditor, Austin, Texas* (retired)

INTRODUCTION

The original edition of this book was written to provide internal auditors with guidance on how to put into practice the *International Standards for the Professional Practice of Internal Auditing* (*Standards*), which became effective Jan. 1, 2002. Since that time, subsequent editions of this book have reflected changes in the *Standards* as well as the updated framework for internal audit guidance, the International Professional Practices Framework (IPPF), which was released in 2009.

In an effort to reflect the most recent changes to the *Standards* and the other components of the IPPF, effective 2011, this third edition of *Implementing the International Professional Practices Framework* has been updated to include the changes noted in this introduction.

Changes to the *Standards*

This book covers *Standards* changes effective in 2011, including:

- Revision to the definition of *Add Value* in the Glossary and elsewhere in the *Standards* to reflect the value proposition that internal auditing adds value to the organization and its stakeholders when it provides objective and relevant assurance and contributes to the effectiveness and efficiency of governance, risk management, and control processes (Standard 2000 and Glossary, Chapter 8).

- Revision to the definition of *chief audit executive*, removing the requirement that the role be inside the organization in full outsourcings of internal auditing (Glossary, Chapter 8).

- Requirement that in full outsourcings of internal auditing that the external service provider be required to make the organization aware that the organization has the responsibility for internal auditing — the responsibility is not removed through outsourcing. Further, in such outsourcing situations, the *Standards* now note that the organization demonstrates its responsibility through the quality assessment and improvement program and its assessments of internal auditing (2070, Chapter 8).

- Clarification that internal auditing's assessment of risk management may be based on multiple engagements taken together, rather than always requiring one specific report covering all of risk management (2120, Chapter 9).

- Requirement that stakeholder expectations for opinions, conclusions, and ratings at the individual engagement as well as overall opinions if any be identified and considered. While not requiring opinions, conclusions, or ratings, such may only be issued if they are supported by sufficient, reliable, relevant, and useful information. Further, if overall opinions are issued, there are now explicit requirements for what they must include (2010.A2, 2410.A1, 2450, Chapter 12).

- Requirement that the internal audit charter define the nature of internal auditing's functional reporting relationship to the board (defined as audit committee for many organizations), including articulating examples of what constitutes functional reporting (1000, 1110, Chapter 4).

- Clarification of the requirements for the external quality assessment team. This includes the requirement that the team demonstrate competence in internal auditing and in performing external quality assessments (1312, Chapter 7).

- Clarification that newer internal audit activities can state they conform with *Standards* solely on the basis of the internal quality assessment and improvement results if they do not yet have an external assessment (1321, Chapter 7).

- Other clarifications in the *Standards* and the Glossary.

Changes to Other Elements of the IPPF

Many Practice Advisories and Practice Guides have been issued since early 2009. Some of the more significant ones referred to in this new edition include:

- Practice Guide: Assessing the Adequacy of Risk Management (December 2010).
- Practice Guide: Measuring Internal Audit Effectiveness and Efficiency (December 2010).
- Practice Advisory 2050-3: Relying on the Work of Other Assurance Providers (October 2010).
- Practice Guide: *GTAG 15: Information Security Governance* (July 2010).
- Practice Guide: CAEs – Appointment, Performance Evaluation and Termination (May 2010).
- Practice Advisory 2200-2: Using a Top-down, Risk-based Approach to Identify the Controls to be Assessed in an Internal Audit Engagement (April 2010).
- Practice Guide: Formulating and Expressing Internal Audit Opinions (April 2009).
- Practice Guide: Internal Auditing and Fraud (December 2009).
- Practice Advisory 2050-2: Assurance Maps (July 2009).

Other Related Changes

Other changes in the last two years impacting this publication include:

- The IIA's articulation of The Internal Audit Value Proposition.
- The IIA's release of the Global Internal Audit Survey, a component of the Common Body of Knowledge (CBOK) Study.
- Enhancements in governance and risk management.
- Changing priorities of internal audit stakeholders.
- Emergence of The IIA's Audit Executive Center.

The information in this book is designed to serve as a practical guide for applying the IPPF. In doing so, it reviews basic information on the essential elements required for providing effective internal audit services, discusses in depth those elements representing significant change, and provides specific practical tools and techniques for delivering high quality internal audit services. We hope you find it useful in your success through internal auditing.

CHAPTER 1

WHY ARE THE IPPF AND THE *STANDARDS* IMPORTANT?

To appreciate the importance of the International Professional Practices Framework (IPPF), it is useful to understand first its history, and then why it is important to internal audit stakeholders, the internal audit profession, and to you, the internal audit practitioner.

A Brief History of Guidance and Standards for the Internal Audit Profession

The practice of internal auditing developed over a long period of time. As organizations grew in size and complexity and developed geographically dispersed operations, managers in the upper echelons of the organizational structure could no longer personally observe operations for which they were responsible nor have significant direct contact with people reporting to them. This distancing of upper-level management from the operations for which they were responsible created a need for other people in the organization to assist by inspecting the operations and providing reports.

With the founding of The Institute of Internal Auditors (The IIA) in 1941, internal audit practice began the move toward becoming a profession, including agreement among practitioners about the role of internal auditing and its basic concepts and practices. The development of guidance for the emerging profession proceeded relatively slowly in the early years of The IIA. The first guidance came with the issuance of the Statement of the Responsibilities of the Internal Auditor in 1947. This short document set out to define the objectives and scope of internal auditing. As the profession evolved, the broadening of its scope was reflected in subsequent revisions. For instance, in the original 1947 Statement, the scope was focused primarily on financial matters, but by 1957, it had been broadened to include numerous services to management regarding review and evaluation of operations as well. Over the years, the Statement was periodically revised (1957, 1971, 1976, 1981, and 1990) until it was replaced in 1999 by the current Definition of Internal Auditing.

The IIA provided additional guidance for the profession in 1968 with the issuance of a Code of Ethics for IIA members. This code consisted of eight articles, the basic principles of which are still found in the current code. The IIA also provided specifics on what knowledge and skills internal audit practitioners should possess with the publication of the Common Body of Knowledge in 1972 and implementation of the Certified Internal Auditor (CIA) certification program the subsequent year. Finally, in 1978, The IIA issued the *Standards for the Professional Practice of Internal Auditing*. They consisted of five general and 25 specific guidelines as to how the internal audit function should be managed and how audit engagements should be performed. These standards were widely adopted and translated into a number of different languages. Additionally, they were incorporated into the laws and regulations of various government entities.

The 1978 *Standards* proved relatively robust and were able to accommodate the evolving profession, remaining relatively unchanged for the next 20 years. However, there was a large amount of additional guidance provided to interpret these standards coming from a number of different sources. These ranged from guidelines that accompanied the *Standards*, to a series of Professional Standards Practice Releases, providing IIA staff's response to frequently asked questions (FAQs) in terms of implementing the *Standards*, to IIA Position Papers, as well as a large number of research studies. By the end of the 1990s, the body of guidance that had developed alongside the Code of Ethics and the *Standards* had reached a point where there were no clear levels of authority among the various sources of guidance, as well as instances of conflicting guidance.

The landscape of the profession in the 1990s also had altered in terms of how internal audit services were being provided, with a significant share of the services now being delivered by external service providers. In some internal audit functions, there was a dramatic shift in the amount of time being allocated from the traditional services of audits and reviews of operations to nontraditional audit services such as control self-assessment programs, proactive training on internal control, participation as advisers in system implementation projects, and other consulting activities. Further, since the mid-1980s, the concept of risk management as a method of allocating internal audit resources had rapidly developed within the profession. The 1978 *Standards* did not specifically address these emerging issues.

Recognizing the important role that the Statement of Responsibilities, the Code of Ethics, and particularly, the *Standards* had played in the development of the now global internal audit profession, The IIA established a Guidance Task Force in 1997 to consider the needs and mechanisms for providing guidance to the profession in the future. After more than a year of study, the Guidance Task Force issued its report — *A Vision for the Future: Professional Practices Framework for Internal Auditing*. This report proposed a new definition of *internal auditing* to replace the one found in the Statement of Responsibilities and a new structure for providing relevant and timely guidance to the profession. The proposed definition and structure were approved in 1999. Implementation began with the revision of the Code of Ethics in 2000 and the completion of a new *International Standards for the Practice of Internal Auditing (Standards)* in 2002.

By 2006, the *Standards* had become recognized globally, with authorized translations in 32 languages, and increasingly incorporated into laws and regulations in a number of countries and jurisdictions. However, with the increased recognition and status of The IIA's professional guidance, IIA leadership saw the need to ensure that its authoritative guidance was clear, current, relevant, and internationally consistent, and that the guidance-setting processes were suitably transparent to the profession's stakeholders and sufficiently responsive to the needs of the profession. A task force and steering committee was established to review the existing guidance structure and the guidance development, review, and issuance processes. The result of the review was a new guidance framework (the IPPF) and reengineering of the guidance-setting processes, including the creation of a guidance oversight board, The IPPF Oversight Council, composed predominantly of outside stakeholders, to monitor processes used in establishing the mandatory guidance.

Why Are the IPPF and the *Standards* Important?

The IPPF and its components are key to those who rely on and use the services of the internal audit profession as well as all those working in the profession. The components, as further described later, include mandatory guidance: the Definition of Internal Auditing, the Code of Ethics, the *Standards*, as well as strongly recommended guidance: Position Papers, Practice Advisories (PAs), and Practice Guides. The *Standards* are a fundamental part of the IPPF and provide the basis for discussion of much of the IPPF in this book.

As described in the Definition of Internal Auditing, an effective internal audit function acts as an independent, objective assurance and consulting activity that is designed to add value and improve an organization's operations. It helps an organization accomplish its objectives by bringing a systematic, disciplined approach to evaluate and improve the effectiveness of risk management, control, and governance processes.

Why Is the IPPF Important to Internal Auditing's Stakeholders, Including Audit Committees and Senior Management?

Internal audit stakeholders, including those responsible for overseeing internal auditing, such as audit committees and senior management, need to have a basis by which to measure internal audit effectiveness. The IPPF provides this basis. The emergence of the IPPF and the *Standards* for the internal audit profession provide the audit committee and senior management with a framework with which to set expectations and measure internal audit performance and quality.

In recent years, the responsibilities of governing bodies such as the audit committee have come under scrutiny or been enhanced by regulators around the globe. In addition, audit committees frequently have stated roles related to internal auditing in their charters. The roles typically include monitoring the effectiveness of internal auditing. The IPPF and the *Standards* outline what internal auditing needs to do to be effective. By understanding the *Standards* and how internal auditing complies, audit committees will be in a better position to appoint, appraise, use, and support their internal auditors.

Further, there is a strong link between the role of the audit committee, regulatory requirements regarding audit committees' oversight of internal auditing, and the *Standards*. See Exhibit 1-1 for a mapping of common audit committee roles and the *Standards*. This clearly illustrates that in organizations whose internal audit function complies with the *Standards*, the audit committees will find it much easier to comply with their own charter and regulatory requirements. Key questions that the audit committee can ask to see if they are properly understanding, assessing, and supporting internal auditing are provided in Exhibit 1-2. Chief audit executives may find these exhibits useful in educating the audit committee on the importance of conformance with the *Standards* and the IPPF.

Why Is the IPPF Important to the Internal Audit Profession?

A professional framework and standards are core attributes that differentiate professions from unstructured groups of people who happen to be employed in similar roles. It differentiates a group conforming to a level of performance and quality from a general grouping of people with similar interests, but inconsistent performance. A dictionary definition of what it means to be *professional* states, "characterized by or conforming to the technical or ethical standards of a profession."

The IPPF and its elements define and provide assurance of quality and professionalism in internal auditing. The Definition of Internal Auditing, the *Standards,* and the Code of Ethics, as mandatory elements of the IPPF, are followed by all IIA members and are the foundation of the internal audit profession. The IPPF enables others, including the stakeholders discussed earlier, to rely upon internal auditing.

Further, the IPPF enables other major institutions in society, such as regulatory bodies and governments, to rely upon internal auditing and incorporate it in their regulations and laws. An ever-increasing number of regulatory bodies are recognizing the importance of the *Standards* in ensuring internal auditing is effective. Greater recognition around the world of the importance of internal auditing enhances the stature of the profession and opens the door for internal auditing to deliver greater value.

Why Is the IPPF Important to Each Internal Auditor?

The IPPF for internal auditing is the sole global set of professional requirements for the internal audit profession. At the most basic level, the IPPF exists to help each and every internal audit professional around the world perform at a certain fundamental level.

When you devote your professional career to any cause, it is important that you excel in what you do. The IPPF and the *Standards* are meant for practitioners. The IPPF is here to help the internal auditor and the internal audit activity succeed. It is a road map, uniquely fitted to the needs of internal auditors. It continues to build on the successful history of the profession.

Why Is This Book Important to You?

This book came from the desire in the internal audit profession for:

- Further explanations of meanings behind the principles-based *Standards* in the IPPF and answers to FAQs.

- Practical tools to help implement the *Standards* in the organization.

- Examples of leading practices in implementing the *Standards* and best practice internal auditing.

- Discussion of trends and various points of view on topics core to the profession of internal auditing.

This book is organized and aligned with the *Standards*. It contains more than 30 exhibits of models, tools, and lists that will be useful in implementing the topics discussed in the IPPF and the *Standards*. Through understanding the topics and applying the exhibits, internal auditors will be able to leverage leading thinking and practical real-world applications of the principles-based *Standards*.

The IPPF and the *Standards* Are Fundamental to Adding Value Through Internal Auditing

Each internal audit activity will have to determine how best to add value for its organization given the needs and climate of the organization. To best add value, internal auditing needs to understand the expectations of key stakeholders and their perception of what adds value. This book illustrates how to take those expectations and — through the IPPF, the *Standards*, and leading practices and tools for implementation — embark on the mission to add value.

Exhibit 1-1
Common Audit Committee Charter or Regulatory Requirements Mapped to The IIA's *Standards*

The table below shows common charter or regulatory requirements regarding audit committees' oversight of internal auditing, and the associated IIA *Standards*. This clearly illustrates that in organizations whose internal audit function complies with the *Standards*, the audit committees will find it much easier to comply with their own charter and regulatory requirements.

Common Audit Committee Requirements	IIA International *Standards*
Monitoring and assessing internal audit effectiveness.	"The chief audit executive must develop and maintain a quality assurance and improvement program that covers all aspects of the internal audit activity." (1300)
	"External assessments must be conducted at least once every five years by a qualified, independent reviewer or review team from outside the organization." (1312)
	"The chief audit executive must communicate the results of the quality assurance and improvement program to senior management and the board." (1320)
	"The chief audit executive must effectively manage the internal audit activity to ensure it adds value to the organization." (2000)
	"The internal audit activity must evaluate and contribute to the improvement of governance, risk management, and control processes using a systematic and disciplined approach." (2100)
Reviewing internal auditing's staffing and that it has the necessary resources.	"The chief audit executive must communicate the internal audit activity's plans and resource requirements . . . to senior management and the board for review and approval. The chief audit executive must also communicate the impact of resource limitations." (2020)
	"The internal audit activity collectively must possess or obtain the knowledge, skills, and other competencies needed to perform its responsibilities." (1210)

Exhibit 1-1 (continued) **Common Audit Committee Charter or Regulatory** **Requirements Mapped to The IIA's *Standards***	
Common Audit Committee Requirements	**IIA International *Standards***
Ensuring communication and reporting lines between the head of internal auditing and the board.	"The purpose, authority, and responsibility of the internal audit activity must be formally defined in an internal audit charter, consistent with the Definition of Internal Auditing, the Code of Ethics, and the *Standards*. The chief audit executive must periodically review the internal audit charter and present it to senior management and the board for approval." (1000) "The chief audit executive must report to a level within the organization that allows the internal audit activity to fulfill its responsibilities." (1110) The IIA strongly believes that to achieve necessary independence, the chief audit executive should report functionally to the audit committee and administratively to the chief executive officer. "The chief audit executive must communicate and interact directly with the audit committee." (1111) "The chief audit executive must report periodically to senior management and the board on the internal audit activity's purpose, authority, responsibility, and performance relative to its plan." (2060)
Reviewing and assessing the annual internal audit plan.	"The chief audit executive must communicate the internal audit activity's plans . . . to senior management and the board for review and approval." (2020)
Review periodic reports on the results of the internal auditors' work.	"The chief audit executive must report periodically to senior management and the board . . . Reporting must include significant risk exposures and control issues, including fraud risks, governance issues, and other matters needed or requested by senior management and the board." (2060)

Exhibit 1-1 (continued) Common Audit Committee Charter or Regulatory Requirements Mapped to The IIA's *Standards*	
Common Audit Committee Requirements	**IIA International *Standards***
Reviewing management's responsiveness to internal auditing's findings and recommendations.	"The chief audit executive must establish a follow-up process to monitor and ensure that management actions have been effectively implemented or that senior management has accepted the risk of not taking action." (2500.A1)
Source: Audit Committee Briefing, *Internal Audit Standards – Why They Matter*, The Institute of Internal Auditors, 2005. Adapted from the 2004 Audit Committee Briefing, *Internal Auditing Standards – Why They Matter* © 2005, published by The Institute of Internal Auditors – UK and Ireland Ltd. and used with permission. The term "board" used throughout the exhibit means "audit committee" for many organizations.	

Exhibit 1-2 Questions for the Audit Committee to Ask Related to Internal Auditing, Reinforcing the Importance of Internal Auditing
To be effective, internal audit departments need audit committees to defend their independence, champion their role in corporate governance, and support their access to information and resources.
Audit committee members should ask themselves how much input they have to the leadership and work of their internal audit team: <ul><li>How well do I know the head of internal auditing? How often do I talk to him or her?</li><li>Do I appoint and have a role in the performance evaluation of the head of internal auditing? Does he or she report directly to the audit committee?</li><li>When was the last time I reviewed and approved the internal audit charter? Do I know what it says?</li><li>How do we ensure clear functional reporting of internal auditing to the audit committee, in form and in substance?</li><li>Do I know how the internal audit department sets its plan? Do I review and approve the annual plan?</li><li>How well is the management team doing on implementing actions agreed during internal audit work?</li><li>If the head of internal auditing came to me and expressed concerns based on his or her business judgment, would I listen? How would I act?</li></ul>

Exhibit 1-2 (continued)
Questions for the Audit Committee to Ask Related to Internal
Auditing, Reinforcing the Importance of Internal Auditing

Audit committee members should also examine the internal audit department's attributes and performance:

- Does my internal audit function comply with The IIA's *Standards*?
- Is its position in the organization at a sufficiently high level and sufficiently detached from functional areas to guarantee its independence?
- Does it avoid activities that could undermine its objectivity?
- Is the internal audit plan based on the organization's risk profile?
- How well is the internal audit department doing in completing its plan this year?
- Does it have a quality assurance program? Does internal auditing have a plan to get an external quality assurance review once every five years as required by the *Standards*? What are the results of the most recent external quality assurance review? Does internal auditing report to the audit committee the results of its internal quality program?
- Is internal auditing sufficiently resourced to provide the objective assurance I need on risk and control?
- Are there any inappropriate scope or resource limitations put upon internal auditing?
- How does the head of internal auditing respond to probing by the audit committee?

If audit committees do not know the answers to these questions, now is the time to ask.

Source: Based upon Audit Committee Briefing, *Internal Audit Standards – Why They Matter*, The Institute of Internal Auditors, 2005. Adapted from the 2004 Audit Committee Briefing, *Internal Auditing Standards – Why They Matter* © 2005, published by The Institute of Internal Auditors – UK and Ireland Ltd. and used with permission.

Chapter 2

THE IPPF

The goal of the IPPF is to provide a structure that organizes the full range of internal audit professional guidance promulgated by The IIA's international technical committees in a way that makes it easily accessible to the profession globally and to provide guidance timely as new issues arise. The authoritative guidance provided in the IPPF elaborates on and supports The IIA's Definition of Internal Auditing. As the shell that holds the information outlining the appropriate practice of internal auditing, the IPPF embodies the core elements of the profession. It provides a consistent, organized method of looking at the fundamental principles and procedures that make internal auditing a unique, disciplined, and systematic activity.

The IPPF contains two categories of authoritative guidance: mandatory and strongly recommended. Mandatory guidance is developed following a rigorous due process, including a period of public exposure. Conformance with the principles set forth in mandatory guidance is considered to be essential for the effective delivery of internal audit services. Strongly recommended guidance describes practices for effective implementation of the principles found in the Definition of Internal Auditing, the Code of Ethics, and the *Standards*. Conformance with this guidance is strongly encouraged by The IIA, but it is recognized that there may be other, equally effective practices that may be used to implement the principles found in the mandatory guidance. While the specific processes are followed in the development and issuance of recommended guidance, the development and issuances processes are shorter and there is no public exposure of the guidance before it is issued.

The components of the IPPF are: the Definition of Internal Auditing, the Code of Ethics, the *Standards*, Position Papers, Practice Advisories, and Practice Guides (Exhibit 2-1). The Definition, the Code of Ethics, and the *Standards* provide mandatory guidance in the sense that these principles must be followed for the effective delivery of internal audit services. As noted in The IIA's Code of Ethics, all IIA members and CIAs, as well as anyone claiming to provide internal audit services, are expected to adhere to the principles outlined in these guidelines. The Position Papers, Practice Advisories, and Practice Guides provide strongly recommended, endorsed, but non-mandatory guidance.

The IPPF is available in several forms. The printed book provides all the mandatory guidance as well as the Practice Advisories. A CD-ROM that contains all elements of the IPPF, including the Practice Guides and Position Papers, accompanies the book. The CD also contains an interactive version of the IPPF, which provides significant efficiencies in researching practice issues. The IPPF also is available at The IIA's website (www.thieiia.org). The mandatory portion of the IPPF is available to all free of charge. The strongly recommended portion requires IIA membership. For members, the website also provides an interactive version so that the same research capabilities are available on the Web and on the CD. The IIA may issue a new edition of the IPPF book and CD annually depending on the amount of change in the IPPF contents. The Web version of the IPPF is updated immediately upon the issuance of any guidance.

Mandatory Guidance

The Definition of Internal Auditing

The IIA's Definition of Internal Auditing is key for understanding the role and depth of internal auditing today. It is also the foundation for the structure and content of the *Standards* and the guidance contained in the IPPF. The definition is:

> *Internal auditing is an independent, objective assurance and consulting activity designed to add value and improve an organization's operations. It helps an organization accomplish its objectives by bringing a systematic, disciplined approach to evaluate and improve the effectiveness of risk management, control, and governance processes.*

The definition of internal auditing used today is quite different from the one penned six decades ago as part of the *Statement of Responsibilities of Internal Auditing.** According to research conducted in the late 1990s by The IIA Research Foundation and the Guidance Task Force responsible for examining the value of IIA guidance, the old terminology failed to "adequately reflect the evolution of practice [or] effectively promote the internal audit profession in the competitive marketplace." The Guidance Task Force therefore drafted a new definition, resulting in the definition used today that more accurately depicts the profession's broadened focus and proactive stance.

Today's definition focuses the image of internal auditing in six significant ways.

1. An Objective Activity

The definition describes internal auditing as "an independent, objective activity."

It is useful to compare the current definition to the previous definition to understand some key points. Today's definition uses the term "activity" rather than "function" and eliminates the phrase "within an organization." The revised terminology allows for internal audit services to be provided by individuals not employed by the organization. In doing so, the new definition acknowledges that outsourcing has become a viable alternative for organizations seeking quality internal audit services.

Adding the word "objective" to the definition is also significant in that it allows auditors to be more responsive to their customers than did the sole reference to the restrictive concept of independence. According to the Guidance Task Force, the auditor adds value through his or her objective analyses and recommendations for improvement. Therefore, objectivity can be considered a defining characteristic of the profession. The reference to "independence" was retained, but not in an effort to limit who could provide internal audit services and what those services could entail. Instead, independence in the current definition reflects the audit activity's freedom to determine audit or assurance scope, to perform the work judged necessary to achieve the engagement objectives, and to communicate the results.

---

*   The 1990 version of the statement stated:
    Internal auditing is an independent appraisal function established within an organization to examine and evaluate its activities as a service to the organization. The objective of internal auditing is to assist members of the organization in the effective discharge of their responsibilities . . .

2. Assurance and Consulting

Explicit recognition of internal auditing's consulting role means that the full range of services being provided by most internal audit functions is acknowledged. While the mix of assurance and consulting work varies greatly across functions, there would be very few functions that do not spend at least some of their time directly meeting their organization's needs for some level of consulting services. By focusing on assurance and consulting work, the definition conveys a proactive, customer-driven approach with a role to play in the governance, risk management and control activities of the organization. The definition allows for internal auditing's increasingly expansive and influential role in organizations.

3. Adding Value and Improving Operations

Adding value is not an option in most organizations. Management expects and demands all functions to create visible value. By stating that internal auditing is *designed* to "add value and improve," the definition further underscores the profession's commitment to serving the needs of the organization. However, because of the nature of the internal audit product, internal auditors have not always clearly articulated how the internal audit activity adds value to their organizations. To assist internal auditors in better communicating the value their work provides the organization, an IIA task force developed a document to concisely convey how internal auditing provides value to governing bodies and senior management. This document, "Value Proposition," succinctly depicts how the concepts contained in the Definition combine to create value (Figure 2-2).

4. Considering the Whole Organization

The definition focuses internal auditing on the whole organization. Internal auditing is charged with helping the *organization* accomplish its overall *objectives*. Such a mandate requires auditors to understand the goals and processes of the organization and to view problems and their solutions from a broad perspective.

5. Broadened Horizons

In stating that internal auditors are to evaluate and improve the effectiveness of risk management, control, and governance processes, the definition presents a broad, though focused, view of the working domain of the internal auditor. Underlying the terminology is the understanding that controls exist only to help the organization manage its risk and promote effective governance processes. The definition charges internal auditors with a broad and involved role to play in the organization's governance and risk management processes.

6. A Unique Franchise

The definition recognizes internal auditing's legacy of delivering services with the tried-and-true systematic, disciplined internal audit approach that results from being a standards-based profession. It is this documented and rigorous methodology that makes internal auditing enduring and unique.

Foundation for the *Standards*

Today's definition of internal auditing is the foundation of the *Standards* and the IPPF. By reflecting the definition, the *Standards* push the character and performance of internal auditing to a higher level.

The Code of Ethics

The purpose of the Code of Ethics (the Code) is to promote an ethical culture in the internal audit profession. The Code does this by setting out four basic principles that reflect the four core values that must be upheld for the customers of internal auditors to have trust in the services provided. While there are varying practices in how specific engagements are carried out, it is hard to imagine there is anyone who would not want the internal audit professional to follow these four principles:

- Integrity.
- Objectivity.
- Confidentiality.
- Competency.

By *integrity* the Code means that internal auditors will do their work with diligence and truthfulness and in accordance with the law and ethical values of their organization. Indeed, who seriously would contend that a report issued by internal auditors that lied about what they found would be of much value to anyone? What trust could the user put in such a report? The Code specifically provides four rules of conduct that guide how the concept of integrity is put into internal audit practice (see Appendix B, rules 1.1 to 1.4). It is the internal auditor's integrity that engenders trust and thus forms the basis for reliance on his or her judgments.

The Definition of Internal Auditing mentions *objectivity* as a fundamental attribute of internal auditing. As the Value Proposition emphasizes, it is an essential ingredient necessary for internal audit services to add value. In conducting their work, it is imperative that internal auditors exercise the highest level of objectivity in gathering, evaluating, and communicating information about the activity or process being examined. They should make a balanced assessment of all the relevant circumstances and not be unduly influenced by their own interests or by others when forming judgments.

This means that in performing their work, internal auditors need to be aware of potential threats to their objectivity such as personal relationships or conflicts of interest. These could be such things as accepting gifts from clients, auditing an operation in which their spouse works, or agreeing with the divisional manager to transfer to the division at the end of the audit. The specific rules are spelled out in the Code as outlined in Appendix B (rules 2.1 to 2.3). Note that the rules do not specify that the auditor's judgment need actually be biased to be an issue, but also that there is an issue if judgment could be presumed to be biased. In addition, rule 2.3 prohibits the potential biasing of the communication of the message in the report of the auditor's work by not disclosing all information critical for the user to correctly understand the report. For example, it is an issue when stating that inventory controls were at the same level of effectiveness as in the last audit, but neglecting to point out that in the previous audit, control activities were found to be unsatisfactory.

In providing internal audit services, the internal auditor will need unrestricted access to all relevant data in the organization. For the organization and clients to grant such access, they need confidence that the internal auditor will not inappropriately disclose or make use of the data. The principle of *confidentiality* requires internal auditors to respect the value and ownership of information they receive and to not disclose information without appropriate authority unless there is a legal or professional obligation to do so. The Code stipulates two rules regarding confidentiality (Appendix B, rules 3.1 and 3.2). The first requires prudence in the use and protection of data obtained in the course of providing internal audit services, and the second prohibits the use of this information for personal gain or in other ways that would be contrary to the law. For instance, this principle would require internal auditors to use passwords and other security measures if they were carrying personally identifiable information of employees or client customers in files on their laptops. This principle would also prohibit internal auditors from making trades in the stock of a company they learned was going to be acquired by their employer (in other words, insider trading).

The Code also requires that the internal auditor have and apply the *competency* necessary to deliver the required internal audit services. One could obtain internal audit services from people who had integrity, were objective, and maintained confidentiality, but those services would be of little value if those persons did not have the necessary knowledge and skills to perform the work. This is required in rule 4.1. In addition, the Code also specifically requires that the work be performed in accordance with the *Standards* and that internal auditors continually work to improve the effectiveness and quality of their services.

The Code is applicable to all individuals and entities that provide internal audit services, not just those who are IIA members or hold IIA certifications. However, The IIA is only able to exercise enforcement over IIA members and recipients of, or candidates for, IIA professional certifications. Breaches of the Code for those in the purview of The IIA are subject to censure, suspension of membership and/or certifications, and expulsion and/or revocation of certification as determined by The IIA's Ethics Committee. It should also be noted that conduct need not be explicitly mentioned in the Rules of Conduct for it to be considered unacceptable or discreditable and thus subject to disciplinary action.

These four principles and the 12 Rules of Conduct thus set expectations for what the customer of internal audit services can expect in terms of behavior from an internal audit professional. Each of the four principles is equally critical. Violation of any of the four will preclude the delivery of value added and, thus, effective internal audit services. Further, although enforcement of the Code by The IIA is relatively limited, in the United States at least, regulators and the courts have looked to the Code as well as the *Standards* in determining cases involving adequacy of the performance of internal audit services.

The *International Standards for the Professional Practice of Internal Auditing* (*Standards*)

The *Standards* serve as the foundation for the internal audit profession and the core of the IPPF. The objectives of the *Standards* are to:

1. Delineate basic principles that represent the practice of internal auditing.
2. Provide a framework for performing and promoting a broad range of value-added internal auditing.

3. Establish the basis for the evaluation of internal audit performance.
4. Foster improved organizational processes and operations.

The *Standards* set out for internal audit practitioners the fundamental concepts on which the internal audit profession is built and established the benchmarks for measuring the performance of internal audit services. In addition, for the customers of these services, the *Standards* allow them to have clear expectations about the nature and quality of the services they are acquiring.

The *Standards* are principles-focused, mandatory requirements consisting of a statement of the basic requirement and, in many cases, an interpretation. The "statement" presents one or more of the basic requirements for the effective practice of internal auditing and is applicable at both the individual and the organizational level. The "interpretation" clarifies terms or concepts used in the "statement." For example, in Standard 2040, Policies and Procedures, the statement is:

> The chief audit executive must establish policies and procedures to guide the internal audit activity.

The interpretation is:

> The form and content of policies and procedures are dependent upon the size and structure of the internal audit activity and the complexity of its work.

In this case the interpretation describes further what is intended by policies and procedures — that the appropriate form and content of the policies and procedures will vary across internal audit functions because of size, organizational structure, and nature of the type of services provided. The *Standards* also include a Glossary that provides definitions of terms that have been given a specific meaning as they are used in the *Standards*. For example, the term *board* is defined as:

> A board is an organization's governing body, such as a board of directors, supervisory board, head of an agency or legislative body, board of governors or trustees of a nonprofit organization, or any other designated body of the organization, including the audit committee to whom the chief audit executive may functionally report.

While in U.S. public companies the term *board* would mean the *audit committee*, in other situations, such as in the case of a government agency, it would be read to mean *agency head*, if there were no additional governing group. The Glossary is an integral part of the *Standards* and is necessary for their correct interpretation. As part of the *Standards*, the Glossary is part of the mandatory portion of the IPPF's authoritative guidance.

The *Standards* consist of three classifications:

*   **Attribute Standards** — the critical characteristics that individuals, teams, and organizations must have to provide effective internal audit services.

*   **Performance Standards** — the description of the nature of internal audit services and the quality criteria against which the performance of these services can be evaluated.

- **Implementation Standard**s — more specific guidance as to how the Attribute and Performance Standards apply to each major type of internal audit activity.

These standards can be found in Appendix A.

The Attribute Standards describe the defining characteristics of organizations and individuals performing internal audit services. They cover such issues as:

- The purpose, authority, responsibility, and charter of the audit activity.
- Independence and objectivity.
- Proficiency and due professional care.
- Quality assurance and improvement.

The Performance Standards describe the nature of internal audit services and provide quality criteria against which the performance of these services can be measured. In other words, they describe what internal auditors do and how they should do it. The Attribute and Performance Standards apply in all types of audit situations. Whether it is a fraud investigation, a control self-assessment exercise, or an accounts payable audit, internal auditors working on the engagement are expected to look the way the Attribute Standards describe and conduct their activities the way the Performance Standards dictate.

Implementation Standards, on the other hand, augment the existing Attribute and Performance Standards by helping employ them in particular types of engagements. As such, they only apply in certain situations.

A numbering system is used to identify each specific type of standard. Attribute Standards make up the 1000 series and Performance Standards the 2000 series. For example, the attribute standard titled "Proficiency and Due Professional Care" is 1200, with more specific discussion of the topic in 1210 (Proficiency), 1220 (Due Professional Care), and 1230 (Continuing Professional Development). The Implementation Standards are covered under the related Attribute and Performance Standards and indicated by a letter. Thus, the Implementation Standards for assurance services are nnnn.A1, nnnn.A2, etc., and for consulting activity, nnnn.C1, etc. An example of how this system applies to an assurance implementation standard is 1220.A3 as shown in Exhibit 2-3. Practice Advisories are similarly organized by reference to a specific standard. For example, PA 1210.A1-1: Obtaining External Service Providers to Support or Complement the Internal Audit Activity is a practice advisory that relates to assurance implementation standard 1210.A.1.

In Chapter 3, we take a closer look at the implementation standards and the distinction between assurance and consulting.

Strongly Recommended Guidance

The Definition, the *Standards,* and the Code are designed to apply to all internal audit activities. However, internal audit activities are performed in a number of very different types of organizations, by persons functioning inside the organization and by outside third parties, centrally and decentrally, and in diverse cultures and legal environments. The Practice Advisories, Practice Guides, and the Position Papers provide more specific guidance, but that guidance is not mandatory — it may not be applicable to all internal audit functions, or it may be just one particular approach out of a number of acceptable alternatives. However, this guidance is authoritative in that it has gone through The IIA's endorsement process, which includes review by the Ethics Committee and the Internal Audit Standards Board for consistency with the mandatory elements of the IPPF.

Practice Advisories. Practice Advisories are designed to assist internal auditors in applying the Definition, the Code of Ethics, and the *Standards,* and to promote good practice. They address internal audit approaches, methodologies, and considerations, but do not provided detailed processes and procedures. The Practice Advisories are the responsibility of The IIA's Professional Issues Committee. However, this committee may work with other IIA committees (such as the Ethics Committee) or a special task force to develop specific advisories. To date, more than 50 Practice Advisories have been issued, but as multiple advisories are issued each year, that number has probably already increased. An up-to-date listing, as well as the text of all issued Practice Advisories, is available at The IIA's website. Only current IIA members are allowed to access them. They are also available in the published edition of the IPPF and the accompanying CD, which is updated annually.

Practice Guides. Practice Guides provide detailed, how-to guidance on procedures and techniques and may range in size from 10 to several hundred pages. The IIA's Professional Practices Council (composed of the chairs of The IIA's international technical committees) oversees the development and issuance of Practice Guides. The concept for a guide may originate with any of The IIA's technical committees. The Professional Guidance Council approves the concept and assigns it to one of the committees to develop. Primarily the development falls to the Professional Issues Committee. The Practice Guides include the Guides to the Assessment of IT Risk (GAIT) and the Global Technology Audit Guides (GTAGs) as well as guides such as *Formulating and Expressing Internal Audit Opinions.* A complete list of the Practice Guides is available on The IIA's website.

Position Papers. The guidance found in position papers addresses issues of concern beyond the specifics of what the internal audit function, the CAE, or the individual internal audit practitioner should do and how they should carry out their work. These papers are written not only for internal auditors but for other interested parties outside the profession. These parties include not only management, the board, and audit committee members, but also external stakeholders such as legislators, regulators and other professionals with whom internal auditors work. The Position Papers deal with such issues as delineating the role of internal auditing in the organization's enterprise risk management system and how the organization sources the internal audit activity. Position Papers also may address significant governance, risk, and control topics with the intent of clarifying and improving both internal auditors' and stakeholders' understanding of the issues.

The Professional Issues Committee usually initiates Position Papers, although any of the international committees or local IIA institutes may do so. Position Papers also may be developed and issued in partnership with other professional associations or not-for-profit organizations. Management of the development and drafting of the Position Papers rests with the Professional Issues Committee. Before issuance, unlike the other types of strongly recommended guidance, Position Papers require a one-month exposure period to the local IIA institutes and the international technical committees.

Strongly recommend guidance also may be developed by local IIA institutes (for example IIA-China or IIA-Germany), which would apply to their specific legal and regulatory environment. This guidance is drafted by the respective institutes and then submitted for review and feedback from the international technical committees to provide assurance that the guidance is consistent with the IPPF.

Using the IPPF with Other Standard Frameworks

The IIA's IPPF is not the only source of guidance and standards that may have relevance for certain specialized aspects of internal audit practice or that apply to particular industries. Other sources of guidance and standards include:

- U.S. Government Accountability Office (GAO).
- International Organization of Supreme Audit Institutions (INTOSAI).
- Information Systems Audit and Control Association (ISACA).
- Board of Environmental, Health & Safety Auditor Certifications (BEAC).
- International Auditing and Assurance Standards Board (part of International Federation of Accountants – IFAC).
- International Standards Organization (ISO).
- Standards Australia.

The IPPF explicitly recognizes that there may be other guidance that may apply to internal audit practice and allows for the possibility that some internal audit activities may need to follow other standards in addition to those of The IIA. For example, it is common for the internal audit functions in many state and local government agencies in the United States to have incorporated both The IIA's *Standards* and the *Government Auditing Standards* (*Yellow Book*) issued by the GAO in their internal audit charters. Specialty groups within some internal audit functions also often adopt the more specialized standards for information technology (IT) auditing or environmental auditing to guide work in those specialized areas.

In cases where multiple standards apply, the introduction to the *Standards* provides the following directive as to how to handle such situations:

> If the *Standards* are used in conjunction with standards issued by other authoritative bodies, audit communications may also cite the use of other standards, as appropriate. In such a case, if inconsistencies exist between the *Standards* and other standards, internal auditors and the internal audit activity must conform with the *Standards,* and may conform with the other standards if they are more restrictive.

Because the *Standards,* are principles-based and intended for use by a wide range of organizations in a variety of legal and cultural environments, there is little, if any, direct conflict between other professional standards discussed in this section and the *Standards.* What differences exist are usually a matter of one set of standards being more stringent than another regarding a particular requirement. For example, ISACA standards for IS auditing (Standard S9.10) require the IS auditor to obtain written representation from management, at least annually, acknowledging management's responsibility for the design and implementation of internal controls to prevent and detect illegal acts. The *Standards* have no specific requirements for management representation, but obtaining such representation does not conflict in any way with the *Standards.*

The Continuing Evolution of the IPPF

The IPPF is not intended to be a static body of guidance, but to evolve along with the internal audit professional as the profession responds to a continually changing environment. The responsibility of maintaining the relevance of the IPPF falls to The IIA's Professional Practices Advisory Council, which consists of The IIA's vice chairman of professional practices and the chairs of The IIA's international guidance committees, the Internal Audit Standards Board, and the Professional Issues Committee.

The Professional Practices Advisory Council is responsible for coordinating the initiation, development, issuance, and maintenance of the authoritative guidance that makes up the IPPF. Annually, the Council develops a work plan for the next year as well as a tentative plan for the two following years that lays out the work for the Standards Board and the Professional Issues Committee. The Council also coordinates the review of all existing guidance on a three-year cycle.

The IIA's three international technical committees responsible for portions of the IPPF are:

The Ethics Committee — A five-member committee charged with developing and promoting ethical values and standards for the profession. Any changes in the Code of Ethics, such as adding additional rules, would be initiated by this committee. Adoption of new rules requires a 90-day exposure period allowing for public comment. Final approval rests with The IIA's Board of Directors. The committee is required to complete a formal review of the existing Code every three years. This committee also evaluates conduct of members and candidates for, or recipients of, IIA professional certifications, when necessary.

Internal Audit Standards Board — Its mission is to develop, monitor, and promote the *Standards*. New standards or modifications are considered and created by this board and, if changes receive at least a two-thirds vote of the board, they are then exposed for public comment for 90 days. Exposure includes translation into Spanish and French, and often into other major member languages (Chinese, Italian, German, Japanese, and potentially others). After considering the responses, a two-thirds vote of the board is required for the final issuance. The Standards Board is required to complete a review of the existing *Standards* every three years.

Professional Issues Committee — The mission of this committee is to provide timely guidance to the members of the profession on concepts, methodologies, and techniques included in the IPPF and to comment on, or develop positions on, other matters that directly or indirectly impact the profession of internal auditing. This committee has specific responsibility for initiating, developing, and maintaining the Practice Advisories, including reviewing the existing Practice Advisories on a three-year cycle. It also is a primary initiator and developer of Practice Guides and Position Papers. Drafts of proposed Practice Advisories, Practice Guides, and Position Papers are circulated to the Ethics Committee and the Standards Board for a review of consistency with existing mandatory guidance before being issued. Position Papers also require a 30-day exposure period to local IIA institutes.

As mentioned in Chapter 1, in 2006 The IIA established the second Vision for the Future Task Force, which recommended the current restructuring of internal audit guidance. In addition to developing the current IPPF structure, the Task Force also proposed changes to improve the transparency and increase the trust that legislators, regulators, and users of internal audit services have in the profession's professional guidance. One of the recommendations was the establishment of an "independent" guidance oversight council to provide assurance that The IIA follows its stated processes in developing, issuing, and maintaining the IPPF and represents the interests of stakeholders outside the profession.[1] The majority of the members of the IPPF Oversight Council are from the global user community. Representatives from this council observe the guidance-setting process and sign off that appropriate processes have been followed before mandatory guidance is finally issued.

A Living Framework for You to Leverage for Your Success

The IPPF provides the structure that organizes the full range of internal audit professional guidance essential for internal audit activities and individual internal auditors. The IPPF provides a consistent, organized method of looking at the fundamental principles and procedures that make internal auditing a unique, disciplined, and systematic activity. As can be seen in this chapter, the IPPF continues to expand and evolve with the internal audit profession and its stakeholders' needs. Looking to the future, you can expect the IPPF to continue to change to help drive quality and value throughout the internal audit profession. Now that you understand the overall structure of the IPPF, you are ready to fully explore the precise elements of internal auditing as captured in the *Standards*, as well as related guidance, insights, and examples of leading practices. By developing this deeper appreciation and understanding, you will be positioned for greater success in delivering internal auditing through your organization's internal audit activity.

Exhibit 2-1
The International Professional Practices Framework

Source: www.theiia.org

Exhibit 2-2
The Internal Audit Value Proposition

Internal Auditing's Value to Stakeholders

What should the governing bodies and senior management expect from internal auditing?

To help internal audit activities effectively communicate the value of their work to primary stakeholders — such as audit committees, boards of directors, management, and audit clients — The IIA has developed an easy-to-understand message tool. It's memorable and adaptable.

Communicated visually by three intersecting circles, the "value proposition" is based on the three core elements of value delivered by internal auditing to an organization: assurance, insight, and objectivity. Focusing on these three core internal audit concepts within your communication with stakeholders will enable them to understand the core value the internal audit activity provides.

INTERNAL AUDITING = Assurance, Insight, & Objectivity

Governing bodies and senior management rely on internal auditing for objective assurance and insight on the effectiveness and efficiency of governance, risk management, and internal control processes.

To expand the explanation of internal auditing's value, it can be defined by sub-values.

ASSURANCE = Governance, Risk, & Control

Internal auditing provides assurance on the organization's governance, risk management, and control processes to help the organization achieve its strategic, operational, financial, and compliance objectives.

INSIGHT = Catalyst, Analyses, & Assessments

Internal auditing is a catalyst for improving an organization's effectiveness and efficiency by providing insight and recommendations based on analyses and assessments of data and business processes.

Exhibit 2-2 (continued)
The Internal Audit Value Proposition

OBJECTIVITY = Integrity, Accountability, & Independence

With commitment to integrity and accountability, internal auditing provides value to governing bodies and senior management as an objective source of independent advice.

Source: www.theiia.org

Exhibit 2-3
Illustration of the Numbering System Used in the *Standards*

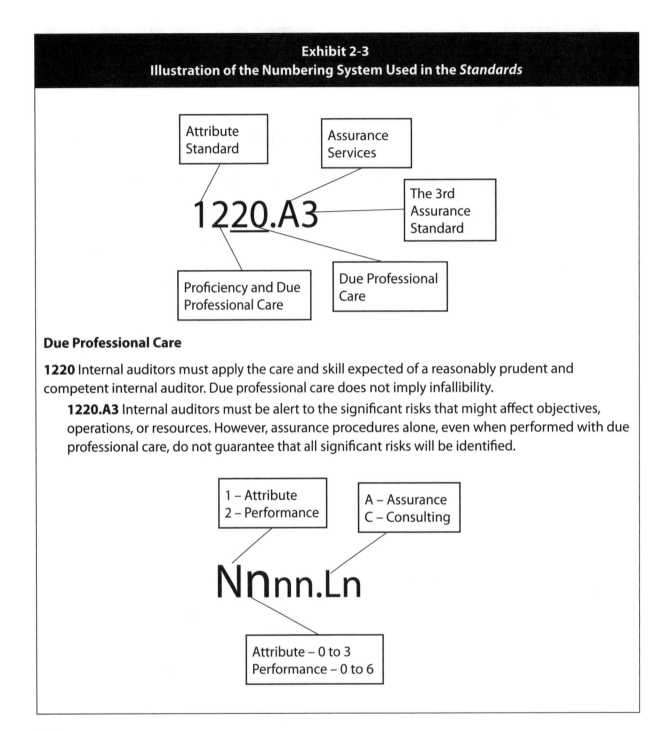

Due Professional Care

1220 Internal auditors must apply the care and skill expected of a reasonably prudent and competent internal auditor. Due professional care does not imply infallibility.

1220.A3 Internal auditors must be alert to the significant risks that might affect objectives, operations, or resources. However, assurance procedures alone, even when performed with due professional care, do not guarantee that all significant risks will be identified.

Reference

[1] The Institute of Internal Auditors, *A Vision for the Future: Guiding the Internal Audit Profession to Excellence*, Report from The IIA's Vision for the Future Task Force (Altamonte Springs, FL: The Institute of Internal Auditors, 2007), p. 11.

Chapter 3

ASSURANCE AND CONSULTING

The Internal Audit Value Proposition (Exhibit 2-2) asserts that the value internal auditing provides its customers comes from the intersection of the three core elements of assurance, insight, and objectivity. These conceptual elements combine in a wide range of potential services — from conducting financial, performance, compliance, and system security audits to participating on committees to select new accounting software, or to revising the organization's code of conduct to benchmarking processes with leading practices inside and outside the organization to teaching training courses in internal control to new managers. In limiting internal auditing to just the traditional auditing of internal controls, a significant part of the valuable contributions being made by internal auditing in many organizations would be missing.

The definition of internal auditing recognizes this broad range of services by dividing internal audit activities into two basic types: assurance and consulting services.

More specifically, the Glossary to the *Standards* defines them as:

Assurance Services — An objective examination of evidence for the purpose of providing an independent assessment on governance, risk management, and control processes for the organization.

Consulting Services — Advisory and related client service activities, the nature and scope of which are agreed with the client, are intended to add value and improve an organization's governance, risk management, and control processes without the internal auditor assuming management responsibility.

This distinction is just the basic recognition of two types of work performed. However, it is an extremely important clarification because it empowers internal auditors to specifically focus on the needs of the users of their services and enhance their ability to add value to their organizations.

From the Value Proposition perspective, however, the distinction between these two types of services can be confusing. In thinking about assurance services and consulting services, remember that the three conceptual core elements — assurance, insight, and objectivity — are present in both types of services, though potentially to different extents. In both types of services the internal auditor provides objective assurance that the organization is operating as intended and insight in the form of recommendations based on the analyses and assessment of data and business processes.

The Internal Audit Customers

Who are the customers of internal audit services? In most organizations the internal audit activity provides service to a number of users with distinctly different needs. Among the various groups of customers are:

- The audit committee and the board.
- Senior management.

- Financial management.
- Line management and operating management.
- External auditors.
- Regulators.
- Suppliers.
- Vendors and the consumers of the organization's products or services.

The IIA's Guidance Task Force provides an analysis of internal auditing's customers and the products these customers value.[1] For example, operating line managers (often the client) are interested in the ways internal auditing can improve the efficiency and effectiveness of their operations. The external auditor looks to internal auditing as a key component of the organization's overall system of control, which, if operating effectively, can reduce the extent of work the external auditor must perform to issue an opinion on the organization's financial statements and internal controls. Suppliers and customers are looking for internal auditing to provide assurance on the reliability and security of the information in the systems forming the interface between them and the organization. The staff members working in the area being audited are looking for internal auditing to bring them innovations and best practices from across the organization. These various value propositions not only differ, but often can be in conflict in terms of allocation of audit resources and, in some cases, tasks.

Balancing the demands from these various customers is up to the chief audit executive (CAE) in each organization. The right balance will depend on the organization's environment, the nature of its governance processes, and the maturity of its internal audit activity. For example, in some government audit environments, the internal audit activity focuses almost exclusively on assurance work with very limited consulting. In other organizations, the internal audit activity may offer a very broad range of both assurance and consulting service products. For example, the audit function of a large utility offers its customers 21 distinct services ranging from investigation into alleged fraud, to surveying customers to determine satisfaction, to facilitation of groups to arrive at process improvements as well as the standard audit of internal controls.[2]

The IPPF does not prescribe a particular mix. It depends on how the audit committee, senior management, and the CAE position the internal audit activity. The balance between the assurance and consulting activities should be clearly understood by these parties and ultimately reflected in the audit department charter.

Adding Value as Viewed by Key Stakeholders

As internal auditing evolves to meet the needs of organizations, many of the changes in the profession in recent years have been driven by the importance of adding value based on stakeholder expectations. Assurance services are often provided with a core focus on serving the needs of the audit committee and others senior in the organization. Consulting services are provided generally at the specific request of a member of management or a process owner in the organization. These consulting, or advisory, services have evolved as organizations have seen that the skill sets and objectivity of internal auditing are ideal in helping serve the needs of the organization. Through providing service beyond the assurance service responsibilities, internal auditing is valued as it does more to add value and improve the organization's operations.

That being said, CAEs realize that the most important stakeholders of internal auditing, usually the audit committee, require that internal auditing's fundamental assurance mission be achieved, and that consulting services, while helpful, should not cannibalize the internal audit resources necessary to fulfill the assurance role.

Assurance or Consulting: What Makes Them Different?

To understand the difference between these types of services and appropriately apply the Attribute and Performance Standards, we must remember two key phrases: (i) in the definition of consulting services — "the nature and scope of which are agreed with the client," and (ii) in the definition of assurance services — "independent assessment." These phrases reflect a fundamental difference in the structure and relationships involved in the delivery of the two types of services (see Exhibit 3-1). Consulting services generally involve two parties: (1) the person or group offering the advice — the internal auditor, and (2) the person or group seeking and receiving the advice — the customer. In assurance services, there are typically three parties involved: (1) the person or group directly involved with the process, system, or other subject matter — the client, (2) the person or group making the independent assessment — the internal auditor, and (3) the person or group relying on the independent assessment — the user. Exhibit 3-2 shows some differences in the characteristics of assurance and consulting internal audit services.

This structural difference is critical to the need for standards in the delivery of the respective services. In consulting, the internal audit service provider typically has direct contact with an identifiable customer from the start of discussion of the potential engagement. Thus, the two parties are able to work together to assess and tailor the work to the customer's needs. The work product is advice and recommendations, which ultimately may or may not be followed by the customer.

However, in assurance services the relationships are different and more complex. First, the service is an independent assessment, not just advice. Users are expecting an objective assessment, a higher standard than consulting advice. Second, often key parties using the internal auditors' assessment, such as the audit committee, are remote from any direct involvement with the audit engagement and rely on the auditors' work without any direct involvement. Accordingly, the expectations of these parties must be protected if the service is to meet their needs effectively. Because certain of the client's interests may have actual or potential conflicts with the interests of the users, it is critical that the provider of assurance services ensure that the nature and scope of the engagement and the reporting of the results are appropriate. Many of the attributes and practices required by the *Standards* and code of conduct are particularly concerned with keeping the interests of assurance service providers and third-party users aligned. Because of this issue, we find considerably more stringent requirements and number of implementation standards for the delivery of assurance as compared to consulting services.

Ensuring Internal Auditing Maintains Its Objectivity and Independence

In some organizations, concerns of external regulators or of the organization's board about maintaining objectivity and independence have resulted in strictly limiting the level of consulting services that internal auditors may perform. This has particularly been the case for internal audit functions in governmental organizations.

Two key elements of ensuring that by providing consulting services internal auditors do not impair their ability to perform internal audit activities effectively in the future are:[3]

- Ensuring internal auditing does not assume management responsibilities. Internal auditors should not make ultimate decisions or execute transactions as if they were part of management. This element is highlighted in the *Standards* in the Glossary definition of consulting services, where it is emphasized that in any of the examples of consulting services properly provided by internal auditing, they are provided *without the internal auditor assuming management responsibility.*

- Ensuring that internal auditors do not audit their own work. Application of this principle requires some judgment, as the prohibition is not life-long. The restriction is not over internal auditing providing consulting services, but rather over assurance services. While there is no explicit rule in the *Standards*, Standard 1130.A1 notes that objectivity is presumed to be impaired if internal auditors *provide assurance services for an activity for which they had responsibility within the previous year.* While providing advice is not as significant as having management responsibility, the consideration of objectivity given past roles of the internal auditors is important. Yet, internal auditors are allowed to provide assurance services to an activity even if they previously provided assurance services over the same activity.

You can see that judgment is required to ensure that the objectivity is maintained. One way the *Standards* ensure there is complete transparency of internal auditing's past roles in serving the organization is by requiring in Standard 1130 that *if independence or objectivity is impaired in fact or appearance, the details of the impairment must be disclosed to appropriate parties.*

Internal auditors should be independent and avoid relationships and situations that compromise their objectivity. In addition to the two core elements above, other threats to auditor independence have been identified, including the conduct of nonaudit (consulting) work that:

- Creates a mutuality of interest; or
- Places internal auditors in the role of advocate for the organization.

To address the expectations of the organization as to the internal auditor's role in consulting, Standard 1000.C1 requires that *the nature of consulting services must be defined in the internal audit charter.*

The internal audit activity should make sure it takes appropriate steps to avoid potential compromises. For example, providing advice on appropriate controls during system design with the clear understanding that management has responsibility for accepting or rejecting the advice would have a limited impact on the auditor's objectivity toward that system in the future. By contrast, if the auditor led the system design team, decided which controls to select, or oversaw the implementation of the recommended controls, the auditor's future ability to objectively evaluate that system would be significantly impaired. However, other nonaudit assignments may not be as clear-cut.

The internal audit function can implement a number of controls that assist in reducing the potential for consulting projects to compromise objectivity of individual auditors, or the independence of the audit function as a whole, and provide the following example of techniques:

a.   Charter language defining consulting service parameters.

b.   Policies and procedures limiting type, nature, and/or level of participation in consulting projects (Exhibit 3-3 provides examples of sample policies).

c.   Use of a screening process for consulting projects, with limits on accepting engagements that might threaten objectivity.

d.   Segregation of consulting units from units conducting assurance engagements within the same audit function.

e.   Rotation of auditors on engagements.

f.   Employing outside providers for carrying out consulting engagements, or for conducting assurance engagements in activities where the audit function's prior involvement in consulting work has been determined to impair objectivity/independence.

g.   Disclosure in audit reports where objectivity may be impaired by participation in a prior consulting project.

Maintaining the balance between consulting and assurance activities and internal audit objectivity is the CAE's responsibility. The CAE should periodically review the nature of the activities and the level of internal audit resources involved with senior management and the audit committee to ensure that there is continued agreement on the focus and balance of these activities. A discussion on this topic may fit well as part of the periodic review of the charter of the audit department.

Reporting on Consulting — the Internal Auditor's Continued Alertness to Risk

While internal auditors on consulting engagements are tasked with serving the needs of the process owner, generally without an expectation of communication being necessary to other users such as the audit committee, there are elements of the internal auditors' role that result in their always needing to be alert to governance, risk management, or control issues that may arise during the engagement. When such issues are significant to the organization, internal auditors must *communicate the issues to senior management and the board* (2440.C2).

Blended Engagements

Another issue involves determining how best to provide consulting services to the organization. In some environments and situations, it may be appropriate to conduct a "blended" engagement that incorporates aspects of both consulting and assurance activities into one consolidated method.[4] Other circumstances may render it necessary to distinguish between the assurance and consulting elements of the engagement, in which case *a specific written understanding as to the objectives, scope, respective responsibilities, and other expectations should be reached and the results of the consulting engagement communicated in accordance with consulting standards* (2220.A2). If the decision is made to consolidate engagements, the audit team must take care to follow the standards for assurance work for those engagements. Exhibit 3-4 provides a framework that can guide the audit team in conducting these blended engagements while protecting the interests of each stakeholder in the engagement. Protecting the interests of assurance customers in these blended engagements will usually necessitate the full engagement to be conducted as an assurance engagement even if a significant consulting component is present.

Some would note that nearly every internal audit engagement has some elements of consulting and nearly all consulting engagements provide at least some degree of assurance. This is clearly recognized in the Internal Audit Value Proposition. In providing assurance, most internal audit groups, to generate appropriate action to address issues, go beyond simply factually stating that operations are or are not working as intended. They also make recommendations and discuss options with process owners as to how the issue can be addressed based on the experience and expertise of internal auditors. While not taking responsibility for the solution, internal auditors frequently suggest solutions during engagements (including assurance engagements), going beyond core assurance. This is clearly what the Value Proposition has in mind by the term "Insight," providing a catalyst for change through the assessments and analyses made by the internal audit engagement team. Similarly in performing consulting engagements, the audit team obtains some limited assurance regarding the management of risks for the area in which the consulting is conducted, which can be of use to the audit function in fulfilling its assurance service responsibilities.

Therefore, even those who are sensitive to the potential threat to independence and objectivity from consulting often are not suggesting internal auditors should stay silent when they can provide advice on the right way to address the issue to help the organization. From this view, the role of internal auditing in providing both assurance and consulting services may be viewed more as a continuum rather than two discrete sets of services.

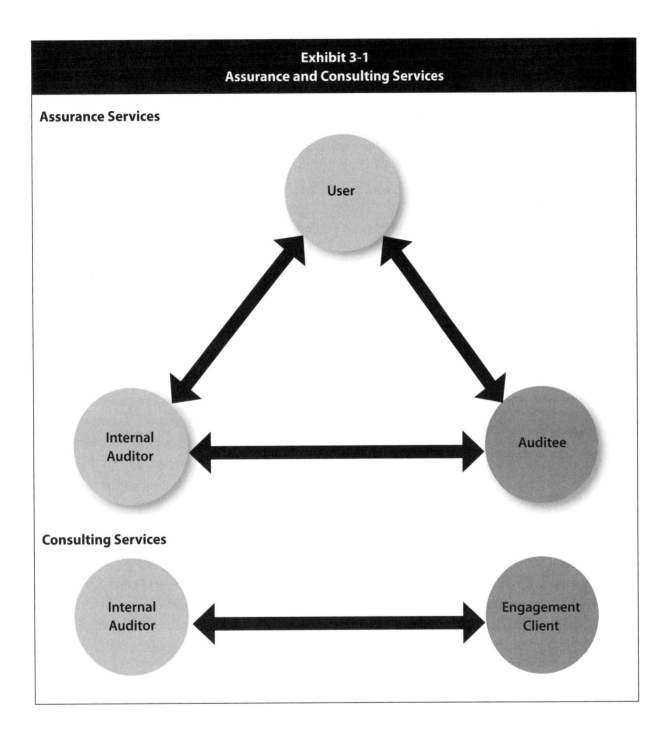

Exhibit 3-1
Assurance and Consulting Services

Assurance Services

User

Internal Auditor

Auditee

Consulting Services

Internal Auditor

Engagement Client

**Exhibit 3-2
Assurance or Consulting?**

Assurance

Assurance involves:

- The auditor, the process owner/activity manager, and the third party to whom assurance is being provided.

Assurance assesses:

- Adequacy of entity internal control.
- Adequacy of process or sub-entity internal control.
- Adequacy of enterprise risk management.
- Adequacy of governance process.
- Compliance with laws or regulations.

The client may be:

- Internal — the board, senior management, the audit committee.
- External — customers, shareholders, regulators, stakeholders.

Results are:

- An "opinion," if appropriate.
- Formal and explicit.
- Reported to the third party (mandatory).
- Followed up on (mandatory).

Assurance work is:

- Mandatory for the internal audit activity — full competence is either present in the audit staff or acquired from outside parties.

Consulting

Consulting involves:

- The auditor and the client.

Consulting provides:

- Improvement of efficiency or effectiveness.
- Assistance in design of corrective actions.
- Controls needed for new systems design.
- Benchmarking.
- Similar services requested due to internal auditing's skill sets.

The client usually is:

- Operating management.

Exhibit 3-2 (continued)
Assurance or Consulting?

Results are:

- A recommendation.
- Often informal.
- Reported as agreed upon with client.
- Followed up on to the extent specified in the consulting arrangement.

Consulting work is:

- Optional — The engagement can be declined if competencies required to perform the engagement are not present in the audit staff.

Exhibit 3-3
Sample Policies for Consulting Services

Example A: The following draft policy statement for consulting services was developed by the internal audit department at a governmental entity. The policy provides a useful model for other audit activities attempting to codify their approach to consulting work.

Acceptance of Consulting Engagements

1. Some consulting projects are specifically identified in the board-approved annual plan. For these projects, the CAE will collaborate with appropriate managers to develop a preliminary statement of work to be performed. This statement will include a general description of work, estimated hours, and projected time frame.

2. Most consulting projects are initiated by managers communicating directly with the CAE. For these requests, the CAE will:

   - Collaborate with managers to develop a preliminary statement of work to be performed. The statement will include a general description of work, estimated hours, and projected time frame.
   - Evaluate whether the internal audit team can perform the work. Considerations include:
     - Knowledge, skills, and disciplines of auditors.
     - Expected resource commitment.
     - Risk of activities.
     - Impact on the audit activity's independence and objectivity.
     - Other appropriate considerations.
   - If the evaluation reveals that the audit activity can perform the work, the CAE will seek senior management approval for the request.
   - If the evaluation reveals that the audit activity should not perform the work, the CAE will notify the appropriate managers. The CAE will also discuss options, such as assisting with the selection of outside consultants.

Exhibit 3-3 (continued)
Sample Policies for Consulting Services

Determining the Approach

Using the preliminary statement of work, the CAE will determine the model that will be used to conduct the work. There are two possible models:

- Assurance Model — Using this model, the consulting project will be performed using the already established standards, policies, and procedures that apply to any audit. The decision to use the assurance model is based on several factors, including:
  - Will project objectives or sub-objectives be determined using a risk/vulnerability assessment?
  - Are resources for the project primarily under the internal audit activity's control?
  - Will at least 80 hours of internal auditing's time be required for the project?
  - Will preparing the report be primarily the responsibility of the CAE?
  - Does the work easily fit into the survey/fieldwork/reporting paradigm?
- Consulting Model — The consulting model is used for requests that do not fit the assurance model. Under the review model, the consulting project is performed using policies and procedures that differ from those used in a traditional audit.

Procedures for the Consulting Model

1. When the internal audit commitment totals 40 or more hours:
    - A project file will be maintained. This file should contain documents such as the preliminary statement of work, meeting agendas, status reports, notes, and other pertinent information.
    - Internal audit staff assigned to the project should document their work as appropriate.
    - Internal audit staff will obtain background information concerning the area in which the work will be performed.
    - Internal audit staff assigned to the project will prepare a memo, which requires the signatures of the assigned staff and the CAE. The memo should provide a general description of the project, including:
      - A revised statement of work, if necessary.
      - Summary of background information.
      - Revised estimates of hours and time frame, if necessary.
      - Description of methodologies and types of evidence to be used.
      - Expected impact of work; for example, expected impact on control activities.
      - Other information as appropriate.
    - Periodic status reports will be prepared according to a schedule agreed upon by the assigned staff and CAE. However, status reports will be prepared at least every three months.

Exhibit 3-3 (continued)
Sample Policies for Consulting Services

- At the end of the project, internal audit staff assigned to the project will prepare a closeout memo. The memo will be reviewed by the CAE and should contain:
  - Discussion of the actual objective if significantly different from the preliminary description of work.
  - Description of scope and methodologies used.
  - Discussion of benefits that resulted from the project.
  - Discussion of any information that can be used in the annual risk assessment.
  - Conclusions, if any, that can be based on work performed.
  - Impact of the project on internal auditing's independence and objectivity.
  - Impact on the objectivity of the staff assigned to the project.
  - Other information as appropriate.
- If issued, any final report or memo will be included in the project file.
- When completed, the project file will be stored in the internal audit activity's workpaper files in order of its assigned project number.

2. When the audit commitment totals less than 40 hours:
  - A project file will be maintained. This file should contain documents such as the preliminary statement of work, meeting agendas, notes, and other pertinent information.
  - Internal audit staff assigned to the project should document their work as appropriate.
  - At the end of the project, internal audit staff assigned to the project will prepare a closeout memo, which includes:
    - Discussion of the original and actual objectives, if significantly different.
    - Discussion of benefits that resulted from the project.
    - Discussion of any information that can be used in the annual risk assessment.
    - Impact of the project on internal auditors' independence and objectivity.
    - Impact on the objectivity of the staff assigned to the project.
    - Other information as appropriate.
  - The closeout memo will be reviewed by the CAE and included in the project file.
  - If issued, any final report or memo will be included in the project file.
  - When completed, the project file will be stored in the internal audit activity's workpaper files in order of its assigned project number.

| **Exhibit 3-3 (continued)** |
| **Sample Policies for Consulting Services** |

Example B: The example policy and procedure below describes consulting services and includes language that limits the services to within parameters that minimize threats to objectivity and independence of the auditors.

Policy

In addition to audit services, internal auditors provide three other types of services to managers of the organization: Quality assurance services for projects in process, consulting services and training, and control self-assessment facilitated workshops. Parameters for each type of service are detailed below.

Quality Assurance Services

In providing quality assurance services, internal auditing will monitor and assist ongoing projects by assessing whether: project objectives will be achieved and are reasonable; all options have been identified and thoroughly analyzed; quantitative and qualitative analyses are complete and accurate; a project plan has been established and project staff are adhering to the plan; and best practices used by other parts of the organization to accomplish project objectives might be adopted in the organization.

Consulting Services and Training

Audit staff is available to provide assistance and training to the organization's staff in designing management accountability systems and reengineering operations. Audit staff is advisory only and management must accept responsibility for implementing any suggestions.

Control Self-assessment Facilitated Workshops

In this audit process an employee team meets with auditors to hold structured discussions on how to achieve its objectives in the most efficient and effective way. Action plans, rather than a formal audit report, are developed to address any obstacles to the objective(s). Employee team members are responsible for implementing action plan steps.

The example procedures below contain language that clarifies actions to be taken by the audit function when consulting engagements are accepted that threaten independence and objectivity on future assurance engagements.

When the audit function is requested by the audit committee to conduct consulting engagements that are determined by the CAE to impair the audit function's independence or an individual auditor's objectivity for conducting subsequent audit work, the following procedures will be carried out:

1. Before starting the nonaudit engagement, the CAE will communicate in writing with the audit committee that the requested engagement will impair independence or objectivity; describe the nature of the impairment; and indicate the consequences of the impairment for future audit engagements (e.g., that the audit function must decline future audits in the area, or the audit committee will need to contract with a third-party provider to conduct future audits). The CAE should request a response in writing from the audit committee, directing the audit function either to proceed with the nonaudit engagement or decline it.

Exhibit 3-3 (continued)
Sample Policies for Consulting Services

---

2. If the audit committee directs the audit function to proceed with the consulting engagement, the CAE will document the impairment in: the consulting engagement's documentation, with a copy to management responsible for the consulting engagement; the audit function's annual project planning procedures; and the audit function's communications with external quality assurance providers at its next quality assurance review. If the audit committee directs the audit function to conduct an audit that includes in its scope activities or operations that were part of a prior nonaudit engagement conducted by the audit function, about which the CAE previously determined that the nonaudit engagement would create an impairment for future audit work, the following procedures should be carried out:

    a. Before starting the audit engagement, the CAE will communicate in writing with the audit committee, provide notice and description of the impairment, and indicate options for carrying out the work with a maximum of objectivity (e.g., contracting with a third-party provider, or requesting the assistance of auditors from partner or regulatory entities).

    b. If the audit committee directs the audit function to proceed with the audit engagement, the CAE will document the impairment in the audit engagement's planning documentation and final report.

    c. In addition, the CAE shall disclose the occurrence and provide full documentation to the audit function's external quality assurance providers at its next quality assurance review.

Example C: The following draft policy's purpose is to document the internal auditors' rationale for providing consulting services and demonstrate their judgment that the services do not violate the core elements of the audit role. One example policy for screening follows:

1. Upon receipt of a request for consulting services, the internal audit department will consider whether providing such services would create a personal impairment either in fact or appearance that would adversely affect either the assigned auditor's objectivity or to the department's independence for conducting subsequent audits within the same area. If the engagement is determined to constitute an impairment to independence or objectivity, the request should be declined. If declined, the factors and final conclusion will be documented in a memorandum addressed to the requestor of the services.

2. Before performing consulting services, the auditor in charge will document an understanding with the requestor(s) that the requestor(s) is responsible for the outcome of the work and therefore has a responsibility to be in a position in fact and appearance to make an informed judgment on the results of the consulting work. The internal audit department will establish an agreement with the requestor(s) concerning the objective, scope, and limitations imposed on the consulting engagement services.

Source: Materials supplied by Colleen Waring and Mark Higdon from The IIA's Austin Chapter and from suppressed PA 1000.C1-3: Additional Considerations for Consulting Engagements in Government Organizational Settings.

Exhibit 3-4 **Framework for Conducting Blended Engagements**
A PRINCIPLES-BASED FRAMEWORK

Definition

Blended engagement: An engagement that includes both an assurance component and a consulting component.

Defining Characteristics

1. The objectives of both components are formalized at the beginning of the engagement. The consulting objectives are more likely to evolve during the engagement than the assurance objectives.

2. The scope of the assurance component is determined by the internal audit function; the scope of the consulting component is agreed on with the customer.

3. The two components focus on the same business process (or function, system, etc).

4. Assurance results are communicated to the process owner and applicable users. Consulting results are communicated only to the customer and parties approved by the customer unless the internal auditor identifies significant issues that must be communicated to senior management and the board.

Guiding Principles

1. **Point of View:** Each stakeholder in the blended engagement process may have a different perspective on how the services provided by the internal audit function will add value and improve the organization's operations. The "point of view" of the auditor, process owner, customer, and users must be synthesized.

2. **Standards:** Both the assurance component and the consulting component must be performed in accordance with The IIA's Attribute and Performance Standards. In addition, each component must be performed in accordance with the applicable IIA Implementation Standards.

3. **Scope:** The process owner and customer must clearly understand the scope of the engagement and the specific assurance and consulting services to be provided.

4. **Communication:** The process owner, customer, user, and internal auditor must all agree on how and in what form the results of the engagement will be communicated:
    *   *The internal auditor must ensure that assurance and consulting results are clearly delineated.*
    *   *The assurance results must be communicated in accordance with the protocol established by the internal audit function, senior management, and the board.*
    *   *The Internal auditor must ensure that the process owner and customer know when assurance results will be relied on by users.*
    *   *The internal auditor must ensure that the customer authorizes consulting results to be shared with other parties.*

Exhibit 3-4 (continued)
Framework for Conducting Blended Engagements

5. **Independence and Objectivity:** The internal audit function must ensure that neither independence nor objectivity is compromised on subsequent assurance and consulting engagements in areas of the organization that have been subject to a blended engagement.

6. **Proficiency:** The audit team performing a blended engagement must collectively possess the knowledge, skills, and other competencies needed to successfully complete both the assurance component and the consulting component of the engagement.

7. **Due Professional Care:** Internal auditors must exercise due professional care when performing a blended engagement. They must, for example, give due consideration to the relative complexity and extent of work needed to achieve both the assurance and consulting objectives of the engagement and the nature and timing of assurance and consulting communications.

Source: Head, Michael, Kurt Reding, and Cris Riddle, "Blended Engagements," *Internal Auditor* (October 2010), pp. 40–44.

References

[1] *A Vision for the Future: Professional Practices Framework for Internal Auditing* (Altamonte Springs, FL: The Institute of Internal Auditors, 1999), pp. 79–81.

[2] Roth, James, *Adding Value: Seven Roads to Success* (Altamonte Springs, FL: The Institute of Internal Auditors, 2002), pp. 168–169.

[3] These two principles are incorporated in section 3.22 of *Government Auditing Standards*, July 2007 Revision (GAO-07-731G).

[4] Head, Michael, Kurt Reding, and Cris Riddle, "Blended Engagements," *Internal Auditor* (October 2010), pp. 40–44.

Chapter 4

YOU MUST HAVE A BOARD-APPROVED CHARTER (1000-1010)

The purpose, authority, and responsibility of the internal audit activity must be formally defined in an internal audit charter, consistent with the Definition of Internal Auditing, the Code of Ethics, and the Standards. *The chief audit executive must periodically review the internal audit charter and present it to senior management and the board for approval* (1000). In using the term "board," the *Standards*, and thus this handbook, are referring to the designated governing body of an organization, such as the board of directors, the audit committee of the board, a supervisory board, the head of an agency, a legislative body, or the board of governors or trustees of a nonprofit organization to whom internal auditors functionally report.

To be "consistent with the Definition of Internal Auditing, the Code of Ethics, and the *Standards*," the charter's tenets must not contradict or conflict with the various requirements of the *Standards*. For example, the charter must indicate the need for independence and objectivity, as discussed in the 1100 series of standards. Including in the charter the requirement that the CAE must confirm annually to the audit committee the organizational independence of the internal audit activity (1100) is another example of how to align the charter with the *Standards*.

If the charter outlines how the internal audit activity fits into the organizational structure, it should follow Standard 1110, which states that the CAE must report to a level within the organization that allows the internal audit activity to fulfill its responsibilities (see Chapter 5). It is also appropriate to include that the CAE reports functionally to the audit committee, and what this functional reporting line means. The Interpretation to 1110 notes that examples of internal auditing's functional reporting include the audit committee:

- Approving the internal audit charter.
- Approving the risk-based internal audit plan.
- Receiving communications from the CAE on the internal audit activity's performance relative to its plan and other matters.
- Approving decisions regarding the appointment and removal of the CAE.
- Making appropriate inquiries of management and the CAE to determine whether there are inappropriate scope or resource limitations.

The charter may include requirements such as that the CAE be an officer of the organization, and that the audit committee be involved in the CAE's performance evaluation and compensation decisions.

Standard 1000 requires that the internal audit charter be periodically reviewed and presented to senior management and the audit committee for approval. Use of the phrase "periodically" provides some flexibility in the frequency of review and approval. Many CAEs review and ask for approval of the internal audit charter annually, often in alignment with the requirement for many organizations that the audit committee's charter be reviewed and approved annually. While the approval comes from both senior management and the audit committee, the Interpretation to Standard 1000 makes clear that final approval resides with the audit committee.

Internal audit shops need to ensure their charter reflects the tenets of internal audit practice as outlined in the definition and in the 2000 and 2100 series of standard's describing the managing and nature of internal audit work. *All charters, therefore, should describe internal auditing's purpose in terms of:*

- *Adding value to the organization.*
- *Improving the organization's operations.*
- *Improving the effectiveness and efficiency of risk management, control, and governance processes.*

According to the Interpretation to Standard 1000, the charter also:

- *Is formally documented.*
- *Establishes the internal audit activity's position within the organization.*
- *Authorizes access to records, personnel, and physical properties relevant to the performance of engagements.*
- *Defines the scope of internal audit activities.*

Two Implementation Standards require *the nature of assurance and consulting services provided to the organization to be defined in the audit charter* (1000.A1 and 1000.C1). It is essential that the board and senior management be made aware of and authorize the kinds of work internal auditors are performing.

It is often appropriate for the CAE to confirm that the audit committee understands and approves the consulting concept before offering such services. Some find the use of the word "advisory" to be more appropriate than "consulting" in the discussion. The charter should reflect the results of this discussion and the direction of senior management and the audit committee. The charter should be clear regarding authority and responsibilities for consulting activities, and the internal audit activity should consider the types of consulting activities to be offered and develop appropriate policies and procedures for conducting such engagements. Sample categories used by organizations to describe the types of consulting services they perform are shown in Exhibit 4-1. Exhibit 4-2's example internal audit charter also has example wording for internal audit consulting.

The *Standards* further mandate that *the nature of assurances provided to parties outside the organization also be defined in the charter* (1000.A1). Suppliers and joint venture partners, for example, are increasingly requesting the opportunity to review internal audit reports as part of their decision-making and due diligence processes. Providing such assurance to outside parties can create additional liability exposures for the organization, and the audit committee should know when such activity is taking place.

While not explicitly required by the *Standards*, the audit charter should include expectations of stakeholders, most importantly the board/audit committee. It should be aligned with the audit committee charter, particularly when the audit committee charter has certain expectations of internal auditing.

The internal audit charter is an important document, since it helps direct the efforts of the audit staff and defines what the board and senior management can and do expect from the audit activity. As a result, much care should be taken when reviewing and updating it. The revision process presents an ideal opportunity for CAEs to introduce new concepts that may need to be negotiated with senior management and the audit committee.

The internal audit charter should of course be consistent with the discussion of internal auditing found in the organization's audit committee charter. While the discussion of internal auditing in the audit committee charter varies across organizations, Exhibit 4-3 provides an example of suggested wording.

The *Standards* state that *the mandatory nature of the Definition of Internal Auditing, the Code of Ethics, and the* Standards *must be recognized in the internal audit charter. The chief audit executive should discuss the Definition of Internal Auditing, the Code of Ethics, and the* Standards *with senior management and the board* (1010). If not already done, the CAE should consider scheduling time with the audit committee to discuss the mandatory elements of the IPPF as well as changes, particularly revisions of the *Standards* that impact internal auditing's role or its communications with the audit committee.

The periodic review of the internal audit charter provides a good opportunity for discussion of expectations for the role of internal auditing. This includes revalidating internal auditing's role in providing fundamental assurance activities, as well as discussing existing and potential proposed use of internal audit resources for consulting and advisory activities. Further impacts of changes in business risks or regulatory requirements impacting internal auditing's role, such as internal auditing's responsibilities related to the U.S. Sarbanes-Oxley Act internal controls compliance, if applicable, as well as internal auditing's role related to sustainability reporting and other external reporting of key nonfinancial information.

A sample charter that complies with the *Standards* is shown in Exhibit 4-2. Your actual charter should be reflective of actual expectations and practices. By comparing existing charters with this example, internal audit staffs may identify specific additions, deletions, or other modifications that they may need to make.

Exhibit 4-1
Types of Consulting Work

Sample categories used by organizations to describe the types of consulting work they provide include:

- Formal engagements — those that are planned and subject to written agreement.

- Informal engagements — routine activities such as participation on standing committees, limited-life projects, ad hoc meetings, and routine information exchange.

- Special engagements — participation on dedicated teams such as a mergers and acquisitions team or system conversion team.

- Emergency engagements — participation on a team established for recovery or maintenance of operations after a disaster or other extraordinary business event, or a team assembled to supply temporary help to meet a special request or unusual deadline.

- Assessment services — the timely examination of a past, present, or future aspect of operations that renders information to assist management in making decisions. Examples include estimating savings from outsourcing processes or assessing the adequacy of internal controls over proposed systems.

- Facilitation services — assistance to management in the examination of organizational performance for the purpose of promoting change by helping management to identify organizational strengths and opportunities for improvement. Examples include control self-assessment, benchmarking, strategic planning support, and business process reengineering support.

- Remediation services — the assumption of a direct role designed to prevent or remediate known or suspected problems on behalf of clients. Examples include developing and delivering training courses on risk management, internal controls, regulatory compliance, etc; drafting proposed policies; and augmenting operating personnel.

Source: From the U.S. Department of Agriculture Graduate School Model.

Exhibit 4-2
Sample Internal Audit Charter

Mission and Scope of Work

The mission of the internal audit department is to provide independent, objective assurance and consulting services designed to add value and improve the organization's operations. It helps the organization accomplish its objectives by bringing a systematic, disciplined approach to evaluate and improve the effectiveness of governance, risk management, and control processes.

The scope of work of the internal audit department is to determine whether the organization's network of governance, risk management, and control processes, as designed and represented by management, is adequate and functioning in a manner to ensure:

- Risks are appropriately identified and managed.
- Interaction with the various governance groups occurs as needed.
- Significant financial, managerial, and operating information is accurate, reliable, and timely.
- Employees' actions are in compliance with policies, standards, procedures, and applicable laws and regulations.
- Interactions and arrangements with third parties, including contractors and joint ventures, are in compliance with policies, standards, procedures, and applicable laws and regulations.
- Resources are acquired economically, used efficiently, and adequately protected.
- Programs, plans, and objectives are achieved.
- Quality and continuous improvement are fostered in the organization's control process.
- Legislative or regulatory compliance issues impacting the organization are recognized and addressed appropriately.

Additional consulting services may be provided where consistent with the mission of the internal audit department. Such consulting services will generally be related to assessing the impact of changes being considered or implemented in the organization's risk management, control, and governance processes.

Opportunities for improving management control, profitability, and the organization's image may be identified during audits. They will be communicated to the appropriate level of management.

Accountability

The chief audit executive (CAE), in the discharge of his/her duties, shall be accountable to management and the audit committee to:

- Provide coverage of the adequacy and effectiveness of the organization's processes for controlling its activities and managing its risks in the areas set forth under the mission and scope of work.
- Report important issues related to the processes for managing risk and controlling the activities of the organization and its affiliates, including potential improvements to those processes, and provide information concerning such issues through resolution. This includes coverage of risk management and governance practices.

**Exhibit 4-2 (continued)
Sample Internal Audit Charter**

- Periodically provide information on the status and results of the annual audit plan and the sufficiency of department resources. This includes ensuring the resources are sufficient in amount and competency, through in-house staff and co-sourcing, to cover the risks in the annual audit plan.
- Coordinate with and provide coverage of other control and monitoring functions (risk management, governance, compliance, security, legal, ethics, environmental) and the external audit.
- Establish a follow-up process to track and monitor the effective implementation of management actions related to important issues and recommendations.

Independence and Objectivity

To provide for the organizational independence of the internal audit department and the objectivity of its personnel, internal audit personnel report to the CAE, who reports functionally to the audit committee and administratively to the CEO. The CAE shall be an officer of the organization. Internal auditing will include as part of its reports to the audit committee a report annually on the independence of internal auditing and any unwarranted restrictions on internal audit scope, communications, access, and resources, including personnel and externally contracted resources.

Because of the importance of audit committee visibility to internal auditing to support independence and objectivity of the internal audit activity, the audit committee should be involved in:

- Approving the internal audit charter.
- Approving the risk-based internal audit plan.
- Receiving communications from the CAE on the internal audit department's performance relative to its plan and other matters.
- Approving decisions regarding the appointment and removal of the CAE.
- Conducting the CAE's performance evaluation and deciding compensation.
- Making appropriate inquiries of management and the CAE to determine whether there are inappropriate scope or resource limitations.

Responsibility

The CAE has the responsibility to:
- Develop a flexible annual audit plan using an appropriate risk-based methodology, including any risks or control concerns identified by management, and submit that plan along with any subsequent periodic changes to senior management and the audit committee for review and approval.
- Align internal audit coverage with the organization's strategic, operational, compliance, and financial risks, including important areas of emerging risk.

| **Exhibit 4-2 (continued)** |
| **Sample Internal Audit Charter** |

- Implement the annual audit plan, as approved, including, as appropriate, special tasks or projects requested by management and the audit committee.
- Maintain professional internal audit resources with internal audit staff and, where appropriate, other internal or external resources with sufficient knowledge, skills, experience, and professional certifications to meet the requirements of this charter.
- Evaluate and assess important merging/consolidating functions and new or changing services, business units, processes, systems, operations, and control processes coincident with their development, implementation, and/or expansion.
- Issue periodic reports to the audit committee and management summarizing results of audit activities.
- Keep the audit committee informed of emerging trends and successful practices in internal auditing.
- Provide internal audit measurement goals and results to the audit committee.
- Assist as appropriate in the investigation of suspected fraudulent activities within the organization and notify management and the audit committee of the results.
- Consider the scope of work of the external auditors and regulators, as appropriate, for the purpose of providing optimal audit coverage to the organization at a reasonable overall cost.
- As appropriate, provide consulting and advisory services to management that add value and improve an organization's governance, risk management, and control processes without the internal auditor assuming management responsibility.
- Execute a quality assurance and improvement program by which the CAE assures effective operation of internal audit activities and annually report the results of the program to the audit committee.

Authority

The CAE is authorized to:
- Ensure the internal audit personnel and contracted resources have unrestricted access to all functions, records, property, and personnel.
- Have full and free access to the audit committee.
- Allocate resources, set frequencies, select subjects, determine scope of work, and apply the techniques required to accomplish audit objectives.
- Obtain the necessary assistance of personnel in units of the organization or those contracting with the organization where they perform audits, as well as other specialized services from within or outside the organization.
- Provide consulting services to management as deemed appropriate.

Exhibit 4-2 (continued)
Sample Internal Audit Charter

The CAE and internal audit personnel are not authorized to:

- Perform any operational duties for the organization or its affiliates.
- Initiate or approve accounting transactions external to the internal audit department.
- Direct the activities of any organization employee not employed by the internal audit department, except to the extent such employees have been appropriately assigned to internal audit teams or to otherwise assist the internal auditors.

Standards of Internal Auditing

The internal audit profession is covered by the International Professional Practices Framework of The Institute of Internal Auditors. This framework includes mandatory elements consisting of the Definition of Internal Auditing, the Code of Ethics, and the *International Standards for the Professional Practice of Internal Auditing*. The internal audit department will meet or exceed these mandatory requirements of the profession.

The CAE will annually discuss with the audit committee the results of the internal audit quality assurance and improvement program by which the CAE assures effective operation of internal audit activities.

_____

Chief Audit Executive

_____

Chief Executive Officer

_____

Audit Committee Chair   Date

Exhibit 4-3
Audit Committee Charter: Suggested Wording Related to Internal Auditing

Purpose

The Audit Committee ("Committee") shall assist the Board of Directors (the "Board") in the oversight of the performance of the Company's internal audit function.

The Committee shall provide a forum for communication among the independent auditor, the internal audit function, management, and the Board.

Authority and Responsibilities

The Committee shall provide assistance to the Board in fulfilling its oversight responsibility to the shareholders relating to the internal audit function.

The Committee shall maintain free and open communication with the internal auditors.

Statement of Processes

The following shall be the principal recurring processes of the Committee in fulfilling its responsibilities:

a.   The Committee shall ensure that the Company establishes, resources, and maintains a professional internal audit function to serve the interests of the Committee, the Board, and the Company.

b.   The Committee shall review and approve annually the Internal Audit Charter.

c.   The Committee shall review with management and the senior internal audit executive the internal audit risk assessment, internal audit plan, and annual budget of the internal audit function, including adequacy of its budget, internal and external resources, and compensation.

d.   Regarding structural objectivity and stature of internal auditing, the senior internal audit executive officer shall be an officer of the Company and report directly to the chair of the Committee and to the Chief Executive Officer of the Company.

e.   The Committee shall ensure there are no unjustified scope or resource restrictions or limitations on the internal audit function.

f.   The Committee shall review and approve the following activities relating to the senior internal audit executive: (a) appointment, replacement, or dismissal, and (b) performance appraisals along with related base and incentive compensation.

g.   The Committee shall review the effectiveness of the internal audit activity, including conformance with The Institute of Internal Auditors' *International Standards for the Professional Practice of Internal Auditing*.

Exhibit 4-3 (continued)
Audit Committee Charter: Suggested Wording Related to Internal Auditing

h.   The Committee shall receive from the senior internal audit executive reports on the internal audit activity's performance relative to its plan, important observations, and recommendations. The Committee shall review with the senior internal audit executive management's response and status of action on important internal audit recommendations.

i.   The Committee shall meet separately with the senior internal audit executive at least quarterly to discuss any matters that the Committee or the senior internal audit executive believes should be discussed privately.

j.   The Committee shall discuss with management, the internal auditors, and the independent registered public accounting firm the adequacy and effectiveness of the accounting and financial controls, including the Company's system to monitor and manage business risk, and legal and ethical compliance programs.

k.   The Committee shall obtain reports from management, the Company's senior internal audit executive, and the independent auditors concerning whether the Company and its subsidiary/ foreign affiliated entities are in conformity with applicable legal requirements and the Company's Code of Business Conduct.

Chapter 5

YOU MUST BE INDEPENDENT AS A FUNCTION AND OBJECTIVE AS AN AUDITOR (1100-1130)

Independence and objectivity refer to two distinct, yet related, concepts that are fundamental to the value of audit services. The IPPF and the Internal Audit Value Proposition (Exhibit 2-2) use the terms in a very precise manner that has evolved as the internal audit profession has developed. A research study sponsored by The IIA Research Foundation, *Independence and Objectivity: A Framework for Internal Auditors,* provided the profession with much needed clarity regarding these concepts.[1] Unfortunately, this precision is not always similar to the use of the terms in everyday language or even the use in much of the audit literature. However, to implement the IPPF effectively, it is essential to clearly understand these two concepts. Internal auditors still need to recognize that in external audit standards, and in other areas as well, the word *independence* is used with a different meaning and for different purposes.

Standard 1100 makes it clear that *the internal audit activity must be independent*, while *internal auditors must be objective*. This is a subtle, yet extremely important, distinction. Independence is viewed as an attribute of the audit function; whereas objectivity is an attribute of the individual auditor. The attribute of the internal audit function really relates to its organizational independence. At its most basic level, we are talking about independence as the ability to conduct internal audit activities without undue influence or control. Standard 1120 describes the attribute of the individual auditors and states that individual auditors achieve this objectivity when they *"have an impartial, unbiased attitude and avoid any conflict of interest."* The *Standards* reflect the notion found in the Research Foundation study that objectivity alone is what directly produces the value of the audit. The value that independence brings to the audit table is based on its creation of "an environment that maximizes the likelihood of auditor objectivity."[2] The fact that an internal auditor is an employee of an organization or has financial instruments or incentives does not in itself impact independence and objectivity.

In other words, in the audit environment depicted by the *Standards,* the Value Proposition, and related research, independence is significant because it gives the audit activity a level of autonomy that facilitates a major determinant of internal audit value — the individual auditor's objectivity. By acknowledging that it is the individual auditor's impartial state of mind that renders value to the audit product, not his or her abstinence from involvement in management and organizational activities, the internal audit team is free to assume a more proactive, preventive, and profitable role in the organization.

Ensuring Independence

Key to internal auditing's independence as described in the *Standards* is the appropriate placement and status of the internal audit activity. Standard 1110 states *"the CAE must report to a level that allows the internal audit activity to fulfill its responsibilities."* The Interpretation to 1100 notes that to have the degree of independence necessary, internal auditing needs to have direct and unrestricted access to senior management and the board. This can be achieved by a dual reporting relationship, administratively to senior management and functionally to the board.

Interpretation 1110 notes that organizational independence is achieved effectively when internal auditing reports directly to the board. The *Standards* do require that *the CAE must communicate and interact directly with the board* (1111). Direct communication occurs when the CAE attends and participates in board meetings. Benefits of attending these meetings also include that the CAE can absorb strategic business and operational developments as well as raise high-level risk, systems, procedures, or control issues at an early stage. Such communication and interaction occurs when the CAE meets privately with the board, at least annually (PA 1111-1). It is not unusual for these private meetings between the head of internal auditing and the board to be quarterly. Remember that this communication and interaction in most situations will be through the audit committee.

While no specific list of suitable administrative reporting structures within management is given in the *Standards*, common sense suggests that the higher the reporting level of the CAE, the more autonomous the activity will be. The IIA strongly believes that to achieve necessary independence, the CAE should report functionally to the audit committee and administratively to the CEO.

The Practice Advisories and the aforementioned Research Foundation report offer more specific guidance regarding effective positioning of the internal audit activity:

The Minimum
- At a minimum, the CAE should report to an individual in the organization with sufficient authority to promote independence and to ensure broad audit coverage, adequate consideration of engagement communications, and appropriate action on engagement recommendations (PA 1110-1).
- The CAE must communicate and interact directly with the audit committee, board of directors, or other appropriate governing authority (PA 1111).

The Ideal

The CAE reports:
- Functionally to the audit committee, board of directors, or other appropriate governing authority, and
- Administratively to the CEO of the organization (PA 1110-1).

Reporting Line
- As a general rule, the internal audit activity should be organized in a way that affords a higher organizational stature consistent with its role in assessing and improving the governance, risk management, and control of the organization. Functions with a narrowly defined role perhaps may report to an appropriate lower level of management, as long as the placement assures the audit team will obtain cooperation from the activity being reviewed and free access to required information.[3] In such situations, it will be important to ensure that appropriate visibility on issues and action on results occurs.

- Whatever the reporting level, internal auditors should have the support of senior management and the board so that they can gain the cooperation of engagement clients, perform their work without interference, provide broad audit coverage, receive adequate consideration of engagement communications, and have appropriate action on engagement recommendations result (PA 1110-1).

Enhancing Independence

- Independence, and therefore ultimately objectivity, is enhanced when the CAE reports functionally to the audit committee or board (Interpretation to 1110 and PA 1110-1). In this context, reporting functionally to the governing authority can include:
  - Giving the CAE unrestricted access to the governing authority.
  - Having private meetings between the audit committee and the CAE without management present.
  - Having the audit committee receive the CAE's annual confirmation of internal auditing's independence.
  - Approving the internal audit risk assessment and related audit plan.
  - Approving the internal audit charter.
  - Approving the risk-based internal audit plan.
  - Receiving communications from the CAE on the internal audit activity's performance relative to its plan and other matters. This includes receiving results of internal as well as external quality assessments of the internal audit activity.
  - Approving decisions regarding the appointment and removal of the CAE.
  - Making appropriate inquiries of management and the CAE to determine whether there are inappropriate scope or resource limitations.
  - Being involved in and approving performance evaluation of the CAE.
  - Approving the salary and annual compensation adjustment of the CAE.
  - Taking part in drafting, reviewing, and approving the internal audit charter.
  - Providing appropriate positive influence over the importance of, budget for, and scope of internal audit activities.
  - Exhibiting active involvement, oversight, review, and follow-up. (PA 1110-1)
- Administrative reporting to senior management typically includes:
  - Budgeting and management accounting.
  - Human resource administration, including personnel evaluations and compensation.
  - Internal communications and information flows.
  - Administration of the internal audit activity's policies and procedures. (PA 1110-1)

While much emphasis is put on the role of the audit committee in ensuring independence and objectivity of internal auditing, senior management also plays a major role in setting the tone and substance of the internal audit activity. Including the CAE in senior leadership team meetings, periodic one-on-one meetings, and periodic presentations to the senior leadership team by internal auditing is frequently seen in internal audit activities with the highest stature. Of course, this is a two-way street. When internal auditing is included in such activities, it must perform and communicate appropriately to earn the respect and appreciation of senior management.

Independence and Assurance

The organizational independence and autonomy of the internal audit activity is particularly important when providing assurance services. In these types of reviews, the auditor serves to protect the interests of the audit committee, senior management, or other outside parties who are relying on internal auditing's objective examination to make wise business decisions.

For non-assurance engagements, like consulting or control self-assessment facilitation, management of the activity under review is usually the driving force behind engagement decisions. Management often plays a crucial role in developing the scope and deciding how and what information is communicated. Management may even participate in performing the audit work.

Direct interference by management in decision-making over scoping in these areas is inappropriate, however, particularly when the goal is to provide assurance. When performing an assessment designed to assure absent, third-party customers of the quality and effectiveness of a particular area, Implementation Standard 1110.A1 specifies that *the internal audit activity must be free from interference in determining the scope of internal auditing, performing work, and communicating results.*

Allowing activity management to control which areas the auditors examine and what information they communicate in an assurance engagement represents a disservice to the individuals relying on the auditor's work, because the users of the auditor's work assume the auditor is making those determinations independently. Because they are not privy to the engagement interactions between auditor and client, they have no way of knowing the degree to which management has influenced the scope of the audit. Such management control fails to meet the needs of those seeking assurance and could cause users to make poor, possibly devastating, business decisions.

Confirming Independence to the Audit Committee

Independence is so fundamental to the unique nature of internal auditing that Standard 1110 states that *the CAE must confirm to the board, at least annually, the organizational independence of the internal audit activity.* Note that this requirement is similar to one that has emerged in places for external financial statement auditors to confirm annually their independence to the board. The CAE may find that it is appropriate to include the audit activity's independence confirmation as part of the audit committee's periodic review of the internal audit charter or in the audit committee communications package that covers other reports internal auditing makes to the audit committee on internal audit performance and on quality assurance and improvement activities.

Maintaining Objectivity

The *Standards* emphasis on objectivity should compel internal auditors and their managers to review the attributes that render someone objective. According to the Interpretation to Standard 1100, objectivity is *an unbiased mental attitude that allows internal auditors to perform engagements in such a manner that they believe in their work product and that no quality compromises have been made.* It also states that objectivity requires internal auditors not to subordinate their judgment on audit matters to others.

The study from The IIA Research Foundation describes objectivity as "a state of mind ... expressing or involving the use of facts without distortions by personal feelings or prejudices." It goes on to characterize objectivity in an audit situation to mean that "given appropriate audit scope and professionalism, relevant and sufficient evidential matter will be effectively analyzed and results will be completely and honestly reported to the appropriate parties, without the auditor's judgment being skewed."[4]

Maintaining this impartial state of mind and avoiding conflicts of interest is prerequisite to any value being gained from internal audit work. Without it, internal audit services may fail to render the reliable and trustworthy information that is needed by users of its services. Trust in the internal audit engagement results is fundamental to the perception by stakeholders of internal auditing's value. Fortunately, audit staffs can take several specific steps to help preserve objectivity, even in the most difficult situations:

Preserving Objectivity

- Internal auditors should not be placed in situations in which they feel unable to make objective professional judgments. (PA 1120-1)
- The CAE should periodically query the internal audit staff concerning potential conflicts of interest and bias and make staff assignments accordingly to avoid potential problems. (PA 1120-1)
- Staff assignments should be rotated periodically where practicable. (PA 1120-1)
- Audit results should be reviewed to provide reasonable assurance that the work was performed objectively before communications resulting from the engagement are released. (PA 1120-1)
- Internal auditors should not accept fees or gifts from employees, customers, suppliers, or business associates. To do so is considered unethical and may create the appearance of impaired objectivity. Internal auditors should report the receipt of all material fees or gifts immediately to their supervisors. (PA 1130-1)
- The internal audit activity should adopt a policy that addresses its commitment to conduct activities so as to avoid conflicts of interest and to disclose any activities that could result in a possible conflict of interest.
- People transitioning into internal auditing, or rotating through internal auditing, should not be auditing their prior area for at least a year from being in that area. (PA 1130.A1.1)

One strategy for an individual internal auditor to ensure he or she is acting objectively is to consult with others in internal auditing when addressing potentially sensitive areas. When more than one person is involved with decisions, the pressure on the individual can be decreased or dissipated.

Also key is remaining aware of potential threats to objectivity and employing mechanisms that defuse those threats. The following eight-phase process may help auditors proactively manage threats to objectivity.[5]

Managing Threats to Objectivity

The internal audit policy and procedures manual should specifically address identifying potential issues, policies, and how people should consult on this important topic. Some suggestions include:

1. **Identify the threat.** Any situation or circumstance that causes internal auditors to question their ability to act without bias must be identified as a threat. Identified threats should be conveyed to the unit or engagement manager so that he or she can proactively participate in the process of managing the threats. Seven categories of threats to auditor objectivity are shown in Exhibit 5-1.

2. **Assess the significance of the threat.** Internal auditors should determine the likelihood that the identified threats will compromise their objectivity and that seemingly insignificant threats could intensify during the conduct of the audit.

3. **Identify mitigating factors.** Specific mitigating factors present in the environment or inherent in the process that might alleviate the threats should be identified. A list of possible mitigating factors appears in Exhibit 5-2.

4. **Assess residual threat.** The auditor should determine whether the identified factors sufficiently mitigate the threats so that the assigned audit work can be performed without bias. If not, then residual threat exists. Blindly assuming that the factors have adequately mitigated all objectivity risk is a mistake. Instead, the auditor should consider whether the factors are effective enough that he or she can represent the customer's interests in spite of the existing threats. In cases of significant residual threats or where the auditor is uncertain about his or her objectivity, the assessment should be made or reviewed by the CAE and, when necessary, senior management or the audit committee. A tool for documenting this assessment can be found in Exhibit 5-3.

5. **Proactively manage residual threat.** Threats to objectivity that are not sufficiently offset by the inherent mitigating factors should be proactively managed. Several tools the audit team can use to manage residual threats are shown in Exhibit 5-4.

---

6. **Assess presence of unresolved threats.** As audit procedures are performed, the auditor should assess whether or not objectivity can in fact be achieved by considering any remaining threats that either were not previously identified or that could not be adequately resolved. If significant threats remain, the auditor and other appropriate parties should determine whether it is necessary or practical to continue with the audit. If the decision is made to continue despite unresolved threats to objectivity, reporting implications should be carefully considered.

7. **Consider the reporting and documentation implications.** It is recommended that identified mitigating factors and steps taken to manage threats be adequately documented to provide an accurate record of auditors' efforts to achieve objectivity. In the case where work continues in the presence of material, unresolved threats to objectivity, auditors should report the details of the situation to the appropriate level, such as senior management or the board, on a continuing or periodic basis. Unresolved threats should also be disclosed in final engagement communications.

8. **Perform ex post facto reviews and monitoring activities.** The individual auditor should conduct a self-review at the end of the engagement to determine whether judgments were made in the most objective manner possible. Questions could include "Do I honestly believe in the work I have produced? Did I make any quality compromises? Did I subordinate my judgment to others? Did my personal feelings play any part in my analysis and decisions?" The audit team should also perform a comprehensive analysis, and the CAE should examine the overall audit program for the time period in question to determine whether objectivity was effectively managed on every audit engagement. Evaluating whether staffing was appropriate, gauging the compatibility of accepted engagements with internal auditing's role in the organization, and monitoring the process for managing threats to objectivity are other key elements of the CAE's review effort. Internal and external quality assessment and improvement processes, as well as audit committees, can also be used for reviewing and monitoring purposes. The annual confirmation of the independence of the internal audit activity can help in the audit committee's monitoring.

The effectiveness of this process-based approach depends to a great extent on the professionalism of the audit team. Audit staffs should find the descriptions of the threats, mitigating factors, and threat management tools presented at the end of this chapter useful as they try to protect their audit decisions from bias and prejudice.

It should be noted, however, that the most crucial ingredient for ensuring auditor objectivity is the organizational independence of the internal audit activity. Organizational independence will not *guarantee* auditor objectivity, since someone could always choose to act inappropriately, regardless of the evidence presented during an engagement. But a lack of organizational independence will almost always make true objectivity impossible to achieve.

Dealing with Impairments

The *Standards* recognize that the expectations of and demands upon the internal audit activity may occasionally result in organizational independence and individual objectivity not being achieved, at least in appearance if not in fact. For example, internal auditors from small shops who have been involved in problem-solving or process improvement initiatives with line management may have little choice but to review areas for which they have had past operational input. Or, occasionally, the controls expertise of the audit staff might result in an auditor being asked to fill an operations role, such as that of treasurer, local unit controller, or accounts payable manager, until problems are corrected or a replacement is hired. Auditors may even be charged with developing operating policies and procedures, particularly in areas where controls are weak.

While such incidents are undesirable and should be avoided whenever possible, the *Standards* provide instructions for addressing these types of anomalies. First, *if independence or objectivity is impaired in fact or appearance, the details of the impairment must be disclosed to appropriate parties. The nature of the disclosure will depend upon the impairment* (1130). Such communication gives internal auditors the opportunity to perform the requested service and provide the needed audit information, but at the same time empowers the customers to determine for themselves whether or not to rely on the audit results. Disclosure statements also prevent users from unknowingly placing undue confidence in potentially biased audit findings.

The Interpretation to Standard 1130 states that impairment to objectivity and independence may include, but is not limited to, *personal conflict of interest; scope limitations; restrictions on access to records, personnel, and properties; and resource limitations, such as funding.* A sample statement disclosing an impairment is presented in the discussion on communicating impairments in Chapter 12.

The Implementation Standards for assurance and consulting services (1130.A1, 1130.A2, 1130.C1, and 1130.A2) further aid auditors in their efforts to address and report impairments to objectivity. When providing assurance to third parties, the *Standards* note that, while *internal auditors must refrain from assessing specific operations for which they were previously responsible, objectivity is presumed to be impaired if an internal auditor provides assurance services for an activity for which he or she had responsibility within the previous year* (1130.A1). If more than a year has passed, objectivity can be presumed to be intact unless evidence indicates otherwise.

In addition, independence and objectivity may be impaired if assurance services are provided within a period after a formal consulting engagement. Given the assurance standards in this area, a one-year period again may be reasonable for assessing potential objectivity issues. However, steps can be taken to minimize the effects of the impairment by assigning different auditors to perform each of the services, establishing independent management and supervision, defining separate accountability for the results of the projects, and disclosing the presumed impairment.

Exhibit 5-5 presents several guidelines that internal auditors should consider when asked to assume such responsibility for nonaudit work. In addition, PA 1130.A1-2 offers guidance to auditors who find themselves having responsibility for or being considered responsible for other nonaudit functions.

The *Standards* call for audits of any *functions over which the CAE has responsibility to be overseen by a party outside the internal audit activity* (1130.A2). One obvious solution is to use outside service providers to do any assurance work in these areas. In such a case, appropriate oversight of the engagement should be provided by an independent member of management, such as from human resources, the legal department, or even a member of the board. Alternatively, the audit staff could perform the assurance engagements in these areas. As in the case of the service provider, oversight should be provided by a member of management independent of the activity under review or a board member.

The *Standards* do allow *internal auditors to provide consulting services relating to operations for which they had previous responsibilities* (1130.C1). In fact, auditors possessing operational experience in an area may be best equipped to serve in a consulting capacity for that area. It is still necessary, however, to discuss the auditor's past history and potential participation on the engagement with the client before the work begins. *If internal auditors have any potential impairments to independence and objectivity relating to proposed consulting services, disclosure must be made to the engagement client prior to accepting the engagement* (1130.C2). Impairments that develop during the engagement should also be communicated promptly to management. For some, including some government organizations, internal auditors performing consulting services creates heightened awareness of potential objectivity and independence situations. Exhibit 5-6 provides guidance on addressing these situations.

Worth Ensuring

Given the auditor's growing sphere of influence in the organization, the significance of internal auditing's organizational independence and the individual objectivity it enables cannot be overlooked. If the internal audit function lacks sufficient organizational status and autonomy, its ability to manage conflicts of interest and generate objective work and communications is called into question. On the other hand, a properly positioned internal audit activity can offer individuals within and outside the organization objective, effective, and reliable information in which they can have unquestionable confidence.

Exhibit 5-1
Seven Threats to Objectivity

Audit staffs should consider the following threats to objectivity when planning an engagement. Applicable self-review questions have been added that can be used to identify potential threats.

1. Self-review

Self-review threats may arise when an auditor reviews his or her own work. For example, an auditor may audit a department repeatedly, reviewing operations in one year that were also reviewed in a prior year. The auditor may provide consulting services in connection with a system implementation that he or she must subsequently audit; or, the auditor may provide recommendations for operational improvements, and subsequently review the operations that were revised in accordance with those recommendations. All of these examples represent situations where the auditor could conceivably become less critical or observant of errors and deficiencies due to the difficulty of maintaining objectivity when reviewing one's own work.

Questions to ask include:

- *Did I ever work in this area?*
- *Does a spouse, a close relative, or a close friend work in the area?*
- *How many times have I reviewed this area in the past five years?*
- *Have I made past recommendations resulting in significant procedural changes in this area?*
- *Have I been involved in system implementations or the development of policies and procedures for this area?*
- *Have I had any personal disputes with the management of this activity?*

2. Social Pressure

Social pressure threats may arise when an auditor is exposed to, or perceives that he or she is exposed to, pressures from relevant groups. This situation may occur when the auditor, for example, has inadvertently cried "wolf" in the past when there were no problems. Pressure from the audit customer or group could drive the auditor to overlook suspicious items. Another form of social pressure could occur when an audit team member is reluctant to oppose a generally held view on the part of the audit team itself (a phenomenon labeled as "groupthink" in behavioral literature).

Questions to ask include:

- *Has management tried to influence scope adversely?*
- *Were my previous findings addressed?*
- *Were there any opposing views within the audit team on a particular finding?*
- *Are company practices efficient and economical, or is there a better way to accomplish goals and objectives?*

Exhibit 5-1 (continued)
Seven Threats to Objectivity

3. Major Economic Interest

This threat may arise when the auditor has a major direct economic stake in the performance of the client. An auditor may fear that significant negative findings, such as discovery of illegal acts, could jeopardize the entity's future and hence the auditor's own interests as an employee. Or, an auditor may have performance incentives directly related to the area under review or other significant financial interests that might be threatened by negative audit findings. This threat also arises when the auditor audits the work or department of an individual who may subsequently make decisions that directly affect the auditor's future employment opportunities or salary. The simple fact that an employee has some economic interest in the organization in which he or she serves does not in and of itself indicate a conflict. However, if the interest is so direct and significant as to impair the auditor's objectivity, the auditor should steer clear of the situation.

Questions to ask include:

- *Does this audit significantly impact the financial interest of the auditor?*
- *Were appropriate levels of management, including legal, involved in reviews of questionable practices?*
- *Was the board appropriately informed of any reviews of questionable practices?*
- *Am I due to rotate to this activity in the foreseeable future?*

4. Personal Relationship

This threat may arise when an auditor is a close relative or friend of the manager or an employee of the audit customer unit. The auditor may be tempted to overlook, soften, or delay the reporting of negative audit findings to avoid embarrassing the friend or relative. An internal auditor also can be influenced by inappropriate negative personal feelings toward individuals.

Questions to ask include:

- *Does a spouse or other close relative or friend work in this area?*
- *Are any former members of the audit staff working in this area?*
- *Are there unusual adverse relationships among those in an audit customer unit and the internal auditor?*

5. Familiarity

This threat may arise due to an auditor's long-term relationship with the audit customer. Familiarity may lead an auditor to lose perspective on an audit by making the auditor overly sympathetic to the customer. Alternatively, familiarity may lead an auditor to prejudge an audit customer on the basis of previous problems (or non-problems) and assume a posture consistent with the prejudgment rather than taking a fresh, objective look.

Questions to ask include:

- *How many times has another member of the audit staff reviewed this activity?*
- *How many times have I reviewed this activity?*

Exhibit 5-1 (continued)
Seven Threats to Objectivity

6. Cultural, Racial, and Gender Biases

This threat may arise from cultural, racial, or gender biases. For example, in a multidivisional entity, a domestically based auditor may be biased or prejudiced against audit customer units located in certain foreign locations. Or, an auditor may be unduly critical of different practices and customs or of units managed or staffed by employees of a particular race or gender.

Questions to ask include:

- *Do I have negative feelings toward people of different cultures, races, or gender?*
- *Does this audit require interaction with these groups?*

7. Cognitive Biases

This threat may arise from an unconscious and unintentional psychological bias in interpreting information, depending on one's role in a situation. For example, if one takes a critical audit perspective, one may overlook positive information and, conversely, if one takes a positive, facilitative perspective, one may discount negative information. In addition, an auditor may come in with certain preconceived notions and tend to see evidence confirming such notions.

Questions to ask include:

- *Were sampling techniques valid?*
- *Is this opinion valid considering the things that went right versus the things that went wrong?*
- *Have I discussed my findings with other members of the audit team?*
- *Were we called in because of a previous audit failure?*
- *Do I have a tendency to overlook positive or negative information?*

Source: *Independence and Objectivity: A Framework for Internal Auditors* by The Auditing Section Task Force of The American Accounting Association. Copyright 2001 by The IIA Research Foundation, Altamonte Springs, FL. Reprinted with permission. The self-review questions were added by the authors of this book and did not come from the Research Foundation study.

Exhibit 5-2
Factors that Mitigate Threats to Objectivity

The following factors, which are often inherent in the processes and environments under review, can serve to lessen the impact of identified threats to objectivity.

Organizational Position and Policies

The auditor/audit activity's organizational position and policy statements at various levels addressing auditor/audit customer relations may bolster the auditor's position in the organization and create disincentives for audit customers to influence or intimidate auditors.

Environment — Strong Corporate Governance System

A supportive environment, in both the internal audit activity and the organization as a whole, that encourages learning and continuous improvement may reduce the perceptions of failure associated with flaws in recommendations, system implementation processes, and other advice. Thus, auditors and audit customers are less fearful of potentially negative outcomes and of reporting on possible prior mistakes. A significant component of a supportive environment is the audit committee. A strong audit committee is of crucial importance in assuring auditor objectivity and professionalism.

Incentives (Rewards, Discipline)

A system of rewards and disciplinary processes in both the internal audit activity and in the organization as a whole can reduce threats to objectivity. For example, an environment that rewards critical and objective thinking or penalizes bias or prejudice can encourage objectivity in the face of these types of threats.

Use of Teams

A key aspect of objectivity involves corroboration of judgments by others. The use of teams rather than individuals to conduct audits can help diffuse cognitive biases, familiarity, personal relationship threats, and self-review threats. One caution that must be raised here is the risk that social pressures may cause a team member to be fearful of expressing a view opposing the generally held team view (i.e., due to "groupthink") or the view of a socially powerful team member.

Supervision/Peer Review

Studies of accountability in auditing indicate that review processes and their attendant impact on audit judgments through performance incentives, justification requirements, and feedback can mitigate individual biases. The anticipation of peer and supervisory review also may increase an auditor's self-awareness and help to avoid potential biases or other threats to objectivity.

Exhibit 5-2 (continued)
Factors that Mitigate Threats to Objectivity

Elapsed Time/Changed Circumstances

The passage of time can reduce the potential self-review threats arising when an auditor reviews his or her own recommendations made during previous audits. Elapsed time also may lead to changes in circumstances and changes in personnel in the audit customer area, leading to a reduction or elimination of potential threats such as familiarity, social pressure, and self-review.

Limited Scope Audit

Limited-scope audits may reduce fears of significant effects from negative findings due to the limited scale of such audits and thus may encourage objective thinking in a very focused context. On the other hand, this could be considered a threat since it may limit the evidence available to be considered by the auditor.

Internal Consultations

This mitigating factor is related to the use of teams and supervision/peer review. In a situation of doubt, the auditor manages threats to objectivity by, voluntarily and on his or her own initiative, asking a colleague for input or feedback. The internal audit activity itself could develop a formal process, setting out criteria that establish when an internal auditor would be encouraged or required to seek consultation.

Source: *From Independence and Objectivity: A Framework for Internal Auditors* by The Auditing Section Task Force of The American Accounting Association. Copyright 2001 by The IIA Research Foundation, Altamonte Springs, FL. Reprinted with permission.

Exhibit 5-3
Auditor's Objectivity and Ethics Statement*

Engagement Team Member _____

Personal Impairments to Objectivity

There are circumstances in which auditors cannot be objective because of their views or circumstances. These circumstances include, but are not limited to:

- Previous involvement in a decision-making or management capacity that impacted the current operations of the process or entity being reviewed.
- Predetermined views toward individuals, groups, organizations, or objectives of a particular program or activity that could bias the review.
- Subsequent performance of an audit by the same individual who had previously been involved in performing or managing the activity or process under audit (for example, approving payrolls or purchases).
- Subsequent performance of an audit by the same individual who previously maintained the accounting records.
- Financial interest, direct or indirect, in the area or process to be audited or its major suppliers or customers.
- Professional, personal, or financial relationships that might cause the auditor to limit the extent of inquiry, to limit disclosure, or to weaken audit findings in any way.

If you have any relatives employed in the area to be reviewed, complete the following:

Name of Relative   Relationship   Position
_____

By my signature below, I certify that I have disclosed below or by attachment to this statement any personal impairment of which I am aware and which might be perceived to impair my objectivity in relation to the engagement. In addition, I have been informed of the independence and objectivity standards of the *International Standards for the Professional Practice of Internal Auditing* issued by The Institute of Internal Auditors. In the event that my objectivity or independence in relation to the area under review becomes impaired, I understand it is my responsibility to inform my immediate supervisor of the relevant circumstances.

In addition, I have knowledge of and will abide by The Institute of Internal Auditors' Code of Ethics.

_____
Signature   Date

---

*To be completed for each engagement team member.

Exhibit 5-4
Tools for Managing Objectivity

Some of these tools, such as the use of teams and supervision/peer review, overlap with the mitigating factors listed in Exhibit 5-2 This is because in one situation, objectivity management may require new procedures to be implemented to mitigate the existing threats, while in another the mitigating factors may already be an inherent part of the process. For example, some audits are of a size that teams are always used, whereas in another context, a team may be used specifically to reduce or eliminate a threat to objectivity. While the following list is not exhaustive, it does illustrate the range of management tools available for counteracting threats to objectivity.

Hiring Practices

Although hiring practices relate primarily to managing professionalism, they also can relate to managing objectivity. For example, screening to assure that potential employees do not have conflicts of interests that threaten objectivity is the starting point for building an objective audit function.

Training

Training in scientific methods and approaches improves objectivity itself. Training also can help auditors recognize potential threats to objectivity so that they can avoid them or effectively manage them in a timely fashion.

Supervision/Review

Close supervision of auditors and careful review of their work beyond what is customary can encourage them to approach audit issues objectively since they are accountable for their judgments. As mentioned previously, research indicates that accountability is an important factor in improving judgments and reducing biases in an audit context.

Quality Assurance Reviews

Internal and external reviews of the internal audit function, its activities, processes, and procedures, can help assure that threats to objectivity are effectively managed and professionalism is maintained.

Use of Teams

Assigning an additional team member to an audit can diffuse or eliminate potential threats to objectivity by bringing an additional perspective to bear on the audit. This additional perspective can counterbalance threats due to familiarity, personal relationships, self-review, or other possible threats to objectivity on the part of one or more audit team members. In addition, appropriate assignments within teams can be made to maximize the mitigating effects of the team approach.

Exhibit 5-4 (continued)
Tools for Managing Objectivity

Rotation/Reassignment

Rotating audit assignments can reduce the degree of familiarity and self-review. There are different types of rotation, including rotating all the staff from one audit to another so that new staff always do the audit, rotating some of the staff but not all, and keeping the audit staff on a repeated audit but rotating the work performed by the staff.

Use of Third Parties

When internal tools cannot be effectively used to manage threats to objectivity, sourcing to an external service provider can help ensure that objective judgment is rendered in a specific circumstance. Such decisions, however, will require additional financial resources and may lead to unease among internal audit staff.

Source: *Independence and Objectivity: A Framework for Internal Auditors* by The Auditing Section Task Force of The American Accounting Association. Copyright 2001 by The IIA Research Foundation, Altamonte Springs, FL. Reprinted with permission.

Exhibit 5-5
Internal Audit Responsibility for Nonaudit Functions

As a general rule, internal auditors should not assume operating responsibilities or oversee other nonaudit functions or duties that are subject to periodic internal audit assessments. However, as organizations are pressured to develop more efficient and effective operations using fewer resources, internal auditors cannot always avoid such situations. The following guidelines from PA 1130.A2-1 present several factors that CAEs need to consider at a minimum when asked to accept responsibility for a nonaudit function:

- If management directs internal auditors to perform nonaudit work, it should be understood that they are not functioning as internal auditors.
- Expectations of stakeholders, including regulatory or legal requirements, should be evaluated and assessed in relation to the potential impairment. In other words, the third parties who rely upon internal auditing's objective assurance should be aware of the audit activity's participation in nonaudit work.
- The impact of the assignment of nonaudit work on independence and objectivity should be discussed with management, the audit committee, and other appropriate stakeholders. A determination should be made regarding a number of issues, some of which affect one another:
  - The significance of the operational function to the organization (in terms of revenue, expenses, reputation, and influence) should be evaluated.

Exhibit 5-5 (continued)
Internal Audit Responsibility for Nonaudit Functions

- The length or duration of the assignment and scope of responsibility should be evaluated.
- Adequacy of separation of duties should be evaluated.
- The potential impairment to objectivity or independence, or the appearance of such impairment, should be considered when reporting audit results.

- If the internal audit charter contains specific restrictions or limiting language regarding the assignment of nonaudit functions to the internal auditor, then these restrictions should be disclosed and discussed with management and subsequently with the audit committee or other governing body if management insists on the assignment anyway. All guidance below in the Practice Advisory is subordinate to the internal audit charter.
- When the time comes to audit the operation, impairment to objectivity can be minimized by asking a contracted, third-party entity or external auditors to conduct the review.
- If the internal audit activity performs the review, individual auditors with operational responsibility for the area should not participate in the audit of the operation.
- Whenever possible, auditors conducting the assessment should be supervised by and report the results of the assessment to those whose independence and objectivity is not impaired.
- Disclosure should be made regarding the operational responsibilities of the auditor, the significance of the operation to the organization (in terms of revenue, expenses, or other pertinent information), and the relationship of those who audited the function to the auditor assuming an operational role.
- Disclosure of the auditor's operational responsibilities should be made in the related audit report along with disclosure and discussion in internal auditing's communications to the audit committee or other governing body.

While these pronouncements are not mandatory or exhaustive, they should provide useful advice for auditors grappling with the issue of assuming operational responsibilities.

Exhibit 5-6
Independence Considerations Related to Consulting Roles

Independence considerations related to consulting roles for internal auditing are particularly sensitive in some government organizations. This exhibit provides guidance for government audit organizations conducting work in compliance with the *Standards* but whose local governance rules audit standards, policies, and/or legislation more strictly limit nonassurance (consulting) services. The parameters within which an organization plans to provide nonassurance (consulting) services should be included in the internal audit charter and supported by the policies and procedures of the internal audit activity. The guidance and suggestions in this exhibit are based directly on a past practice advisory of The IIA (past PA 1000-C1.3: Additional Considerations for Consulting Engagements in Government Organizational Settings).

Exhibit 5-6 (continued)
Independence Considerations Related to Consulting Roles

1. **Core Elements of the Role of Auditors.** Through their assurance (audit) engagements, auditors help to ensure that management is accountable for meeting organizational objectives and complying with internal and external requirements for how operations and activities are carried out. Although these engagements can include an "assistance" dimension through the inclusion of recommendations for improvement, the auditor does not bear ultimate responsibility for making or authorizing the improvement. Should an auditor take responsibility for implementing or authorizing operations improvements, whether recommended in the course of an audit (assurance) engagement or as a separate nonaudit (consulting) engagement, the auditor is very likely jeopardizing the independence and objectivity that are essential to the role of audit.

   Even when assisting an organization through nonaudit (consulting) activities, auditors should keep their activities within boundaries that define the core elements of the audit function. These core elements include:[6]

   - Auditors should be independent and avoid relationships and situations that compromise auditors' objectivity.
   - Auditors should not audit their own work.
   - Auditors should not perform management functions or make management decisions.

   The elements are "core" because they support the fundamental value proposition of audit, namely, the principle that an objective third party is attesting to (or providing assurance as to) the credibility of management's assertions. Accordingly, to protect their ability to provide assurance, auditors must minimize potential threats to auditor independence that can arise when the same audit function is also providing nonaudit (consulting) services.

   In addition to the core elements above, other threats to auditor independence have been identified, including the conduit of nonaudit (consulting) work that:

   - Creates a mutuality of interest.
   - Places auditors in a role of advocacy for the company.[7]

2. **Governing Rules.** Specific jurisdictional rules that set restrictions on the work of auditors outside the audit (assurance) role may apply only to auditors conducting the external (financial statement or statutory) audit, or they may apply to auditors performing all types of audits. Moreover, the rules may have been established in the audit function's enabling legislation, imposed by oversight or regulatory bodies, or included in codes of ethics or auditing standards required for audits of specific organizations or jurisdictions. It is the CAE's responsibility to ensure that the audit function's charter and its policies and procedures comply with relevant governing rules.

   Moreover, even where the audit function is not subject to governing rules that restrict nonaudit (consulting) services, CAEs will nevertheless need to ensure that the quality assurance system is designed to manage or minimize threats to auditor independence or objectivity. Otherwise,

Exhibit 5-6 (continued)
Independence Considerations Related to Consulting Roles

nonaudit (consulting) assignments could have the long-term effect of compromising the audit function's ability to carry out its audit (assurance) role. In addition, an audit function's engagement in nonaudit (consulting) work that compromises its independence could prevent other auditors from relying on the audit function's work.

3. **Activities That Compromise Objectivity and Independence.** Auditors' ability to engage in nonaudit (consulting) work without compromising their independence depends to some extent on whether they "draw the line" between assisting or consulting in the sense of advising versus assisting by doing work that is the responsibility of management. For example, providing advice on appropriate controls during system design with the clear understanding that management has responsibility for accepting or rejecting the advice would have a limited impact on the auditor's objectivity toward that system in the future. By contrast, if the auditor led the system design team, made the final decision on which specific controls to employ, or managed the actual system implementation, then the auditor's future ability to objectively evaluate that system would be significantly impaired. However, other nonaudit assignments may not be as clear-cut. Accordingly, audit functions need to develop procedures for reviewing potential nonaudit (consulting) assignments and determining whether they present a threat to independence and objectivity. The review used to determine the effect on future independence and objectivity should be documented. This documentation should be provided to external quality control reviewers during the external quality assessment engagement.

4. **Processes for Minimizing Threats to Objectivity or Independence.** The audit function should implement controls that assist in reducing the potential for nonaudit (consulting) projects to compromise objectivity of individual auditors, or the independence of the audit function as a whole. Techniques may include:

    - Charter language defining nonaudit (consulting) service parameters.
    - Policies and procedures limiting type, nature, and/or level of participation in nonaudit (consulting) projects.
    - Use of a screening process for nonaudit (consulting) projects, with limits on accepting engagements that might threaten objectivity.
    - Segregation of nonaudit (consulting) units from units conducting audits (assurance engagements) within the same audit function.
    - Rotation of auditors on engagements.
    - Employing outside providers for carrying out nonaudit (consulting) engagements, or for conducting assurance engagements in activities where the audit function's prior involvement in nonaudit (consulting) work has been determined to impair objectivity/independence.
    - Disclosure in audit reports where objectify was impaired by participation in a prior nonaudit (consulting) project.

References

[1] The research study was conducted by a task force of leading audit researchers from around the globe under the auspices of the Auditing Section of the American Accounting Association and published by The IIA Research Foundation in 2001.

[2] Ibid, p. 8.

[3] Ibid, pp. 18–20.

[4] Ibid, p. 15.

[5] Ibid, pp. 24–26.

[6] These principles have been articulated by numerous standards-setting bodies, including guidance published by IAASB/IFAC in its Code of Professional Ethics and the U.S. Government Accountability Office in the Generally Accepted Government Auditing Standards.

[7] This risk is raised in the January 2003 Smith Report on Audit Committees and Combined Code Guidance, appointed by the Financial Reporting Council, and is addressed in guidance published by ICAEW (Institute of Chartered Accountants in England and Wales), among others.

Chapter 6

YOU MUST BE PROFICIENT AND PROFESSIONAL (1200-1230)

The *Standards* require engagements to be performed *"with proficiency and due professional care"* (1200). Basically, internal auditors must possess the skills necessary to do the job, keep those skills up-to-date, and do what they are supposed to do the way they are supposed to do it. Also implied in this requirement are two related perspectives: the proficiency of the individual auditor and the proficiency across the internal audit activity. The second is a particularly important responsibility of the CAE. The *Standards* requiring proficiency and due professional care are fundamental to ensuring internal auditors have the right skills and do things right, and have been part of internal audit standards since the 1970s when standards were first adopted by The IIA.

Proficiency

Proficiency refers to internal auditors' possession of the knowledge, skills, and other competencies needed to fulfill their individual responsibilities. The internal audit activity collectively is also expected to exhibit proficiency, either through possession of the required abilities or acquisition of them from external sources (1210).

The Interpretation to Standard 1210 adds further that *knowledge, skills, and other competencies is a collective term that refers to the professional proficiency required of internal auditors to effectively carry out their professional responsibilities. Internal auditors are encouraged to demonstrate their proficiency by obtaining appropriate professional certifications and qualifications, such as the Certified Internal Auditor designation and other designations offered by The Institute of Internal Auditors and other appropriate professional organizations.*

The *Standards* generally do not mandate what specific skills or capabilities are essential to achieving proficiency as an internal auditor, thereby giving audit staffs the flexibility to determine those parameters in ways that best meet the needs of their organizations. However, there are many sources of guidelines in this area, including PA 1210-1 on proficiency, research in *The Competency Framework for Internal Auditing* (*CFIA*), the *Common Body of Knowledge – Core Competencies for Today's Internal Auditor,* and The IIA's Internal Auditor Competency Framework (/www.theiia.org/guidance/additional-resources/competency-framework-for-internal-auditors/).

For example, the paradigm shift in internal auditor focus initially suggested by CFIA in 1998, which obviously influences the competencies auditors are expected to demonstrate, is shown on the following page.[1]

Past Focus	Additional Focus
Hard Controls	Soft Controls
Control Evaluation	Self-assessment
Control	Risk
Risk	Context
Risk-threats	Risk-opportunities
Past	Future

Past Focus	Additional Focus
Review	Preview
Detective	Preventive
Operational Audits	Strategy Audits
Auditor	Consultant
Imposition	Invitation
Persuasion	Negotiation
Independence	Value
Audit Knowledge	Business Knowledge
Catalyst	Change Facilitator
Transactions	Processes
Control Activities	Management Controls
Control Consciousness	Risk Consciousness

These shifts in focus introduce new essential competencies, such as negotiation skills, change facilitation capabilities, and business/process knowledge that are crucial to the effective performance of internal auditing.

Further, the definition of internal auditing implies that internal auditors will have proficiency in the areas of risk management and governance as well as control. This is not only for assurance work, but for consulting services as well.

Exhibits 6-1, 6-2, and 6-3 show expectations of internal audit competencies from professional services firms, as well as a comparison of relative competencies needed in the internal audit profession, as compared to the external audit profession.

The IIA's Internal Auditor Competency Framework (www.theiia.org) provides audit functions with a tool that allows them to assess where their function stands in terms of the minimum level of knowledge and skills needed to effectively operate and maintain an internal audit function. The competency framework also offers each auditor the ability to assess their own professional development and plan what knowledge and skills they need to acquire to move to the next level. The assessment tool looks at the competencies needed at six progressive levels, starting with new staff and moving progressively to the CAE level.

CAE	Director	Audit Manager	Audit Senior Supervisor	Internal Audit Staff	New Internal Auditor (Less than 1 year)	Self-assessment
CAE		Experienced		New Internal Audit Staff		

The tool breaks down the competencies into four basic categories:

- Interpersonal Skills
- Tools and Techniques
- Internal Audit Standards, Theory, and Methodology
- Knowledge Areas

Within each of the categories there is a detailed list of specific competencies. For example, for problem-solving tools and techniques:

	CAE	Director	Audit Manager	Audit Senior Supervisor	Internal Audit Staff	New Internal Auditor (Less than 1 year)
	CAE		Experienced		New Internal Audit Staff	
Can apply major problem-solving techniques such as: drill-down technique, cause and effect diagram, systems diagram, SWAT, PEST, five whys, affinity diagrams, chunking, critical success factor, impact analysis, inductive reasoning, the ladder of inference, and reverse brainstorming.	4	4	4	4	3	2
Can apply other problem-solving techniques such as Porter's five forces, value chain analysis, SUP analysis, the Banff matrix, and change curve.	4	4	3	2	2	1

	CAE	Director	Audit Manager	Audit Senior Supervisor	Internal Audit Staff	New Internal Auditor (Less than 1 year)
	CAE		Experienced		New Internal Audit Staff	
Can select the appropriate problem-solving techniques.	4	4	4	4	3	2
Can identify the need for a specific expert/facilitator in the problem-solving field.	4	4	4	3	3	2

The numbers in the cells refer to the minimal competency level:

    1 = Awareness only
    2 = Basic competence and knowledge with support from others
    3 = Independently competent in routine situations
    4 = Independently competent in unique and complex situations

Due Professional Care

The internal auditor's exercise of due professional care is described in terms of *applying the care and skill expected of a reasonably prudent and competent internal auditor* (1220). In other words, internal auditors must take care to conduct themselves in a manner consistent with how other professional internal auditors would act if placed in the same or similar situation.

The *Standards* are careful to point out, however, that *due care does not imply infallibility* (1220). In fact, self-protection is one reason due care is so important. If something were to go wrong in an audit, the burden of guilt assigned to the auditor can be reduced if he or she is shown to have acted as any other internal auditor would when faced with those circumstances.

The obvious question that comes to mind is how to ensure that the auditing staff's conduct is in line with that of other professional internal auditors. The *Standards* require internal auditors to *enhance their knowledge, skills, and other competencies through continuing professional development* (1230), an activity that will obviously educate staff on appropriate procedures and behavior. Adhering to professional standards, such as The IIA's *Standards,* is also one way. Staying up-to-date on the non-mandatory guidance and guidance issued from applicable bodies is another. Additional effective approaches include having peers outside the organization periodically review the internal audit operation (see Chapter 7), or sharing benchmarks on a regular basis with a group of audit shops from the same industry.

Proficient and Professional Assurance Work

The specifics as to what constitutes proficiency and due professional care may vary, depending on the type of engagement. For example, the *Standards* present several Implementation Standards that address proficiency and due professional care when performing assurance services.

The *Standards* make it clear that *the CAE must obtain competent advice and assistance if the internal auditors lack the knowledge, skills, or other competencies needed to perform all or part of the engagement* (1210.A1). Almost by definition, not every person can possess all specialty skills. In practice, it is hard for every function to have the strongest levels of specialty skills. In today's internal audit activity where various areas of complex risk are being addressed, often a CAE needs to assess whether he or she has sufficient skills to address the areas that should be addressed by the internal audit plan. The proficiency standards recognize this challenge in requiring the CAE to obtain competent advice and assistance if the internal audit staff lacks the knowledge, skills, or other competencies needed to perform all or part of the engagement.

Today CAEs commonly co-source with outside specialists to obtain skills and expertise in a number of areas, including:

Information technology skills:	Business process expertise:	Specialist governance, risk, and control needs:

• System development risk
 • IT security risk
    o Application system
    o Network and infrastructure
 • Application systems specialties, such as ERP packages
 • Data analysis and management
	• Supply chain
	 • Treasury
	 • Business process efficiency or better practices expertise
	 • Other based on nature of the industry
		• Enterprise risk management
		 • Fraud assessment and investigation
		 • Governance, ethics, and compliance
		 • Internal controls (the U.S. Sarbanes-Oxley Act of 2002)

Beyond functional expertise, many co-source to enhance the local culture understanding, language skills, and cost effectiveness for locations beyond their home territory. Co-sourcing can bring an internal audit activity quality and agility in resources.

Foregoing an assurance engagement due to a lack of specialized knowledge, as might be the case in a consulting exercise, is not an option. Guidelines for obtaining such support from outside service providers are presented in PA 1210.A1-1 (see Exhibits 8-2 and 8-3 in Chapter 8).

There are two areas of competency where the *Standards* do specifically address the expected competency of the auditor: fraud and information technology. Both are important areas of knowledge, as well as important areas of specialty knowledge. The *Standards* address both the base level of competency expected in these areas by all internal auditors and recognize that not all internal auditors will have the deep knowledge of a specialist.

	Expectations of all internal auditors — have sufficient knowledge:	**Understanding of the limitations in competency of the average internal auditors — not expected to have the expertise of:**
Fraud 1210.A2	To evaluate the risk of fraud and the manner in which it is managed by the organization.	A person whose primary responsibility is detecting and investigating fraud.
Information Technology 1210.A3	Of key information technology risks and controls and available technology-based audit techniques to perform their assigned work.	An internal auditor whose primary responsibility is information technology auditing.

These are not the only areas of specialist skills, including other functional and industry specific skills. However, the *Standards* recognize as important a certain level of proficiency in fraud risk and information technology for any internal auditor to be effective. These two topics are of such importance that Practice Guides have been devoted to them. For instance, the PG Internal Auditing and Fraud focuses on internal auditing's role in fraud risk. The Global Technology Audit Guide series in the Practice Guides focuses on information technology risks and controls.

Finally, internal auditors are expected to exercise due professional care in an assurance engagement by considering five specific issues:

- *Extent of work needed to achieve the engagement's objectives.*
- *Relative complexity, materiality, or significance of matters to which assurance procedures are applied.*
- *Adequacy and effectiveness of governance, risk management, and control processes.*
- *Probability of significant errors, fraud, or noncompliance.*
- *Cost of assurance in relation to potential benefits* (1220.A1).

Similar to the discussion earlier on implementation standards for proficiency, the *Standards* do highlight that to exercise due professional care, today's internal auditor needs to consider the use of technology-based audit and other data analysis techniques. The power of information technology should be used to the internal auditor's advantage. The internal auditor needs to be familiar with the various specialized tools available, such as ACL and Idea, as well as the basic tools, such as Excel.[2] Various ACL discussion papers on continuous monitoring and using data analysis can be accessed at www.acl.com/products/ccm.aspx. In addition, *GTAG 3: Continuous Auditing: Implications for Assurance, Monitoring and Risk Assessment* is a valuable resource.

In addition, the *Standards* stipulate that due care requires the internal auditor *to be alert to the significant risks that might affect organizational objectives, operations, or resources. However, assurance procedures alone, even when performed with due professional care, do not guarantee that all significant risks will be identified* (1220.A3).

Proficient and Professional Consulting Work

Proficiency and due professional care requirements for consulting engagements are a bit different from those associated with assurance work. *If the internal auditors lack the knowledge, skills, or other competencies needed to perform all or part of a consulting engagement, the chief audit executive must decline the engagement or obtain competent advice and assistance* (1210.C1), whereas an assurance engagement must be performed and necessary skills must be acquired.

The list of due care concerns is also different. According to Standard 1220.C1, *internal auditors must exercise due professional care during a consulting engagement by considering the:*

- *Needs and expectations of clients, including the nature, timing, and communication of engagement results.*
- *Relative complexity and extent of work needed to achieve the engagement's objectives.*
- *Cost of the consulting engagement in relation to potential benefits.*

In addition, internal auditors will often want to understand:

- The possible motivations and reasons of those requesting the service.
- The effect on the scope of the audit plan previously approved by the audit committee.
- The potential impact on future audit assignments and engagements.

It is important that the internal audit team determine why management is seeking the proposed consulting service, because internal auditors do not want to be party to any activity that might later be used to circumvent or undermine organizational policies, procedures, or values. In addition, it is important to consider the effect on planned and future engagements, since the acceptance of consulting work may result in some assurance engagements being dropped from the plan or postponed to make room for the assignment or avoid objectivity impairments. The acceptance of any consulting engagement usually represents a trade-off with time devoted to assurance work. The internal audit staff must carefully weigh the reasons for and benefits of the consulting engagement to make sure that their resources are not misspent (see discussion of the CAE's planning responsibilities in Chapter 8).

There are several principles that should guide the performance of professional consulting work. When providing consulting services, the internal auditor should:

- Conduct appropriate meetings and gather necessary information to assess the nature and extent of the service to be provided.

- Confirm that those receiving the service understand and agree with relevant guidance contained in the internal audit charter, internal audit policies and procedures, and other related material governing the performance of consulting engagements. The internal auditor should decline to conduct consulting engagements that are prohibited by the terms of the internal audit charter, conflict with the policies and procedures of the internal audit activity, or do not add value and promote the best interests of the organization.

- Evaluate the consulting engagement for compatibility with the internal audit activity's overall plan of engagements. The internal audit activity's risk-based plan of engagements may incorporate and rely on consulting engagements, to the extent deemed appropriate, to provide necessary audit coverage to the organization.

- Document general terms, understandings, deliverables, and other key factors of the formal consulting engagement in a written agreement or plan. It is essential that both the internal auditor and the consulting engagement customer understand and agree with reporting and communication requirements.

Internal auditors exercising appropriate due care will weigh the results of these various evaluations when determining whether to accept a consulting assignment and when planning the engagement.

Worthy of Review

Many may consider these standards regarding proficiency and professionalism to be stating the obvious. But, as Exhibit 6-1 indicates, the competencies needed by internal auditors are constantly evolving. A review of the guidelines is time well spent, since adherence to these principles helps ensure the integrity, credibility, and reputation of the internal audit activity and the profession as a whole.

Exhibit 6-1 **Competencies Needed in Internal Auditing**
What are the professional skill sets needed to meet this market demand? • Coursework: Business process, internal controls, accounting, systems. • Behavioral/Personal Skills: analytical, problem solving, presentations, communications. • Ability to deal with unstructured business processes and issues. • A holistic, risk-oriented approach. • Internship experience.

Source: Deloitte & Touche LLP, Tools and Techniques to Get the Job Done: How Can We Best Prepare Our Future Audit Leaders to Excel? 2005 EIAP Symposium, Focus on the Future, Chicago, 2005.

Exhibit 6-2 Skill Set Analysis: External Auditing Versus Internal Auditing		
	Internal Auditing	**External Auditing**
Business Process	HIGH	MEDIUM
Internal Controls	HIGH	MEDIUM
Accounting	MEDIUM	HIGH
Systems	MEDIUM	LOW
Analytical	HIGH	HIGH
Problem Solving	HIGH	MEDIUM
Presentation Skills	HIGH	LOW
Communications	HIGH	MEDIUM
Unstructured Problem Solving	HIGH	MEDIUM
Risk Orientation	HIGH	MEDIUM

Source: Deloitte & Touche LLP, Tools and Techniques to Get the Job Done: How Can We Best Prepare Our Future Audit Leaders to Excel? 2005 EIAP Symposium, Focus on the Future, Chicago, 2005.

Exhibit 6-3 Core Competencies				
General Competencies	**Behavioral Skills**	**Technical Skills**	**Knowledge**	**Audit Tools and Techniques**
Common Core	Common Core	Common Core	Importance (Ranked highest importance)	Current Use (Most used)
• Communication skills • Problem identification and solving skills • Keeping up to date with industry, regulation, and professional standards	• Discretion and confidentiality • Clarity of communication	• Understanding business • Risk analysis and control assessment techniques	• Auditing internal audit standards • Ethics • Fraud awareness • ERM • Technical knowledge of industry • Governance • Financial accounting	• Risk-based audit planning • Analytical review • Electronic workpapers • CAATS • Data mining • Statistical sampling • CSA

Exhibit 6-3 (continued) Core Competencies				
Incremental Core	**Incremental Core**	**Incremental Core**		
Internal Audit Staff	Internal Audit Staff	Internal Audit Staff		
• Accounting • IT • IA management • Project and time management • Negotiation skills • CAE • Ability to promote the value of internal auditing within the organization • Negotiation skills	• Objectivity • Judgment • Team player • IA management • Leadership • Staff management • Governance and ethics sensitivity • CAE • Leadership • Governance and ethics sensitivity • Ability to persuade	• Data collection and analysis tools and techniques • Business process analysis • Identification of types of controls • IA management • Project management • Negotiations • Operations and management research skills • CAE • Negotiation • Governance, risk, and control tools and techniques • Project management		

Source: James A. Bailey, CBOK Report II: *Core Competencies for Today's Internal Auditor* (Altamonte Springs, FL: The Institute of Internal Auditors Research Foundation, 2010).

Exhibit 6-4 Importance of Skill Sets Over the Next Three Years				
	Increase	**Stay the Same**	**Decrease**	**Not Applicable**
Critical thinking and analysis	68%	31%	1%	1%
Knowledge of risk management approaches	67%	31%	1%	1%
Communication	63%	36%	0%	0%
Understanding of organization's strategy & business model	61%	39%	1%	0%
Specific technology experience (e.g., security, ERP)	60%	36%	2%	3%
Leadership	54%	44%	1%	1%
Experience in the business outside of internal auditing	53%	42%	3%	3%
Collaboration and teamwork	50%	49%	1%	0%
Qualifications (CPA, CIA, BSA, CISA, etc.)	49%	50%	1%	2%
Other specific industry skills	27%	9%	0%	64%

Source: 2010 State of the Internal Audit Profession Survey: A Future Rich in Opportunity, Internal Audit Must Seize Opportunities to Enhance Its Relevancy. PricewaterhouseCoopers LLP, 2010.

References

[1] From Vision University, an executive development program of The IIA in association with Louisiana State University.

[2] See the article by R. Jackson, "Getting the Most out of Audit Tools," *Internal Auditor* (August 2004), pp. 37–47, for a perspective on the use of various tools.

Chapter 7

YOU MUST MAINTAIN AN EXTENSIVE QUALITY ASSURANCE AND IMPROVEMENT PROGRAM (1300-1322)

The 1300 series of standards on quality assurance and improvement represent a fundamental focus in the *Standards*. Seven standards dictate specific activities that must be part of Quality Assurance and Improvement (QA&I) programs, including an external review that is performed at least once every five years. The quality assurance and improvement standards are core to ensuring the effectiveness of internal auditing, for the benefit of stakeholders of internal auditing, the internal audit profession, and the specific activity's internal auditors.

This is the area of the *Standards* where the profession ranks itself lowest in conformance.[1] It is an area of significant focus in the last decade, and likely further focus in the years ahead. The lower level of conformance is likely because not all internal audit activities are yet receiving external quality assessments once every five years. It appears, however, that the assessments continue to gain wider acceptance and recognition. Many organizations are finding ways to have the reviews done cost effectively, to address any fears they may have of being reviewed by a third party, and to derive value for internal auditing and its stakeholders from the assessments.

Quality programs should be designed to provide reasonable assurance to the various stakeholders of the internal audit activity that it: (1) performs in accordance with its charter, which should be consistent with the Definition of Internal Auditing, the *Standards,* and the Code of Ethics; (2) operates in an effective and efficient manner; and (3) is perceived by stakeholders as adding value and improving the organization's operations (PA 1300-1). As noted in the Interpretation to Standard 1300, the program also *identifies opportunities for improvement* in the internal audit activity. To that end, the *Standards* require that any quality program:

1. Cover all aspects of the internal audit activity (1300).

2. Assure conformance with the Definition of Internal Auditing, the *Standards*, and the Code of Ethics (1300).

3. Include periodic internal reviews (1311).

4. Include ongoing internal monitoring (1311).

5. Obtain an external assessment at least once every five years (1312).

6. Communicate the results of the external and internal quality assurance and improvement program to senior management and the board (1320).

The omission of any of these six elements from the QA&I program represents nonconformance with the *Standards*.

It is the responsibility of the CAE to develop and maintain the quality assurance and improvement program (1300).

Provide Both Assurance and Improvement

The *Standards* specifically include the word "improvement" along with "assurance" in the quality standards. This inclusion of "improvement" is deliberate. The QA&I program is to be an ongoing effort that is used to improve the operations of the internal audit activity, whether a relatively basic activity or a major, well-established, well-respected internal audit activity. In all cases, the QA&I program should contribute to continuous improvement. Achieving quality is not a goal that is achieved through a review. It is more of a continuing journey. Of course, some internal audit activities will be further along on the journey than others.

Ensure All Elements of the QA&I Program Cover the Right Things

PA 1310-1 recommends that assessments of internal audit quality evaluate:

- Conformance with the Definition of Internal Auditing, the *Standards*, and the Code of Ethics.
- Adequacy of the internal audit activity's charter, goals, objectives, policies, and procedures.
- Contribution to the organization's governance, risk management, and control processes.
- Compliance with applicable laws, regulations, and government or industry standards.
- Effectiveness of continuous improvement activities and adoption of best practices.
- The extent to which the internal audit activity adds value and improves the organization's operations. (PA 1310-1)

These elements should be considered in internal monitoring, internal periodic assessments, and external assessments of the internal audit activity.

Assure the Internal Audit Activity is in Conformance with the Definition of Internal Auditing, the *Standards*, and the Code of Ethics (1300)

Because adherence to an established definition of the profession, standards of practice, and a code of conduct are generally accepted as prerequisites to quality work in any profession, assessing conformance with The IIA's Definition of Internal Auditing, *Standards*, and Code of Ethics remains a primary purpose of the quality assurance program. A QA&I program that does not consider the *Standards* cannot meet the definition of a quality assurance and improvement program for purposes of the *Standards*.

Exhibit 7-1 presents a brief exercise that can be completed as a part of every engagement. Its purpose is to assess whether staff members are complying with each of the performance standards. Engagement checklists and other forms of policies, procedures, training, and tools incorporating the *Standards* into the internal audit process at the front end are important to ensuring the internal audit activity will find that it is in conformance when later reviewing its practices.

Reviewing after the fact for conformance is likely to find inadequate conformance if sufficient *Standards*-based guidance, practices, and training are not built into the internal audit process at the beginning.

A checklist can also be a useful tool for assessing overall conformance of the internal audit activity. One type, shown in Appendix C, provides a "total conformance checkup" by asking more than 100 questions based on the *Standards'* mandates. Exhibit 7-2 presents another overall list of questions that can be used both in planning for conformance as well as later as part of assessments.

Include Ongoing Internal Monitoring (1311)

Internal assessments must include *ongoing monitoring of the performance of the internal audit activity, and periodic reviews performed through self-assessment or by other persons within the organization with sufficient knowledge of internal audit practices* (1311).

Ongoing monitoring is primarily achieved through continuous monitoring activities, including the analysis of performance metrics, supervision, standard working practices, automated workpaper procedures and signoffs, and report reviews. The most obvious internal method for continuously assessing quality is management oversight of internal audit work. Adequate supervision from the beginning through the end of engagements is the most fundamental element of a quality assurance program, and specific requirements to supervise audit work is highlighted in Standard 2340, which is supported by advice on how to supervise in PA 2340-1. Additional ongoing review mechanisms include acquiring feedback from audit customers and other stakeholders; using checklists or internal audit automation that ensures certain steps are performed; following audit policies and procedures manuals; using measures of project budgets, timekeeping systems and audit plan completion; and analyses of other performance metrics such as cycle time and recommendations accepted (PA 1311-1).

Establishing the right quantitative and qualitative measures to support reviews of internal audit activity performance can be key to developing an ongoing internal monitoring program. Measures should be tailored to the organization, the expectations of the internal audit function's key stakeholders, and definitions of value from internal auditing as illustrated in Exhibit 7-3. The Practice Guide, Measuring Internal Audit Effectiveness and Efficiency, provides detailed guidance on developing performance measures. Exhibits 7-4, 7-5, and 7-6 provide additional examples of balanced scorecard formats that can be tailored and used to promote internal audit quality assurance and improvement.

PA 1310-1 recommends that quality improvement efforts include a communication process designed to facilitate appropriate modification of and follow up on recommendations for resources, technology, processes, and procedures that arise from the internal and external quality improvement processes.

Include Periodic Internal Reviews (1311)

As noted earlier, in addition to the quality procedures that are part of the ongoing internal audit process, the *Standards* call for the QA&I program to include *periodic reviews performed through self-assessment or by other persons within the organization with sufficient knowledge of internal audit practices* (1311).

Periodic reviews should be designed to assess conformance with the activity's charter, the Definition of Internal Auditing, the *Standards,* and the Code of Ethics, and the efficiency and effectiveness of the activity in meeting the needs of its various stakeholders (PA 1311-1). One way audit departments fulfill this requirement is to routinely subject themselves to self-assessment. Such exercises are conducted by members of the internal audit staff and performed in the same manner as any other engagement. For example, audit shops can undergo a self-assessment review just like or very similar to the exercises performed in their internal auditing. Practices internal auditors use in control self-assessment (CSA) are as useful for ferreting out hidden problems and inefficiencies in the audit process as they are for finding such issues in the operational environment.

As internal quality programs evolve, it is becoming more common for periodic assessments to include elements such as:

- A documented review of conformance with each area of the *Standards*.

- A review of internal auditing in comparison to leading practices and benchmarks.

- Reviews of a selection of engagement workpapers and reporting. These reviews may focus on standards areas 1200 and 2200 to 2500. The reviews may consist of a sample of an engagement from each manager in the activity. Some have managers review the work of other managers so the managers can share perspectives with peers, and learn. Others have a quality group perform all the reviews.

- Continuous improvement programs that celebrate the strengths of the activity and focus on improvement and training in areas where further development is appropriate.

Alternatively, the CAE may assemble a team of assessors employed by the organization, but working in areas outside of internal auditing. The IIA's *Quality Assessment Manual*, or a comparable set of guidance and tools, may serve as the basis for periodic internal assessments. Highly successful former members of the department, for example, or employees in other divisions with CIAs and a proven internal audit track record at another organization can be effective assessors.

Additional initiatives include conducting more in-depth interviews and surveys of stakeholder groups, and benchmarking the internal audit activity's practices and performance metrics against relevant best practices (PA 1311-1). To perform this benchmarking, CAEs may seek out advisory information outside the organization, including from IIA resources, industry forums, and service providers.

Some internal audit groups see the periodic internal audit assessment as an action taken during years when an external assessment is not performed. This complement of ongoing quality activities provides an effective structure for continuous assessment of internal audit quality and improvement opportunities. Others audit groups perform yearly internal assessments. While the *Standards* do not explicitly state the frequency of periodic internal quality assessments, it is natural given the annual cycle of business that there is some annual element of the internal quality program.

Some larger audit shops are capable of establishing a formal internal quality assessment group that is responsible for all QA&I activities. In such environments, a reporting structure should be implemented that helps maintain appropriate credibility and objectivity. In general, those assigned responsibility for conducting ongoing and periodic internal assessments should report to the CAE while performing the assessments, and they should communicate their results and conclusions directly to the CAE (PA 1311-1).

Obtain an External Assessment at least Once Every Five Years (1312)

A visible requirement in the *Standards* is that *an external assessment must be conducted at least once every five years by a qualified, independent reviewer or review team from outside the organization* (1312).

This is one area where many CAEs need to take decisive action. An external assessment of every internal audit shop is required once every five years. Standard 1312 recognizes the potential need for more frequent external assessments. More frequent assessments may be appropriate, particularly when there have been significant changes in the internal audit function or the organization itself. An example would be a change in the CAE or the merger of two audit functions in an acquisition. The CAE *must discuss the need for more frequent external assessments with the board audit committee* (1312).

PA 1312-1 recommends that external assessments consist of a broad scope of coverage that includes:

- Conformance with the Definition of Internal Auditing, the *Standards,* and the Code of Ethics, applicable legislative and regulatory requirements, and the internal audit activity's charter, plans, policies, procedures, and practices.

- The expectations of the internal audit activity as expressed by the board, executive management, and operational managers.

- The integration of the internal audit activity into the organization's governance process, including the attendant relationships between and among the key groups involved in that process.

- The tools and techniques employed by the internal audit activity.

- The mix of knowledge, experience, and disciplines within the staff, including staff focus on process improvement.

- The determination of whether the audit activity adds value and improves the organization's operations. (PA 1312-1)

As appropriate, these assessments should offer recommendations for improvement. This would be expected of a high quality external assessment, given the focus of the 1300 series of *Standards* on both assurance and improvement.

These types of external assessments usually involve a team of qualified reviewers who spend anywhere from several days to several weeks interviewing key stakeholders and staff members and examining the audit process. The end result is a formal written report that provides an overall assessment of the function as well as recommendations for improvement.

Carefully Consider Options for Obtaining an External Assessment

The qualifications of available external reviewers or review teams vary. The quality, capabilities, and competency of the external reviewers, as well as the scope of the external assessment itself, should consider the size, complexity, sector or industry, and technical issues of the organization. The external assessor should be competent in two areas: the practice of internal auditing and the external assessment process. Competence can be demonstrated through a mixture of experience and theoretical learning. While one team member may have all the competencies necessary, the overall team should demonstrate the appropriate competencies matched to the organization being reviewed. Much care should be taken when selecting an external reviewer. Importantly, the reputation and capabilities of the reviewer reflect on the reputation of the internal audit activity being reviewed.

Several options for obtaining resources to perform an external assessment are available. They include:

- The IIA and member volunteers.

- Other industry associations if their review specifically covers the Definition of Internal Auditing, the *Standards,* and the Code of Ethics.

- Internal audit advisory practices of, or generalists from, accounting firms.

- Internal audit staffing firms, other consultants, or retired internal audit professionals.

- The "round robin" method, whereby a group of organizations "trade off" by performing each other's quality assessments. Care should be taken to avoid the appearance of any quid pro quo activity by making sure that each review team assesses an audit department not responsible for performing the QA of its own operation. Accordingly, reciprocal peer reviews between two organizations should be avoided (1312-1).

- Self-assessment with independent validation, for smaller internal audit activities. This approach, discussed in PA 1312-2, was made available for smaller internal audit activities where a full external assessment may be onerous. Some organizations have internal audit activities of only one internal auditor, for instance, and the *Standards* apply to all organizations regardless of size. Insofar as possible, to achieve optimum quality assurance and process-improvement benefits, an internal audit activity should consider the self-assessment with independent validation as an interim measure and endeavor to obtain a full external assessment during subsequent periods.

The need for more frequent external assessments as well as the qualifications and independence of the external reviewer or review team, including any potential conflict of interest, must be discussed by the CAE with the board audit committee (1312).

Interpretations to 1312 note:

A qualified reviewer or review team demonstrates competence in two areas: the professional practice of internal auditing and the external assessment process. Competence can be demonstrated through a mixture of experience and theoretical learning. Experience gained in organizations of similar size, complexity, sector or industry, and technical issues is more valuable than less relevant experience. In the case of a review team, not all members of the team need to have all the competencies; it is the team as a whole that is qualified. The chief audit executive uses professional judgment when assessing whether a reviewer or review team demonstrates sufficient competence to be qualified.

An independent reviewer or review team means not having either a real or an apparent conflict of interest and not being a part of, or under the control of, the organization to which the internal audit activity belongs.

PA 1312-1 advises that the individual or group should be independent of the organization and the audit activity. As such, they are to be free from any obligation to or interest in the reviewed organization or its personnel, and they should not have either a real or apparent conflict of interest. "Independent of the organization" is defined as "not a part of, or under the control of, the organization to which the internal audit activity belongs." Therefore, individuals working in another department of the same organization are not considered independent for the purposes of conducting an external quality assessment. In addition, the Practice Advisory notes that consideration should be given to a possible real or apparent conflict of interest that the reviewer may have due to present or past relationships with the organization or its internal audit activity. This issue might be of concern, for example, if an external quality assessment is performed by a firm to which a significant percent of internal audit services for the organization has been outsourced. Standard 1312 requires that potential conflicts of interest be discussed with the audit committee.

The Practice Advisory goes on to advise that the review team should consist of individuals who are competent in the professional practice of internal auditing and the external assessment process. As such, an individual serving as a reviewer should:

* Be a competent, certified internal audit professional who possesses current, in-depth knowledge of the *Standards*.

* Be well-versed in the best practices of the profession.

* Possess at least three years of recent experience in the practice of internal auditing or related consulting at the management level.

PA 1312-1 suggests additional requirements for the leader of the review team. Standard 1312 notes that the team should align with the size, complexity, sector or industry, and technical issues of the organization. For many organizations, it will be appropriate, for instance, to have information technology auditing expertise on the assessment team.

Areas for Coverage through Assessment

Assessments, whether internal or external, may include coverage of:

- Departmental structure and organization, to determine the effectiveness of the activity's implementation of its charter, mission statement, goals, and similar documents, as well as to evaluate the organizational structure, objectivity, policy manual, roles and responsibilities, and processes to manage the function. This may also include assessment of the direct reporting and communication with the audit committee and senior management, both through appropriate formal reporting lines as well as actual practices. Communication includes understanding of value from the point of view of the key stakeholders.

- Risk assessment and audit planning, to determine the extent to which the activity is aligned with the organization's enterprise risk universe, perspectives of senior management and the board, governance processes, management controls, decision support information, accountability mechanisms, and the management of technology, as well as to determine how effectively the activity applies its planning processes to make optimum use of its resources. Alignment of the risk assessment and audit plan development is key because it defines the focus of the rest of the internal audit program.

- Audit plan execution and project management, including reporting, working practices, use of internal audit automation, accomplishments, and reports issued, to assess the appropriateness of the planning, control, supervision, and use of resources on individual engagements; adequacy of documentation of audit and consulting services; form, content, and effectiveness of audit and consulting communications as compared to stakeholder expectations; and implementation follow-up.

- Information technology, to determine the adequacy of the internal audit activity's understanding of the organization's technology risks, use of available technology-based audit techniques and continuous auditing, and the activity's capability to cover those important functions.

- Human resources, including staffing skills and experience, to assess the sources, numbers, skills mix, continuing professional education, communications with staff, empowerment and management development practices, knowledge management and resources, performance evaluation, use of sourcing, and other elements of the management of human resources. It is important that the skills mix matches the risk coverage of the internal audit activity.

- Feedback surveys and interviews, to determine the opinions of operating management, the board and audit committee, and senior management on internal audit effectiveness and value added by internal auditing.

- Communications, reporting, and performance measures to understand how internal auditing ensures issues lead to action plans that serve the organization, adds value, improves operations, and communicates on matters of governance, risk management, and control.

A useful tool for preparing for any type of quality assessment is The IIA's *Quality Assessment Manual*. This publication, which was originally developed for use as a training and procedures manual for The IIA's own quality assurance review teams, contains several tools and worksheets for assessing various elements of the internal audit activity. Even with this guide, most internal audit activities will see that significant knowledge of the organization, industry, definitions of added value, and best practices is required for a quality assurance and improvement program.

In addition to the manual, there are now software tools that can help internal audit activities bring structure and documentation to their internal quality programs and their preparation for an external quality assessment. Examples include the ARC Logistics' CCH TeamMate Teamstore addressing internal audit quality and YCN Group's QAR Infocus for QAIP.

It is natural to assume that internal audit activities with more mature and advanced internal quality programs will find preparation for the external quality assessment much easier and their performance results more positive.

Reporting on Conformance (1321)

Internal auditors can report that their activities are conducted in conformance with the *Standards only if the results of the quality assurance and improvement program support this statement* (1321). Such notations are often made in the internal audit charter, as well as in engagement reports.

Inclusion of the statement of conformance is only allowed *if the results of the quality assurance and improvement support this statement* (1321). Identified problems should be corrected, and the quality assurance system should document that the correction is working before conformance can be claimed. In addition, *when nonconformance with the Definition of Internal Auditing, the Code of Ethics, or the* Standards *impacts the overall scope or operation of the internal audit activity, the chief audit executive must disclose the nonconformance and the impact to senior management and the board* (1322). This includes failure to obtain an external assessment, or failure to obtain an external assessment within five years of the previous assessment.

An Interpretation to Standard 1321 effective in 2011 states:

The internal audit activity conforms with the Standards *when it achieves the outcomes described in the Definition of Internal Auditing, Code of Ethics, and* Standards. *The results of the quality assurance and improvement program include the results of both internal and external assessments. All internal audit activities will have the results of internal assessments. Internal audit activities in existence for at least five years will also have the results of external assessments.*

The interpretation emphasizes that the results of internal as well as external quality assessments provide a basis for assessing internal auditing's conformance. Further, the *Standards* now clarify that for newer internal audit activities, they can state that they conform if this is supported by internal quality assessment results, even when they are new enough to not yet require an external assessment.

It is important to note that Standards 1321 and 1322 address overall, systemic nonconformance of the audit department, not isolated instances of nonconformance that may occur during a particular engagement. Internal auditors who find themselves unable to comply with a particular standard during a specific audit may still claim that their work is conducted in accordance with the *Standards* as long as they note the particular nonconformance issue in their final engagement communications (see the discussion of Standard 2430 in Chapter 12) and quality assessments have demonstrated the overall conformance of the activity.

Help Internal Auditing Add Value and Improve Organizational Operations

Quality is not solely about complying with policies and procedures. In fact, under the *Standards* a boilerplate conformance assessment of the audit department's operations is insufficient. The QA&I process must also assess the degree to which the activity is adding value to the organization and improving its operations, and it should identify specific opportunities to enhance internal audit services (PA 1310-1).

This is obviously one of the most challenging requirements. It is easier to determine conformance with rules and required tasks, but how does one assess the degree to which audit operations add value and improve the organization? While this is a challenge in building a high quality QA&I program, the issue is more fundamental than that. This is a key challenge of leading and participating in a high-quality internal audit activity.

Adapting to today's internal audit challenges requires leadership, vision, and agility. Leveraging lessons from other high performing internal audit activities into the assessment of internal audit quality can help identify breakthrough insights that drive impact through internal audit performance. Exhibit 7-7, Eight Attributes of a Maximized Internal Audit Function, can be useful to CAEs and their quality programs in identifying and assessing how their internal audit function can leverage lessons of others. Internal audit QA&I programs, when optimally designed, drive internal audit quality, value, and stakeholder satisfaction.

It is important that the QA&I process consider added value, effectiveness, and efficiency from the perspective of senior management, the board, and other key stakeholders. Internal auditors should clearly understand and articulate key stakeholders' perspectives on internal audit value. Similarly, the organization's overall strategic objectives and core values should be a starting point for identifying opportunities to add value and for improvement. It is best if this definition of value is put in the internal audit charter. Internal auditors then must plan to deliver this value. A QA&I process that begins with the perspective of key internal audit customers and the organization as a whole will go a long way toward helping internal auditors add more value and enhance operations, and thereby enhance the stature of internal auditing.

When it comes to actually assessing the contributions of the audit staff, the CAE will have to determine how best to measure the value of internal auditing's work. One important way is through customer satisfaction surveys. Another gauge is the number of management requests for audit involvement. If no one is asking for internal auditing's assistance, it may be because audit services are not seen as helpful or beneficial. Assessing the degree to which internal audit best practices and new procedures are adopted because they are perceived to add value provides a useful indicator. Additionally, the level of positive change in the organization that has been generated through internal audit activities is a metric that some executives hold as the core measure of added value. Finally, healthy dialogue between the CAE and senior management and the board is sure to reveal how well the audit activity is meeting the needs of its customers.

One tool that can assist the CAE in assessing and improving internal audit's effectiveness in adding value to the organization is the recently developed internal audit capability maturity model (Internal Audit Capability Model (IA-CM) for the Public Sector, The IIA Research Foundation, 2009). While the model was developed for internal audit functions in governmental organizations, it is equally relevant to internal auditing in all organizations. The model looks at the internal audit activity as being composed of six essential elements:

- Services and role of internal auditing.
- People management.
- Professional practices.
- Performance management and accountability.
- Organizational relationships and culture.
- Governance structures.

An audit function will be at various stages of development in regard to each of these elements. Exhibit 7-8 presents a matrix of these stages of development. CAEs can use this model to help structure their QA&I program.[2]

The Importance of Quality

The Guidance Task Force of The IIA recognized that consistent high quality across the internal audit profession was essential for broader marketplace recognition and competitiveness of the profession — two of the driving forces behind their recommendations that led to the complete rewrite of the *Standards* that became effective Jan. 1, 2002, and provide the framework for today's *Standards*. By requiring all internal auditors to maintain a comprehensive quality assurance and improvement program, the new *Standards* help ensure dependable, high caliber internal audit services throughout the profession's ranks, and hence greater recognition and competitiveness for the internal audit profession.

Exhibit 7-1
Performance Standards Checklist

This simple "performance standards checklist" can be a valuable tool for training staff members and encouraging conformance with the *Standards* regarding performance of internal audit work (2200-2500). The checklist also can help audit executives meet the quality assurance requirement mandating ongoing reviews of internal audit performance.

To be effective, a performance standards checklist must include necessary information, but be brief enough to allow efficient completion during every audit engagement. Customized checklists can be created for specific types of audits. For example, separate checklists for consulting engagements and for assurance engagements might be in order. Checklists also can be customized to include additional mandatory items specific to the organization's policies and procedures. The goal is not to include every possible standard, policy, or regulation, but to include fundamental items that should be considered during each engagement.

IAS Management Review Document

Audit:

Lead Auditor:

Audit Period:

Activity	Workpaper Reference	Comments/Review Notes OR Manager Approval (Initials)
PLANNING:		
1. The following issues were considered when planning the engagement:		
• The objectives of the activity being reviewed and the means by which the activity controls its performance.		
• The significant risks in the activity, its objectives, resources, and operations and the means by which the potential impact of risk is kept to an acceptable level.		
• The adequacy and effectiveness of the activity's risk management and control systems compared to a relevant control framework and model.		
• The opportunities for making significant improvements to the activity's risk management and control systems.		

	Activity	Workpaper Reference	Comments/Review Notes OR Manager Approval (Initials)
	**Exhibit 7-1 (continued)** **Performance Standards Checklist**		
2.	Risks relevant to the activity were identified and assessed. The engagement objectives reflect the results of the risk assessment.		
3.	The probability of significant errors, fraud, nonconformance, and other exposures were considered when developing the engagement objectives.		
4.	Relevant systems, records, personnel, and physical properties, including those under the control of third parties, were considered when establishing the engagement scope.		
5.	Appropriate resources (e.g., staff) were allocated to achieve engagement objectives.		
6.	Work programs were developed, establishing the procedures for identifying, analyzing, evaluating, and recording information during the engagement.		
FIELDWORK:			
1.	Sufficient, reliable, relevant, and useful information was identified to achieve the engagement's objectives.		
2.	Conclusions and engagement results were based on appropriate analyses and evaluations.		
3.	Relevant information to support the conclusions and engagement results was documented.		
4.	Access to engagement records was controlled by the CAE, and approval of senior management was obtained prior to releasing such records to external parties.		
5.	Retention requirements were developed by the CAE and were consistent with the organization's guidelines and any pertinent regulatory or other requirements.		

Exhibit 7-1 (continued) Performance Standards Checklist		
Activity	**Workpaper Reference**	**Comments/Review Notes OR Manager Approval (Initials)**
6. The engagement was properly supervised to ensure objectives were achieved, quality was assured, and staff was developed.		
COMMUNICATIONS:		
1. Engagement results were communicated promptly.		
2. Communications included the engagement's objectives and scope as well as applicable conclusions, recommendations, and action plans.		
3. The final communication of results contained the internal auditor's overall opinion, if appropriate.		
4. Engagement communications acknowledged satisfactory performance.		
5. Communications were accurate, objective, clear, concise, constructive, complete, and timely.		
6. The final results were communicated to individuals who can ensure that the results are given due consideration.		
MONITORING PROGRESS:		
1. A system to monitor the disposition of results communicated to management was established and is maintained.		
2. A follow-up process was established to monitor and ensure that management actions have been effectively implemented or that senior management has accepted the risk of not taking action.		

Source: Derived from The IIA's electronic newsletter, *CAE Bulletin*, Oct. 3, 2001.

Exhibit 7-2
Questions for Gap Analysis

This exhibit includes suggested questions that should be addressed in each of the 11 sections of The IIA's *Standards*. These questions can serve as a useful tool when conducting a preliminary gap analysis to assess conformance with the *Standards*.

1000
Purpose, Authority, and Responsibility

The purpose, authority, and responsibility of the internal audit activity must be formally defined in an internal audit charter.

- Are the purpose, authority, and responsibility for internal audit formally defined in an internal audit charter?
- Has the charter been recently reviewed and presented to senior management and the audit committee for approval?
- Is the mandatory nature of the Definition of Internal Auditing, the Code of Ethics, and the *Standards* recognized in the charter?
- Are the Definition of Internal Auditing, the Code of Ethics, and the *Standards* discussed with senior management and the audit committee?
- Is the nature of any consulting services being offered by internal auditing defined in the charter?
- Is the nature of internal auditing's functional reporting relationship to the audit committee articulated in the charter, such as the audit committee:
  - Approving the internal audit charter?
  - Approving the risk-based internal audit plan?
  - Receiving communications from the CAE on the internal audit activity's performance relative to its plan and other matters?
  - Approving decisions regarding the appointment and removal of the CAE?
  - Making appropriate inquiries of management and the CAE to determine whether there are inappropriate scope or resource limitations?

1100
Independence and Objectivity

The internal audit activity must be independent, and internal auditors must be objective in performing their work.

- Does internal auditing report to an appropriate level?
- Does the CAE communicate and interact directly with the audit committee?
- Is the internal audit organization free from interference?
- Do corporate policies foster individual objectivity?
- Is internal auditing's independence confirmed with the audit committee annually?

Exhibit 7-2 (continued)
Questions for Gap Analysis

1200
Proficiency and Due Professional Care

The purpose, authority, and responsibility of the internal audit department must be clearly defined. Engagements must be performed with proficiency and due professional care.

- Is the internal audit staff proficient?
- Is the fraud risk expertise of the internal audit function sufficient?
- Is the IT expertise of the internal audit function adequate?
- Does internal auditing seek outside expertise when warranted?
- Do internal audit policies foster due professional care?
- Does internal auditing deploy IT tools when warranted?
- Are members of the internal audit staff adequately trained and educated?

1300
Quality Assurance and Improvement Program

The CAE must develop and maintain a quality assurance and improvement program that covers all aspects of the internal audit activity.

- Are there ongoing internal audit quality monitoring processes?
- Does internal auditing perform its own periodic internal quality reviews?
- Are external quality assessments performed at least once every five years?
- Are the results of internal and external quality assessments communicated to senior management and the audit committee?

2000
Managing the Internal Audit Activity

The CAE must effectively manage the internal audit activity to ensure it adds value to the organization.

- Have policies and procedures been prepared for internal auditing?
- Does internal auditing under take a comprehensive annual risk assessment?
- Is the annual plan for internal auditing based on an annual risk assessment?
- Is the annual internal audit plan approved by the audit committee?
- Does the CAE consider during planning the expectations of senior management, the audit committee, and other stakeholders, including the form and levels of assurance desired?
- Does the CAE coordinate with other oversight activities, such as risk management or compliance?
- Does the CAE inform senior management and the audit committee about internal auditing's resource requirements and limitations?

Exhibit 7-2 (continued)
Questions for Gap Analysis

2100
Nature of Work

The internal audit activity must evaluate and contribute to the improvement of governance, risk management, and control processes using a systematic and disciplined approach.

- Within your organization, does internal auditing:
  - Assess corporate governance?
  - Promote appropriate ethics and values?
  - Ensure effective organizational performance management and accountability?
  - Communicate about risk and control issues?
  - Facilitate the exchange of information among the board, external and internal auditors, and management?
- Does internal auditing evaluate the effectiveness of risk management in the organization?
- Does internal auditing contribute to the improvement of risk management processes?
- Does internal auditing evaluate fraud risk and how the organization manages fraud risk?
- Does internal auditing foster effective controls in:
  - Reliability and integrity of financial and operational information?
  - Effectiveness and efficiency of operations?
  - Safeguarding of assets?
  - Compliance with laws, regulations, and contracts?

2200
Engagement Planning

Internal auditors must develop and document a plan for each engagement, including the engagement's objectives, scope, timing, and resource allocations.

- Is there an engagement work program for each internal audit engagement?
- Is a preliminary risk assessment conducted when planning each engagement?
- Are engagement objectives a logical extension of a risk assessment process?
- Does the engagement scope adequately address engagement objectives?
- Do engagements have appropriate and sufficient resources?

Exhibit 7-2 (continued)
Questions for Gap Analysis

2300
Performing the Engagement

Internal auditors must identify, analyze, evaluate, and document sufficient information to achieve the engagement's objectives.

- Do internal audit workpapers appropriately document information?
- Are engagements properly supervised?
- Do auditors identify, analyze, evaluate, and record sufficient information to achieve engagement objectives?
- Has the engagement team identified a sufficient amount of reliable, relevant, and useful information to achieve engagement objectives?

2400
Communicating Results

Internal auditors must communicate the engagement results.

- Are engagement results properly communicated to management?
- Are the communications pertaining to internal audit engagements accurate, objective, clear, concise, constructive, complete, and timely?
- If opinions, conclusions, or ratings on engagements are issued, is the communication supported by sufficient, reliable, relevant, and useful information?
- Are engagement communications properly supported by workpapers?
- Are engagement results disseminated to appropriate parties?
- If an overall opinion or conclusion on the organization is issued:
  - Is it supported by sufficient, reliable, relevant, and useful information?
- Does the communication and reporting include:
  - The scope, including the time period to which the opinion pertains?
  - Scope limitations?
  - Consideration of all related projects, including the reliance on other assurance providers?
  - The risk or control framework or other criteria used as a basis for the overall opinion?
  - The overall opinion, judgment, or conclusion reached? If an unfavorable overall opinion is reached, are the reasons for it stated?

2500
Monitoring Progress

The CAE must establish and maintain a system to monitor the disposition of results communicated to management.

- Has a process been established to monitor the implementation of internal audit recommendations?
- Are engagement results followed up in a timely manner?

Exhibit 7-2 (continued)
Questions for Gap Analysis

2600
Resolution of Senior Management's Acceptance of Risks

When the CAE believes that senior management has accepted a level of residual risk that may be unacceptable to the organization, the CAE must discuss the matter with senior management. If the decision regarding residual risk is not resolved, the CAE must report the matter to the board for resolution.

- When management disagrees with the recommendations of internal auditing, is there a process in place to resolve such disagreements with the board of directors?

- If such a resolution process exists, does it allow for escalation of disagreements until resolved by the audit committee or the board?

Source: PricewaterhouseCoopers LLP, *How Quality Assurance Reviews Can Strengthen the Strategic Value of Internal Auditing,* 2006, modified for recent *Standards* changes.

Exhibit 7-3
A Framework for Developing Performance Measures

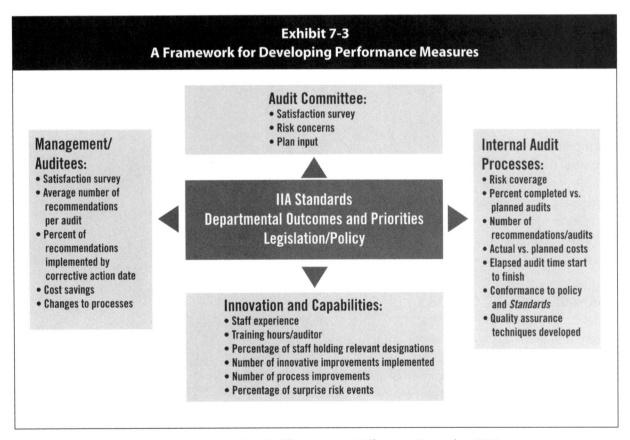

Source: Practice Guide, Measuring Internal Audit Effectiveness & Efficiency, December 2010.

Exhibit 7-4
Performance Measures

Exhibit 7-3 was extracted and adapted from an IIA publication titled *A Balanced Scorecard: Framework for Internal Auditing Departments.* This exhibit provides a point-in-time snapshot of performance measurements that were considered important to a limited number of CAEs. Specific performance measures should be selected that meet the unique needs of the internal audit activity.

Professional Practices Framework
Corporate and Internal Audit Strategies
Laws and Regulations

INNOVATION AND CAPABILITIES:
Staff experience
Training hours per internal auditor
CAE reporting relationship — functional
Percent of certified staff

BOARD/AUDIT COMMITTEE:
Audit committee satisfaction survey
Role of internal auditing viewed by audit committee
Audit committee risk concerns

INTERNAL AUDIT PROCESS:
Importance of audit issue
Completed vs. planned audits
Number of process improvements
Number of major audit findings
Amount of audit savings
Quality assurance techniques developed
Number of repeat findings
Days from end of fieldwork to report issuance

MANAGEMENT AND CLIENTS:
Client satisfaction survey results
Percent of audit recommendations implemented
Number of management requests
Management expectations of internal auditing
Number of complaints about audit

Exhibit 7-5
Building a Balanced Scorecard — Measure Results

To be effective, your internal audit team must demonstrate results. You must have a performance measurement system tied to the stakeholder value drivers you have identified. It is important to regularly track and measure internal audit performance against broad management expectations to meet — and then exceed — the expectations of key stakeholders.

To measure value, consider using "balanced scorecards," an effective tool that goes well beyond numbers to examine important, broad-based activities. The balanced scorecard concept was created by Drs. Robert S. Kaplan and David P. Norton based on the simple premise that "measurement motivates." Today, it has been used by thousands of corporations, organizations, and government agencies worldwide.

The balanced scorecard allows organizations to implement strategy rapidly and effectively by integrating measurement with the management system. It allows you to assess a detailed set of objectives and activities on an ongoing basis, as well as to measure links between incentive compensation and individual performance. Each organization should build its specific internal audit scorecard based on the first three steps of the framework: Define Stakeholder Expectations, Articulate the Mission, and Develop a Formal Strategic Plan. A sample scorecard is shown below.

Example Internal Audit Balanced Scorecard	
25% People	**25% Internal Audit Process Effectiveness**
Quality of professional staff	Rapid and effective startup
Ability to address specialized and technical needs	Effective and timely communication
Understanding of the business and the global business environment	Development and delivery of practical recommendations to improve internal controls and corporate governance
Interaction and communication with line management executives	Results of client satisfaction questionnaires
Development of management talent for the organization	

Example Internal Audit Balanced Scorecard	
25% Risk Management	**25% Value Added to the Business**
Timely and effective identification of key business risks	Protection of shareholder value through an improved control environment
Percentage of audit activities and resources allocated to addressing key business risks	Enhanced shareholder value through:
Adaptability and responsiveness to emerging risks	– Cost reductions
	– Reduced revenue leakage
	– Reduced working capital
	– Enhanced cash flow

Source: PricewaterhouseCoopers LLP, *Building a Strategic Internal Audit Function: A 10-step Framework*, 2003.

Exhibit 7-6
Create the Performance Scorecard

A maximized internal audit function demonstrates results, improvement, and value. Unfortunately, many internal audit functions today do not have a robust set of meaningful targets and metrics.

To measure performance, many for- and not-for-profit enterprises have adopted balanced scorecards based on the premise that what gets measured gets done. An internal audit balanced scorecard should comprise four dimensions: financial, stakeholder, process, and learning and growth enablers. However, these dimensions are only one aspect that needs to be balanced. Goals also should be balanced among:

- Strategic goals that align to the main themes in internal auditing's strategic plan for achieving its two-year to three-year vision. An example would be implementing a rotational staffing model.

- Improvement goals that address areas requiring shorter-term focus and visibility, in effect, remediation efforts such as improving the percentage of audits completed on time and on budget from 60 percent to 90 percent within one year.

- Operational goals or standards that track the key drivers of day-to-day efficiency and effectiveness such as reporting cycles, stakeholder satisfaction, staff utilization, staff certification, and turnover.

Finally, metrics can relate to either efficiency or effectiveness. The following graphic outlines a holistically balanced approach for designing metrics and a scorecard.

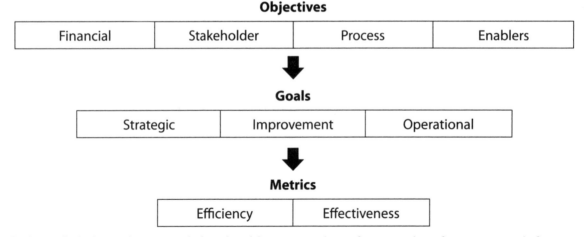

Objectives

Financial	Stakeholder	Process	Enablers

Goals

Strategic	Improvement	Operational

Metrics

Efficiency	Effectiveness

A holistically balanced scorecard also should serve as a basis for annual performance goals for everyone within the audit organization so they can be held accountable for results and rewarded for successes.

What this means for your business: Internal auditing's value will be measured by its ability to drive positive change and improvement.

Source: PricewaterhouseCoopers LLP, *Maximizing Internal Audit: A 10 Step Process for Thriving in a Challenging Economy*, 2010.

| **Exhibit 7-7** |
| **Eight Attributes of a Maximized Internal Audit Function** |

The following list of attributes has been gathered from working with leading internal audit activities and their stakeholders to understand what differentiates these functions from others.

A. Align value proposition with stakeholder expectations.
   1. Engage audit stakeholders to determine needs and goals.
   2. Create and update a charter that defines the audit mandate.
   3. Define the internal audit activity's scope of services.
   4. Affect the audit charter with a detailed strategy document.
   5. Devise a strategy to continually improve the audit function.
   6. Use a balanced scorecard and performance measures to assure ongoing alignment.

B. Target the most critical risks and business issues.
   1. Focus on critical risks and business issues with a top-down approach.
   2. Adopt a formal risk analysis framework.
   3. Identify key strategic risks enterprisewide.
   4. Define internal auditing's enterprise risk management role and contribute to enhancing risk management maturity.
   5. Create and update rolling, risk-based audit plans.
   6. Deploy resources in accordance to critical need and strategic importance.

C. Engage stakeholders and deliver on expectations.
   1. Build key stakeholder relationships and align reporting hierarchies.
   2. Position internal auditing as an efficiently managed business partner.
   3. Define internal auditing's role related to governance, risk, and compliance functions.
   4. Deliver insightful, impactful, and constructive communications and reports.

D. Deliver services cost-effectively.
   1. Determine the appropriate staffing composition and management-to-staff ratio.
   2. Use lean and consistent audit processes companywide.
   3. Apply technology strategically to achieve positive return on investment and enhanced efficiency.
   4. Identify the appropriate mix of core versus noncore services.
   5. Expand staff capabilities with guest auditor programs.
   6. Define and monitor tangible productivity standards and metrics.

E. Align the internal audit talent model to the value proposition.
   1. Specify the desired skill and business experience mix of core and specialist auditors.
   2. Establish formal training and professional development programs aligned to the talent model.
   3. Establish clearly defined career paths.
   4. Boost auditor development with a formal performance management system.
   5. Leverage rotational auditor programs to develop managerial talent.
   6. Embed a virtual resource model to enhance excellence in skills, coverage, and talent.

Exhibit 7-7 (continued)
Eight Attributes of a Maximized Internal Audit Function

F. Enable a client service culture.
1. Provide training and development in soft skills and business acumen.
2. Recruit and retain experienced auditors with relevant business experience.
3. Foster an environment that encourages independence, objectivity, and adding value.
4. Make communication skills a core competency of the internal audit staff.
5. Communicate the value added by internal auditing.
6. Use formal mechanisms to gauge stakeholder and audit customer satisfaction.

G. Promote quality improvement and innovation.
1. Adhere to The IIA's *International Standards for the Professional Practice of Internal Auditing.*
2. Establish a closed-loop system of continuous quality review and improvement.
3. Promote a culture of innovation and process improvement.
4. Apply quality improvement and lean techniques to audit processes.
5. Establish technology, policies, and processes to create a knowledge management capability.
6. Implement a robust, ongoing internal quality assessment program.

H. Leverage technology effectively.
1. Implement an audit management platform for efficiency and effectiveness.
2. Use data analytics and business intelligence technology to deliver the internal audit mission.
3. Use automated controls monitoring software.
4. Leverage enterprise resource planning (ERP) capabilities to realize continuous auditing.
5. Use internal auditing as a knowledge resource for risk, controls, and best practices.
6. Align audit technology with companywide governance, risk, and compliance (GRC) tools.

Note: Effective communication is key throughout the internal audit process.

Source: PricewaterhouseCoopers, *Global Best Practices for Managing Internal Audit,* 2011.

Exhibit 7-8
Internal Auditing — Capability Model Matrix

	Services and Role of IA	People Management	Professional Practices	Performance Management and Accountability	Organizational Relationships and Culture	Governance Structures
Level 5 – Optimizing	IA Recognized as Key Agent of Change	Leadership Involvement with Professional Bodies Workforce Projection	Continuous Improvement in Professional Practices Strategic IA Planning	Public Reporting of IA Effectiveness	Effective and Ongoing Relationships	Independence, Power, and Authority of the IA Activity
Level 4 – Managed	Overall Assurance on Governance, Risk Management, and Control	IA Contributes to Management Development IA Activity Supports Professional Bodies Workforce Planning	Audit Strategy Leverages Organization's Management of Risk	Integration of Qualitative and Quantitative Performance Measures	CAE Advises and Influences Top-level Management	Independent Oversight of the IA Activity CAE Reports to Top-level Authority
Level 3 – Integrated	Advisory Services Performance/Value-for-Money Audits	Team Building and Competency Professionally Qualified Staff Workforce Coordination	Quality Management Framework Risk-based Audit Plans	Performance Measures Cost Information IA Management Reports	Coordination with Other Review Groups Integral Component of Management Team	Management Oversight of the IA Activity Funding Mechanisms

Exhibit 7-8 (continued)
Internal Auditing — Capability Model Matrix

	Services and Role of IA	People Management	Professional Practices	Performance Management and Accountability	Organizational Relationships and Culture	Governance Structures
Level 2 – Infrastructure	Compliance Auditing	Individual Professional Development Skilled People Identified and Recruited	Professional Practices and Processes Framework Audit Plan Based on Management/ Stakeholder Priorities	IA Operating Budget IA Business Plan	Managing within the IA Activity	Full Access to the Organization's Information, Assets, and People Reporting Relationships Established
Level 1 – Initial	Ad hoc and unstructured; isolated single audits or reviews of documents and transactions for accuracy and compliance; outputs dependent upon the skills of specific individuals holding the position; no specific professional practices established other than those provided by professional associations; funding approved by management, as needed; absence of infrastructure; auditors likely part of a larger organizational unit; no established capabilities; therefore, no specific key process areas					

Source: *Internal Audit Capability Model (IA-CM) for the Public Sector*, IIA Research Foundation, 2009

References

[1] See James A. Bailey, CBOK Report II, *Core Competencies for Today's Internal Auditor* (Altamonte Springs, FL: The Institute of Internal Auditors Research Foundation, 2010), pp. 35–39, for the current state of quality assurance program practices and the reasons firms have difficulty.

[2] MacRae, Elizabeth, "A Framework for Audit Evolution," *Internal Auditor* (February 2010), pp. 68–69.

Chapter 8

YOU MUST MANAGE THE INTERNAL AUDIT ACTIVITY FOR THE ORGANIZATION, ENSURING IT ADDS VALUE (2000-2060)

The *Standards* assign management responsibility for the internal audit activity to a CAE. According to the Glossary, the CAE is *a senior position responsible for effectively managing the internal audit activity in accordance with the internal audit charter and the Definition of Internal Auditing, the Code of Ethics, and the* Standards. In a traditional in-house audit shop, the CAE often has a title such as internal audit director, general auditor, chief internal auditor, head of internal audit, or inspector general. In outsourced environments, the CAE may be inside the organization, such as a senior official who has ultimate responsibility for overseeing the internal audit service contract. In other situations, the CAE may be designated to be from the service provider, such as the partner over the relationship. The extent of the roles assumed by the service provider will depend on the specifics of the outsourcing arrangement. In smaller organizations and in those that outsource the activity, the CAE could have other responsibilities as well. He or she could serve, for example, as the chief compliance or ethics officer, the chief risk officer, the chief legal officer, the chief administrative officer, or potentially even the chief financial officer. Whatever the title, the *Standards* require that *the CAE report to a level within the organization that allows the internal audit activity to fulfill its responsibilities* (1110 — see Chapter 5).

The *Standards* assign specific responsibilities to the CAE, clearly delineating those internal audit management responsibilities that the CAE is responsible for fulfilling. This list of CAE requirements, which is outlined below, may prove particularly useful to newly named CAEs previously from other management areas in the organization.

Manage to Add Value

In keeping with the *Standards'* emphasis on adding value, a key requirement of the CAE is that he or she *effectively manage the internal audit activity to ensure it adds value to the organization* (2000). The Interpretation to Standard 2000 further states that *the internal audit activity is effectively managed when:*

- *The results of the internal audit activity's work achieve the purpose and responsibility included in the internal audit charter;*
- *The internal audit activity conforms with the Definition of Internal Auditing and the* Standards; *and*
- *The individuals who are part of the internal audit activity demonstrate conformance with the Code of Ethics and the* Standards.

This needs to be done in the context of 1110, where the CAE must ensure that the internal audit activity is conducted without undue influence so its responsibilities can be carried out in an unbiased manner. The *Standards* raise the bar for effective management by making the responsibility for ensuring the internal audit activity adds value the primary goal of the CAE. In every management action the CAE takes, he or she is required to foster the value-added nature of internal audit services.

The Glossary to the *Standards* notes that internal auditing adds *value to the organization and its stakeholders when it provides objective relevant assurance, and contributes to the effectiveness and efficiency of governance, risk management, and control processes.* As the Internal Audit Value Proposition (Exhibit 2-2) illustrates internal auditing adds value by bringing positive change to organizations as well as by reducing risk exposure through providing assurance to management and the audit committee. The definition of *adding value* varies by organization and by internal audit stakeholder. Having a good understanding of key stakeholder value drivers is essential to effective management of the internal audit activity.

Each individual CAE will have to determine how best to cultivate a value-added audit activity given the needs and climate of his or her organization. To understand how best to add value, the CAE needs to understand the expectations of key stakeholders and their perception of what adds value. A list of identified best practices for adding value is shown in Exhibit 8-1.

Administer the Activity

One of the primary duties of the CAE is the general administration of the internal audit activity. According to the *Standards*, the CAE is responsible for such administrative issues as resource management, policies and procedures, coordination of work, and quality assurance and improvement.

Resource Management

The CAE must ensure that internal audit resources are appropriate, sufficient, and effectively deployed to achieve the approved audit plan (2030). Resources broadly include in-house resources as well as subject matter experts and third parties from other parts of the organization. The related interpretation further explains the elements of Standard 2030:

- *Appropriate refers to the mix of knowledge, skills, and other competencies needed to perform the plan.*
- *Sufficient refers to the quantity of resources needed to accomplish the plan.*
- *Resources are effectively deployed when they are used in a way that optimizes the achievement of the approved plan.*

Guidelines for allocating resources to a specific audit engagement are discussed in Standard 2230 (see Chapter 10).

The foundation of internal audit resource allocation has to start with the risks and expectations of how internal auditing can add value. It is important that the process not be reversed, with the skill sets of the existing internal audit resources being a constraint to how internal auditing addresses risks of the organization. This is one of the key points in the CAE's role where they can define whether internal audit results will deliver the promise of the Definition of Internal Auditing. Given a strong understanding of the organization's risks and how internal auditing can add value in the eyes of key stakeholders, the CAE can then ensure resources are appropriate and the internal audit activity has sufficient knowledge, skills, or other competencies to address the risks of the organization, whether insourced or outsourced.

As part of resource management, it is recommended that the CAE establish a program for selecting and developing the human resources for the internal audit activity (PA 2030-1). For an internally staffed audit group, this program should include:

- Developing written job descriptions for each level of the audit staff.
- Selecting qualified and competent individuals.
- Training and providing continuing educational opportunities for each internal auditor.
- Appraising each internal auditor's performance at least annually.
- Providing counsel to internal auditors on their performance and professional development.
- Considering succession planning for management of internal auditing.

Across all elements of the internal audit activity, including sourcing of resources, the CAE should define the skill set needs based on the organization's risks and related internal audit plan as well as the value drivers of key stakeholders.

During certain engagements, effective resource management may require the CAE to obtain outside assistance and advice. If the internal auditors lack the knowledge, skills, or other competencies needed to perform all or part of an assurance engagement, for example, then the CAE is responsible for obtaining competent advice and assistance (1210.A1). For consulting engagements, the *Standards* similarly state that *the CAE must decline the consulting engagement or obtain competent advice and assistance if the internal auditors lack the knowledge, skills, or other competencies needed to perform all or part of the engagement* (1210.C1).

Such advice and assistance may be acquired from internal audit service providers, actuaries, accountants, appraisers, environmental specialists, fraud investigators, lawyers, engineers, geologists, security specialists, statisticians, information technology specialists, and other consulting organizations. The level of outside help varies from total outsourcing of the audit activity, to partial outsourcing or "co-sourcing" of selected pieces of audit work. However, the CAE cannot delegate certain audit management activities, such as responsibility for the internal audit plan. Whenever the CAE is considering the use of external assistance, he or she must take care to retain ultimate ownership over those elements that the *Standards* describe as his or her responsibility.

That being said, the *Standards* clearly recognize that the key point is internal audit quality and adding value, not who does the internal audit work. There is an emerging view by many CAEs that seeking stronger overall resources and knowledge through sourcing providers is a sign of strength, not a sign of weakness. PA 1210.A1-1, from which Exhibit 8-2 is derived, provides detailed guidance for the CAE when obtaining services to support or complement the internal audit activity. Exhibit 8-3 provides the elements of a contract to obtain internal audit resources from a third-party provider.

Policies and Procedures

The CAE must establish policies and procedures to guide the internal audit activity (2040). As noted in the related interpretation, *the form and content of policies and procedures are dependent upon the size and structure of the internal audit activity and the complexity of its work.* Some small audit shops, for example, may be managed informally through daily close supervision and written memos that state policies and procedures to be followed. Larger groups may find more formal and comprehensive audit manuals outlining their policies and procedures essential to guide internal auditing. As part of this policy-making role, the CAE should also consider whether existing policies and procedures, including the internal audit charter, accurately reflect the Definition of Internal Auditing and the *Standards*.

Policies and procedures are one set of tools that the CAE has to ensure internal auditing follows a systematic and disciplined approach to its work. The policies and procedures are a set of tools that the CAE can leverage to help everyone involved in the internal audit activity consistently deliver high-quality service.

Coordination of Work

The chief audit executive should share information and coordinate activities with other internal and external providers of assurance and consulting services to ensure proper coverage and minimize duplication of efforts (2050). Groups devoted to internal quality assurance, such as ISO 9000 certifications, environmental health and safety, contract management, security, or consulting, may perform audits. Often these reviews will address areas and issues relevant to internal auditing's scope of work.

Some suggested coordination activities include:

- Ensuring that the audit team relies on, reviews, or leverages the work of other service providers, if possible, when conducting an audit, instead of duplicating it.
- Ensuring a common understanding of audit techniques, methods, and terminology.
- Providing access to one another's audit programs and working papers.
- Exchanging audit reports and management letters. (PA 2050-1)

When sharing information with providers outside the organization, having limits on use and restrictions on sharing of any confidential information is most often appropriate, and with external auditors, it is particularly important. Because board support is crucial to effective coordination, it is recommended that the CAE regularly evaluate the coordination effort between internal and external auditors and communicate the results to senior management and the board. It is especially important that the CAE review such efforts when the internal audit activity is outsourced to a firm other than the one that performs the external audit. Additional guidance on coordination with external auditors is available in PA 2050-1. It is particularly critical today that the CAE encourage good coordination of internal audit and external audit activities. While it is important to maintain the independence of both roles, audit committees today expect a solid, constructive, collaborative relationship.

The CAE's role in coordination of assurance work is rapidly evolving with the increased demands across the organization and from the board and senior management as they are being held ever more accountable for their oversight roles. Likewise, line managers are increasingly suffering from assurance fatigue brought on by an overwhelming and uncoordinated assurance process. It not uncommon for a manager to be dealing with the demands from internal auditing, compliance, information security, fraud, risk management, and EH&S in a given year. We are finding a number of CAEs who are undertaking a more systematic approach to assurance across the organization.

For example in South Africa, the recently issue King III report, *King Code of Governance for South Africa 2009,* introduces the notion of "combined assurance" in its governance principle 3.5. The principle states "the audit committee should ensure that a combined assurance model is applied to provide a coordinated approach to all assurance activities." For the audit committee to meet this requirement, the organization must take a much more structured approach to assurance coordination. This includes the preparation of an "assurance" map or profile of the organization as described in PA 2050-2.[1] Exhibit 8-4 presents an example of such a map.

Quality Assurance and Improvement

The CAE is responsible for developing and maintaining the quality assurance and improvement (QA&I) program that covers all aspects of the internal audit activity (1300). This includes accountability for performing quality work on every single audit project. Cases where there is no CAE within the organization will be discussed later in this chapter. A detailed discussion outlining specific requirements associated with effective QA&I programs, and particularly the responsibility of the CAE to show that the internal audit activity is adding value, is provided in Chapter 7.

Establish Effective Plans

Establishing a plan for performing internal audit work is another primary responsibility of the CAE. According to the *Standards, the chief audit executive is responsible for establishing risk-based plans to determine the priorities of the internal audit activity* (2010). *These plans are to be consistent with the organization's goals* (2010) *and must be approved by senior management and the board* (2020). In the case of planning for assurance engagements, *the risk assessment must be documented and must be performed once a year at minimum. In addition, this risk assessment process must consider input from senior management and the board* (2010.A1).

The planning process includes such activities as establishing goals, developing engagement work schedules, formulating staffing plans and financial budgets, and composing activity reports. Each element of the risk-based plan should be based upon information obtained from the risk assessment (see Chapter 10).

In addition, the audit plan should ensure that sufficient evidence will be obtained to evaluate the effectiveness of control processes. The plan should call for audit engagements or other procedures to gather relevant information about all major operating units and business functions. The audit plan should also give special consideration to those operations most affected by recent or expected changes.

If the CAE designs the audit plan with the intent of providing an overall opinion on the organization's internal controls, Standard 2010.A2 requires the CAE to identify and consider the expectations of senior management, the board, and other stakeholders regarding such an opinion. This also applies to individual engagement opinions or ratings. It is important that the CAE and key stakeholders are aligned on expectations of the level of assurance provided by internal auditing. If stakeholders require greater assurance, then more internal audit resources should be provided up front, if appropriate. It is also important that the level of assurance provided by the opinion or rating be understood by those using the opinion or rating.

To minimize duplication and inefficiencies in coverage, the CAE should consider relevant work that has been, or will be, performed by others. Work associated with management's assessments of controls and quality improvement processes, as well as the work planned by external auditors, should be considered in determining the coverage of the audit plan for the coming year. Assurance maps (PG 2050-2) and an organizational assurance profile (Exhibit 8-4) are tools the CAE can use to improve the efficiency and effectiveness of assurance coverage and help avoid assurance fatigue.

Internal audit plans and nature of work are directly affected by risk. As noted in the Interpretation to Standard 2010, *the CAE is responsible for developing a risk-based plan. The CAE takes into account the organization's risk management framework, including using risk appetite levels set by management for the different activities or parts of the organization. If a framework does not exist, the CAE uses his/her own judgment of risks after consultation with senior management and the board.*

Planning for Consulting Work

The nature of consulting work as a value-added, advisory, and problem-solving service necessitates unique planning considerations. Consulting engagements are often performed on an ad hoc, as needed basis. Therefore, many may not appear on the annual plan of engagements, because the CAE will not have agreed to the consulting work at the time the plan is developed. However, the *Standards require that accepted consulting engagements must be included in the plan* (2010.C1). In other words, the annual plan should not be limited to assurance work. Any consulting engagements that the CAE knows will be undertaken during the year must appear in the plan.

In addition, the *Standards* state that *the CAE should consider accepting proposed consulting engagements based on their potential to improve management of risks, add value, and improve the organization's operations* (2010.C1). All consulting engagements are not equal in terms of their value to the organization, and the CAE must exercise good judgment in determining which ones to accept. As noted above, the *Standards* stipulate that the priorities of the audit activity are to be based on organizational goals and areas of risk. In addition, internal auditing is, by definition, charged with adding value by improving organizational operations, including the risk management system. Any consulting engagement should, therefore, be related to the areas delineated in these mandates. Another element of balance in accepting consulting engagements is being aware that the needs of high priority stakeholders such as the board and senior management may need to be prioritized over those of other stakeholders, particularly when internal audit resources are limited.

Best Practice Planning

Many CAEs are finding opportunities to add more value to their organizations by making sure the risk assessment and resulting audit plan reflect the overall objectives of the business, as required in Standard 2010. Assessing the risks of an operational area in a vacuum without considering the bigger picture does not add much value to the organization as a whole. Even in a narrowly focused consulting engagement, the internal auditor can contribute more to the operating management customer by bringing an organizationwide perspective to the table.

The definition of the audit universe, and how to ensure that is complete, is important in effective risk assessment. You must have a good process to not only define what gets in your audit universe, but also a way to challenge it to ensure it is complete. For instance, have you compared it to your product mix, your general ledger, and your organization structure to ensure it is complete?

One way to accomplish this "big picture" approach is to include components from the organization's strategic plan in the audit universe (PA 2010-1). Strategic plans often reflect the organization's attitude toward risk, and they can serve as useful indicators of the difficulty associated with achieving planned objectives. Such linkage to the strategic plan therefore helps ensure that the audit universe considers and reflects the overall business objectives and remains in line with the organization's risk tolerance level. In "best practice" shops, auditors study the strategic plan and query executives to ascertain where the business is going in the next few years. Armed with that information, it is possible to identify a set of audit projects that support the mitigation of risks to the strategic plan.

Even the establishment of audit work schedules should be linked to risk by basing them on, among other things, an assessment of risk priority and exposure. Resources should be applied according to the likelihood and consequences of identified risks, and repetitive cycle audits that have little link to risk should be minimized or even eliminated.

Many organizations are building flexibility into their audit plan so that they can address risks as they arise throughout the year. Audit shops may leave a percentage of their time unallocated, for example. Some do this by assessing risk and the resulting internal audit plan more frequently than once a year. The frequency of risk assessment may be seen to be dictated by how frequently the underlying risk may change. For risks or organizations that do not change frequently, an annual risk assessment process may be fine. On the other hand, when risks or organizations may change dramatically in the course of a year, it is more appropriate then for risk assessment processes and internal audit plans to not stick to a rigid one-year cycle. When major changes such as major acquisitions or significant changes in global economic conditions occur, that is often a sign for internal auditing to consider more frequent risk assessment and audit plan reprioritization.

Others may commit to spending a certain amount of time in a functional area, like information technology, but stop short of identifying specific projects. When the time arrives to perform one of these conditional engagements, the auditor spends 10 to 12 hours to prepare an engagement specific risk assessment to further define the project that is submitted to audit management. Based on the information acquired during this preliminary planning phase, audit management can determine whether or not the audit is still appropriate. Such approaches give the audit team the versatility to respond to changes and avoid wasting their time on audits that appeared to be necessary 10 months ago, but do not make sense anymore given the "big picture" of the current business environment.[2]

A variety of risk models exist to help the CAE prioritize potential audit subject areas. Such factors as dollar materiality, asset liquidity, management competence, quality of internal controls, degree of change or stability, time since last audit engagement, complexity, and employee and government relations may be used in these risk models to assign priority (see Chapter 10 for additional information on quantifying risk).

It is interesting to note that most leading edge audit shops have lessened or deemphasized the use of automated risk models managed by internal auditing with little input from those outside of internal auditing to assign a numeric weight to various risk factors. Current best practice considers such programs as secondary tools to be used as part of the planning process. In addition, qualitative factors are often emphasized by weighting them as much as three times more heavily than quantitative factors. One organization, for example, starts its risk assessment process by using a model that assigns weights as follows:[3]

Risk Factor	Approximate Weighting
Control environment	3
Business events	3
Size	2
Last audit opinion	2
Time since last audit	1
Time since last control-related activity	1
(e.g., use of another internal audit product)	

The results of the model are then adjusted to reflect additional qualitative management judgments, such as alignment with corporate goals and strategic initiatives, the business unit's financial performance, and the business unit management's areas of concern. PA 2010-1 notes that most risk models use risk factors such as impact, likelihood, materiality, asset liquidity, management competence and stability, quality of and adherence to internal controls, degree of change or stability, timing and results of last audit engagement, complexity, and employee and government relations.

When looking closely at internal audit risk assessments and the risk factors that some develop, one can see that all risk factors, whether the department uses three or 15 risk factors, really are simply indicators of one of two fundamental factors in assessing risk — significance or likelihood. As required by the *Standards*, a fundamental best practice is for the risk assessment to *consider the input of senior management and the board* (2010.A1).

Fortunately, the growing practice of providing consulting services is helping internal auditors stay abreast of the changing risk environment. Consulting work gives internal auditors a perspective on risk that usually cannot be acquired through assurance activities alone. From their participation on steering committees and system implementation projects, to their interactions during control training and self-assessment exercises, internal auditors achieve a "real" understanding of the various risks facing the organization. Consulting work may occur in any nook and cranny of the organization, whether the area is listed on the annual audit plan or not. And, in many organizations, some type of consulting work is occurring all the time, meaning that internal auditors are always in the field acquiring real-time knowledge regarding what is really happening in the organization.

While the stated objectives of a consulting engagement may only tangentially address risk, the *Standards* make it clear that internal auditors can never completely turn off their risk assessment radars. The *Standards* call for internal auditors *to address risk and control consistent with the consulting engagement's objectives* (2120.C1 and 2130.C1), thereby allowing the operating client to retain influence on the scope of the engagement. But, the *Standards* also require internal auditors to *be alert to the existence of other significant risks and control weaknesses* (2120.C1 and 2130.C1), and they state that internal auditors *must incorporate knowledge of risks and controls gained from consulting engagements into their evaluation of the organization's risk management and control processes* (2120.C2 and 2130.C1). In addition, substantial risk exposures identified during consulting engagements should be brought to the attention of management. Certain situations may also necessitate that the auditor's concerns be communicated to executive management, the audit committee, and the board of directors.

The internal auditor's dual purpose in a consulting engagement can lead to problems with the client if not handled carefully. To avoid impressions of betrayal, internal auditors must advise their consulting clients up front that the risk and control lessons resulting from the assignments will be part of internal auditing's growth in knowledge of, and may result on communications to others on, organizational risk.

The focus in the *Standards* on risk-based planning highlights the emphasis on the internal auditor's risk assessment and management role (see Chapter 9).

Communicate, Communicate, Communicate

One of the most important aspects of the CAE's job is communicating with internal auditing's customers, particularly with senior management and the board. The *Standards* outline several specific reporting requirements for the CAE.

Communication of the Audit Plan

The CAE must communicate the internal audit activity's plans and resource requirements, including significant interim changes, to senior management and the board for review and approval. The CAE must also communicate the impact of resource limitations (2020). In addition, as stated in Standard 2010. C1, *any accepted consulting engagements must be included in the plan* and therefore should be covered in these reports.

The reports may include specific information on the organization's risks, linkage of that assessment to the internal audit plan, the audit work schedule, the staffing plan, and the financial budget. These elements should be presented in such a way that they inform senior management and the board of the scope of internal audit work and of any limitations placed on that scope. The communications should also contain sufficient information to enable the board to determine whether internal auditing's objectives and plans support those of the organization and the board (PA 2020-1).

Periodic Communication on the State of the Internal Audit Activity

The CAE must report periodically to senior management and the board on the internal audit activity's purpose, authority, responsibility, and performance relative to its plan. Reporting must also include significant risk exposures and control issues, including fraud issues, corporate governance issues, and other matters needed or requested by senior management and the board (2060).

This standard addresses the various other reports the CAE makes to the board and senior management throughout the year. By requiring the CAE to "report periodically," the *Standards* allow the CAE to establish a reporting schedule that best meets the needs of the board and the organization. As explained in the Interpretation for 2060, *the frequency and content of reporting are determined in discussion with senior management and the board and depend on the importance of the information to be communicated and the urgency of the related actions to be taken by senior management or the board.*

The first part of the standard emphasizes the importance of discussing the internal audit charter with the board and senior management. It is the CAE's responsibility to periodically review the tenets of the charter and determine whether the stated purpose, authority, and responsibility continue to enable the internal audit activity to accomplish its objectives. The CAE should communicate the results of this periodic assessment to senior management and the board. *It is also the CAE's responsibility to present the internal audit charter to senior management and the board for approval* (1000).

In addition, the CAE should update the board and senior management, preferably quarterly but at least annually, on the progress of the audit team in achieving its stated goals for the year. This is the time to report on specific informational requests made by senior management and the board and to bring up any major issues uncovered during engagements (PA 2060-1). Most CAEs report on engagements in one of three ways: (1) providing a summary of audit work by area; (2) discussing only major issues; or (3) distributing copies of all their audit reports. The goal should be to present a balanced, prioritized view of insights from audit work that enables the audit committee to best perform its role. Best practice reporting also provides:[4]

- Executive summaries — These condensed reports on engagements and the total activity for the year focus on key issues and solutions instead of discussing each individual problem.

- Material in advance — Audit committees have limited time during their meetings to devote to the CAE's report, but they do spend time in their own environments reading material that is sent to them in advance.

- Actions, not just issues — Audit committees cannot, and should not in their role, create solutions for every issue identified by internal auditing. For important issues identified by internal auditing, the audit committee needs to be able to see that appropriate solutions are planned and have comfort that those solutions will be implemented. Hence, the internal audit communication of issues should include management's action plans or commitment to implementing recommendations.

- An event matrix — Rather than debate what should be reported to the audit committee after an event has occurred, it is useful to develop a list of pre-agreed reporting protocols for certain situations. For example, in case of a major fraud, would the audit committee prefer a report immediately or at the next meeting? If the fraud involves senior management, does their reporting preference change?

In addition, reporting of the internal audit activity should include reports on the nature, extent, and overall results of formal consulting engagements, along with other routine reporting of auditing activities. Internal auditors are expected to keep senior management and the audit committee informed of how audit resources are being deployed. Detailed reports discussing specific results and recommendations are not required, but appropriate descriptions of consulting engagements and their significant recommendations should be communicated and are essential in satisfying the requirements of Standard 2060. In looking at internal audit reporting, the CAE should look to ensure that internal audit communications are concise and understandable, with a clear communication of the importance or prioritization of issues.

The last part of this standard addresses the CAE's reports on risk, control, and governance, noting that *reporting must also include significant risk exposures and control issues, including fraud issues, corporate governance issues, and other matters needed or requested by senior management and the board.* This is a key role internal auditing has that contributes to transparency, issue resolution, and effective risk management, control, and governance in the organization. Internal auditing's transparent sharing of information is an important part of contributing to good governance in the organization. Communication of results is further discussed in Chapter 12.

Reporting on the Quality Program

The CAE must communicate the results of the quality assurance and improvement program to senior management and the board (1320). This communication might include a written action plan in response to the significant comments and recommendations of the external quality assessment reviewers. It is important that this also include the results and action plans coming from internal auditing's internal quality assurance and improvement program. See Chapter 7 for additional guidance on external quality assessment reports.

Communication of Engagement Results

The CAE must communicate audit engagement results to the appropriate parties (2440). This standard gives the CAE some flexibility in determining who should receive final engagement communications. For example, *when disseminating the final results of an assurance engagement, the* Standards *specifically require the CAE to communicate those results to individuals who can ensure that the results are given due consideration* (2440.A1). To ensure proper action is taken, findings from an assurance engagement should be communicated to those in a position to take corrective action or ensure corrective action is taken (PA 2440-1).

In the case of consulting engagements, however, the *Standards* state that *the CAE is responsible for communicating the final results to clients* (2440.C1). In most cases, it will only be appropriate to disseminate the results to the operating or line management customer. Yet, there may be times when the CAE and his or her staff conclude that engagement results should be communicated beyond those who received or requested the service. In such cases, the CAE should expand the reporting so that the results are communicated to the appropriate parties. One strategy for the CAE is to encourage those receiving or requesting the service to expand voluntarily the communication to the appropriate parties.

Instances requiring additional reporting will most often arise when governance, risk management, and control issues are identified. According to the *Standards, whenever these issues are significant to the organization, they must be communicated to senior management and the board* (2440.C2). Much care should be dedicated to making such disclosures properly to avoid perceived betrayal of the trust of the consulting client. Auditors should be sure to use their best professional judgment to determine the significance of exposures or weaknesses and the actions taken or contemplated to mitigate or correct these exposures or weaknesses, as well as to ascertain the expectations of senior management and the board in having these matters reported. In addition, clients should always be advised prior to the CAE's acceptance of the assignment that the internal auditor's foremost responsibility is adequate control of risk. Therefore, the identification of any significant risk management, control, or governance issues relevant to the organization as a whole will be considered in future risk assessments and may be communicated to senior management and the board, if necessary.

It is recommended that the CAE approve final engagement communications before issuance. In very large internal audit activities, the CAE review may be limited to executive summaries and more important issues. If circumstances warrant, it may be permissible for the auditor-in-charge, supervisor, or lead auditor to approve the communication as a representative of the CAE. PA 2440-1 provides additional guidance on disseminating results.

If a final communication contains a significant error or omission, the Standards *require the CAE to communicate corrected information to all parties who received the original communication* (2421).

Communication on Follow-up

Communication on follow-up is an important part of a fully functioning internal audit process. *The CAE must establish and maintain a system to monitor the disposition of results communicated to management* (2500). This is fully discussed in Chapter 13.

The CAE's Role in Communicating Unacceptable Residual Risks

The CAE has a key role in risk management, control, and governance in the responsibility to communicate unacceptable residual risk to the board where necessary. This is covered in the concluding standard 2600, *when the CAE believes that senior management has accepted a level of residual risk that may be unacceptable to the organization, the CAE must discuss the matter with senior management. If the decision regarding residual risk is not resolved, the CAE must report the matter to the board for resolution.* See Chapter 13 for further discussion of this important role.

When the CAE Role Is Provided by the Service Provider and Does Not Exist Within the Organization

In cases where internal audit services are provided by an in-house staff or an in-house staff supplemented by cosourcing with service providers, the CAE must fulfill all the responsibilities prescribed in *Standards* 2000 to 2060. However, there are situations where the CAE role is provided by the service provider. This might be a case where the audit committee contracts directly for internal audit services or when there is no one within the organization with the necessary skills set to take on these responsibilities. In such situations, most of these responsibilities fall to the lead person on the service provider's engagement team.

However, the organization cannot pass to the service provider the ultimate responsibility for maintaining an effective internal audit activity. Standard 2070 requires that *when an external service provider serves as the internal audit activity, the provider must make the organization aware that the organization has the responsibility for maintaining an effective internal audit activity.* The interpretation to this standard goes on to say that this responsibility is *demonstrated through the quality assurance and improvement program which assesses conformance with the Definition of Internal Auditing, the Code of Ethics, and the* Standards. This means that the service provider needs to (1) educate the board and senior management as to their oversight responsibilities in this regard, and (2) construct a quality assurance and improvement program specifically tailored to the service engagement, including a performance measure that demonstrates that the internal audit services are adding value and conforming with the *Standards*.

While the role of the CAE and internal audit services can be fully outsourced, if appropriate, the ultimate responsibility for internal auditing cannot be outsourced. The *Standards* make clear that the quality assurance and improvement program, including ensuring that an external quality assessment is performed and the results are reported to senior management and the board, is an important tool for the organization to use in exercising its responsibilities over fully outsourced internal audit activities.

Additional CAE Concerns

The *Standards* include a couple of additional Implementation Standards for assurance engagements that are directed to the CAE. Due to the fiduciary nature of assurance engagements, these requirements, which are outlined below, are more detailed and stringent than the general attribute and performance *Standards* from which they are derived.

Independence

If the CAE has responsibility for the area that is the subject of the assurance engagement, then he or she must not oversee that audit. Instead, the engagement must be overseen by a party outside the internal audit activity (1130.A2). Appropriate oversight could be provided by an independent member of management, such as the legal department or risk management; a past audit staff manager employed within the organization; or a board member.

Records

The CAE must control access to assurance engagement records and must obtain the approval of senior management and/or legal counsel prior to releasing such records to external parties (2330.A1). In addition, *it is the CAE's responsibility to develop retention requirements for assurance engagement records regardless of the medium in which each record is stored. These retention requirements must be consistent with the organization's guidelines and any pertinent regulatory or other requirements* (2330.A2). PA 2330.A2-1 notes:

- Record retention requirements vary among jurisdictions and legal environments.

- The CAE develops written retention policies that meet the organization's needs as well as legal compliance needs.

- Record retention requirements need to include appropriate provisions for internal audit work done by external service providers.

Control over access to engagement records may be increased by including applicable statements in the charter and internal audit policies.

- The internal audit charter should address access to and control of organizational records and information that applies, regardless of the type of media used to store the records.

- Internal department policies should cover, among other matters, what should be included in engagement records, how long departmental records should be retained, how outside requests for access to department records should be handled, and what special practices should be followed with legal counsel in an investigation.

When risks of access are more important, the CAE should also educate the board and management about the risks of access to engagement records. In such situations, the policies regarding who can be granted access to engagement records, how those requests are to be handled, and what procedures are to be followed when an audit warrants an investigation should be reviewed by the audit committee.

When engagement records must be disclosed, careful preparation is important. The following steps should be considered:

- Disclose the specific documents that are requested. Engagement records with opinions and recommendations are generally not released. Documents revealing attorneys' thought processes or strategies usually are privileged and not subject to forced disclosure.

- Release copies and keep the originals, especially if the documents were prepared in pencil. If the court requests originals, the internal audit activity should keep a copy.

- Label each document as confidential, and note on each that secondary distribution is not permitted without permission.

- Consult with legal counsel when there are uncertainties on allowing access.

In the case of consulting engagements, the *Standards* require the CAE to *develop policies governing the custody and retention of consulting engagement records, as well as their release to internal and external parties. These policies must be consistent with the organization's guidelines and any pertinent regulatory or other requirements* (2330.C1). Such policies might cover ownership of records, for example. Some organizations consider the end product of a consulting engagement to belong to the management client and therefore relinquish all records to their care. Other audit activities may retain custody of the records, but establish policies that provide copies to the client or grant unlimited access to the originals. Policies may also require client permission before the release of records to third parties, or they may spell out what actions are appropriate given requests from certain individuals, such as the audit committee or senior management. Situations involving legal proceedings, regulatory requirements, tax issues, and accounting matters may also require special handling of certain consulting engagement records.

The Organization's Responsibility for Internal Auditing

No matter who does the work, the *Standards* make it clear that internal auditing is an integral part of the organization's governance structure and that the responsibility for an effective internal audit activity rests with senior management and the board. Senior management cannot outsource this core responsibility; and by assigning key management oversight to the internally assigned role of CAE, the *Standards* make sure that the organization retains responsibility, authority, and accountability for determining the scope and nature of the internal audit activities provided and ensuring the overall quality of audit services.

Exhibit 8-1
Best Practices in Value-added Auditing
Audit Department Structure

1. Align the Audit Department Structure with the Structure of the Organization.

- Organizational units, processes, or product lines — however the organization categorizes itself — are assigned to each audit manager. For example, consider the following structure used at a major retail company:

Audit Managers for:	Audit Manager for:	Audit Managers for:	Audit Managers for:
– Dept. Stores (2) – Catalog – Business Process Review Team – Merchandising & Marketing	– Separate Vitamin and Health Products Subsidiary	– Accounting Center – Credit – Direct Marketing – Finance	– International – IS – Audit Technology

For this tactic to work, the audit department must be large enough to require and support several audit managers.

2. Use Relationship Managers.
- An experienced auditor is assigned to each organizational unit/process/product line.
- Purpose:
  - To stay in touch with unit/process/product line managers.
  - To provide real-time risk assessment.
  - To find opportunities to help: talk about changes taking place and the resulting risks; suggest procedures for managing risk; share best practices and common control weakness being found throughout the organization; etc.
- Activities:
  - A formal call program of once a month or at least once a quarter.
  - Frequent, informal "stopping by."
  - Attendance at staff meetings, planning sessions, conference calls, etc.
- Variations:
  - If the organization is geographically disbursed, an auditor is assigned in each region for each process.
  - The lead auditor fills this role until another auditor leads an audit in the area.

Exhibit 8-1 (continued)
Best Practices in Value-added Auditing

Risk Assessment and Audit Planning

3. Base the Audit Plan on Risk.

- Minimize or eliminate repetitive, cycle audits.
- Use qualitative, participative risk assessment.
- An automated risk model is of secondary importance.
  - If you use one, emphasize qualitative factors.
  - If you use one, use it as the starting point only.
- Management participation is primary.

4. Identify Tomorrow's Risks, Not Yesterday's.

- Once a year is not enough.
- Use "real-time" risk assessment.
- Focus on change, business strategy.
- Build flexibility into the annual plan to address risks as they arise.

5. Select the Best Assurance Service for Each Risk.

- Offer a menu of products/services, including:
  - Risk-based process audits.
  - Pre-implementation reviews.
  - Use of self-assessment.
    - For soft controls (workshops, surveys, questionnaires, structured interviews).
    - For hard controls (operating personnel independent of the area tested perform detailed tests of internal control procedures on a defined schedule and with internal reporting of results; internal audit reviews documentation and sub-tests to verify integrity of the process).
  - Internal control education (formal training programs and ad hoc training during audits).

Value-added Audit Methodologies

6. Ensure Audits Are:

- Risk-based.
  and/or
- Process-based.
  - Meaning #1: audit the entire business process, not organizational units.
  - Meaning #2: focus on process improvement, not just control.

7. Ensure Audits Are Participative.

- Plan the audit with your audit customer.
- Work through the audit with your customer; discover weaknesses together.
- Develop solutions together.

Exhibit 8-1 (continued) **Best Practices in Value-added Auditing**
8. Ensure Audits Include CAATS.

9. Ensure Audits Are Integrated.
  • Consider technology, operation, control, etc. together in the audit.
  • One person ideally should be looking at the composite picture that results.

10. Employ "Stop and Go" Auditing.
  • "Stop" when comfort is acquired, not when the audit plan or program states.
  • "Go" where weaknesses are indicated until comfort is achieved.
  • Avoid spending 99% of audit time reviewing things that are 99% okay.

Staffing and Work Environment

11. Staff with Experts More Than Trainees.
  • High average experience level.
  • Multidisciplinary.
  • Experienced in the business.
  • Skilled in data analysis.
  • Integrated IT/business audit skills.
  • Highly professional (certifications, advanced degrees, active in IIA).
  • Enhanced with selective outsourcing.

12. Create a Positive Work Environment.
  • Challenging work assignments.
  • Creativity encouraged and rewarded.
  • Employee involvement in decision-making.
  • "Fun place to work."

13. Promote a Value-adding Culture.
  • Emphasize partnership more than independence.
  • Serve as an internal control trainer, coach, consultant; not just an evaluator.
  • Make sure everyone always looks for opportunities to improve the business.

Source: Reprinted with permission from Jim Roth, AuditTrends, www.audittrends.com.

Exhibit 8-2
CAE Activities Regarding Use of External Service Providers

- The CAE is required to obtain any competencies and skills that the audit teams lacks, but which are necessary to complete an assurance engagement or any accepted consulting assignment. The following guidelines are designed to assist the CAE when obtaining such advice and assistance from an external service provider.

- The CAE should evaluate the competency, independence, and objectivity of the external service provider as it relates to the particular assignments to be performed, even if the service provider is selected by the board or senior management. Note that the definition of independence is different than that used for external auditors. If the assessment determines that the CAE should not use or rely on the work of the external service provider chosen by senior management and the board, the results of the assessment should be communicated to them, as appropriate.

- When assessing competency, the CAE should consider the following:
  - Professional certification, license, or other recognition of the external service provider's competency in the relevant discipline.
  - Membership of the external service provider in an appropriate professional organization and adherence to that organization's code of ethics.
  - The reputation of the external service provider. This may include contacting others familiar with the external service provider's work.
  - The external service provider's experience in the type of work being considered.
  - The extent of education and training received by the external service provider in disciplines that pertain to the particular engagement.
  - The external service provider's knowledge and experience in the industry in which the organization operates.

- The CAE should assess the relationship of the external service provider to the organization and to the internal audit activity to ensure that independence and objectivity are maintained throughout the engagement. This assessment should consider:
  - The financial interest the provider may have in the organization, if somehow adverse to the goals of the internal audit activity.
  - The personal or professional affiliation the provider may have to the area under review, or perhaps if there is a conflict, then the board, senior management, or others within the organization.
  - Any past conflicting relationship the provider may have had with the organization or the activities being reviewed that conflict with the objectives of the internal audit activity.
  - The extent of other ongoing services the provider may be performing for the organization.
  - Compensation or other incentives that the provider may receive that are adverse to the objectives of the internal audit activity.

Note that relationships with the provider can be important keys to success, are not necessarily negative, and may be strong positives, similar to how internal auditing builds relationships and earns respect in the organization.

Exhibit 8-2 (continued)
CAE Activities Regarding Use of External Service Providers

- If the external service provider is also the organization's external auditor, and the nature of the engagement is extended audit services or total outsourcing of the internal audit activity, the CAE should ascertain that work performed does not impair the external auditor's independence.

- The CAE should obtain sufficient information regarding the scope of the external service provider's work to ascertain that the scope of work is adequate for the purposes of the internal audit activity. It may be prudent to have these and other matters documented in an engagement letter or contract. As part of this exercise, the CAE should review with the external service provider:
    - Objectives and scope of work.
    - Specific matters expected to be covered in the engagement communications.
    - Access to relevant records, personnel, and physical properties.
    - Information regarding assumptions and procedures to be employed.
    - Ownership and custody of engagement working papers, if applicable.
    - Confidentiality and restrictions on information obtained during the engagement.

- The CAE should specify and ensure that the work complies with the *International Standards for the Professional Practice of Internal Auditing*, the Code of Ethics, and the Definition of Internal Auditing.

- The CAE may refer to the use of external service providers in final engagement communications, as appropriate. The external service provider should be informed and, if appropriate, concurrence should be obtained prior to such reference being made in engagement communications.

Source: Derived from PA 1210.A1-1.

Exhibit 8-3
Components of an Internal Audit Sourcing Contract

A.   Items to Look for in an Internal Audit Sourcing Contract

- Addressee, whether the CEO, CFO, CAE, or other senior officer, as appropriate.
- The scope of the engagement and service provider responsibilities, such as risk areas or locations to be covered and length of the agreement. It may cover who from the company will provide the direction for the work. It may cover format of deliverables.
- Professional standards covering the engagement, such as the Standards for Consulting Services established by the American Institute of Certified Public Accountants (AICPA) if the work is performed by a CPA firm, or the *International Standards for the Professional Practice of Internal Auditing*.

Exhibit 8-3 (continued)
Components of an Internal Audit Sourcing Contract

- Inherent limitations of the internal audit process and of internal controls. Provide description of what is and is not covered by the services.
- Who the beneficiaries of the work are, and who can and cannot have access to the deliverables. Cover any restrictions on references to the work.
- Management's responsibilities, such as for establishing and maintaining an effective system of internal control as well as evaluating the effectiveness of that system, final determination and assessment of audit risk and scope of internal audit activity, performing management functions and making management decisions, complying with statutes such as the U.S. Sarbanes-Oxley Act of 2002, and indemnifying and holding harmless the service provider for unauthorized third-party reliance.
- The service provider team leading the work.
- The agreed billing arrangements for fees and expenses.
- Ownership of work product.
- Mechanisms for resolution of disputes.
- The location whose laws apply to the agreement, such as a state in the United States.
- Restrictions on reliance on e-mail and risks of viruses.
- Mutual ability to terminate the agreement.
- Warranties and limitations of warranties.
- Confidentiality of information.
- Indemnification and limitation of liability provisions.
- Procedures for requesting additional services.
- Arrangements and restrictions on soliciting employees of the other party.
- Industry specific provisions.
- The agreement should be signed by both parties.

A similar point of view is seen in this excerpt from regulatory guidance provided to organizations in the financial services industry.

B. Excerpt from Interagency Policy Statement on the Internal Audit Function and its Outsourcing, March 17, 2003

To clearly distinguish its duties from those of the outsourcing vendor, the institution should have a written contract, often taking the form of an engagement letter. Contracts between the institution and the vendor typically include provisions that:

- Define the expectations and responsibilities under the contract for both parties;
- Set the scope and frequency of, and the fees to be paid for, the work to be performed by the vendor;
- Set the responsibilities for providing and receiving information, such as the type and frequency of reporting to senior management and directors about the status of contract work;

Exhibit 8-3 (continued)
Components of an Internal Audit Sourcing Contract

- Establish the process for changing the terms of the service contract, especially for expansion of audit work if significant issues are found, and stipulations for default and termination of the contract;

- State that internal audit reports are the property of the institution, that the institution will be provided with any copies of the related workpapers it deems necessary, and that employees authorized by the institution will have reasonable and timely access to the workpapers prepared by the outsourcing vendor;

- Specify the locations of internal audit reports and the related workpapers;

- Specify the period of time (for example, seven years) that vendors must maintain the workpapers;

- State that outsourced internal audit services provided by the vendor are subject to regulatory review and that examiners will be granted full and timely access to the internal audit reports and related workpapers prepared by the outsourcing vendor;

- Prescribe a process (arbitration, mediation, or other means) for resolving disputes and for determining who bears the cost of consequential damages arising from errors, omissions, and negligence; and

- State that the outsourcing vendor will not perform management functions, make management decisions, or act or appear to act in a capacity equivalent to that of a member of management or an employee and, if applicable, will comply with AICPA, U.S. Securities and Exchange Commission (SEC), Public Company Accounting Oversight Board (PCAOB), or regulatory independence guidance.

*The engagement letter provisions described are comparable to those outlined by the American Institute of Certified Public Accountants (AICPA) for financial statement audits (see AICPA Professional Standards, AU section 310). These provisions are consistent with the provisions customarily included in contracts for other outsourcing arrangements, such as those involving data processing and information technology. Therefore, the federal banking agencies consider these provisions to be usual and customary business practices.

Source: OCC 2003-12, Attachment, The Board of Governors of the Federal Reserve System, Federal Deposit Insurance Corporation, Office of the Comptroller of the Currency, Office of Thrift Supervision.

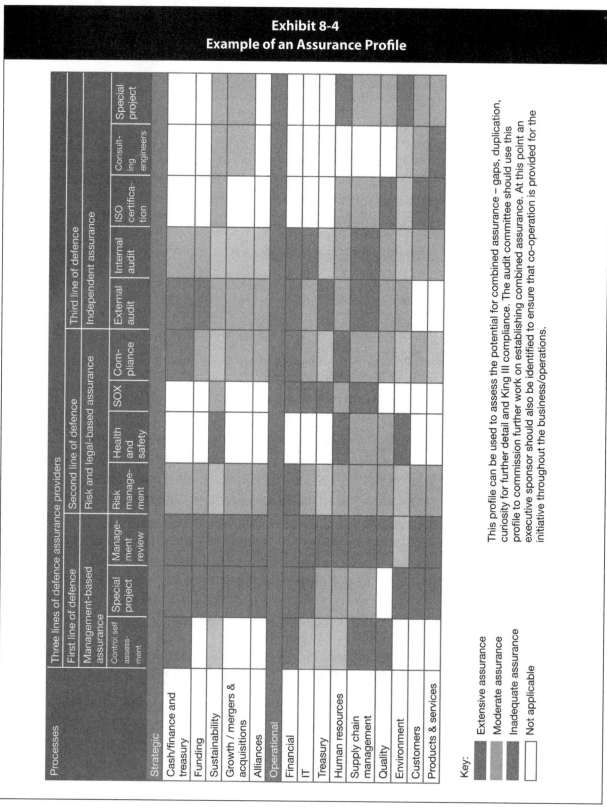

Exhibit 8-4
Example of an Assurance Profile

This profile can be used to assess the potential for combined assurance – gaps, duplication, curiosity for further detail and King III compliance. The audit committee should use this profile to commission further work on establishing combined assurance. At this point an executive sponsor should also be identified to ensure that co-operation is provided for the initiative throughout the business/operations.

Source: *Preparation, Perseverance, Payoff: Implementing a Combined Assurance Approach in the Era of King III*, PricewaterhouseCoopers, 2010.

References

[1] See also *Preparation, Perseverance, Payoff: Implementing a Combined Assurance Approach in the Era of King III*, PricewaterhouseCoopers, 2010.

[2] Roth, James, *Adding Value: Seven Roads to Success* (Altamonte Springs, FL: The Institute of Internal Auditors Research Foundation, 2002).

[3] Roth, James, *Best Practices: Value-Added Approaches of Four Innovative Auditing Departments* (Altamonte Springs, FL: The Institute of Internal Auditors, 2000), p. 12.

[4] In part from Vision University, an executive development program of The IIA in association with Louisiana State University.

Chapter 9

YOU MUST EVALUATE AND CONTRIBUTE TO THE IMPROVEMENT OF GOVERNANCE, RISK MANAGEMENT, AND CONTROL PROCESSES (2100-2130)

The 2100 series of the *Standards* reflects the broad nature, or scope, of internal audit work beyond the traditional areas of internal control assurance and compliance to include governance and risk management initiatives as well.

For most internal audit activities, the area of control is the most mature. It is developed, documented, and understood. Internal audit activities often have a long history of heavily covering control.

Risk management is a developing area. Industries vary in terms of how far they have progressed along the risk management maturity curve, and the level of involvement by internal auditing varies. Some organizations believe they are further along the maturity curve, while for other organizations, risk management or internal auditing's role in it is nearly nonexistent. In light of the financial crisis late in the first decade of the new millennium, the desire has never been greater for organizations to have, and therefore for internal auditing to provide, assessments of the effectiveness of risk management processes. Assessing and contributing to enhancing risk management practices is a key need and thus an opportunity for internal auditing.

For governance, the concept is well-grounded, but it is the least developed of the three areas. For many internal audit activities, governance is the most challenging of the areas in which to define their role. Many internal audit activities still struggle with how to assess, and make appropriate recommendations for improving, governance.

Highly respected management control frameworks like the Committee of Sponsoring Organizations of the Treadway Commission (COSO), Cadbury, and CoCo (see Exhibit 9-1) have exposed the futility of considering control activities in a vacuum. To be most effective, controls should be aligned with the broad objectives of the organization and the risks of not achieving those objectives. The role of control in the organization is, therefore, not limited to ensuring financial integrity and compliance with policies and procedures within functional silos, and neither is the role of the internal auditor. Instead, internal control and the internal audit activity exist to help the organization promote effective governance processes and manage all of its risks.

The Nature of Work

As part of today's internal audit scope, the *Standards* require the following activities to be part of the internal auditor's work.

- Help the organization's governance by:
- Assessing and making appropriate recommendations for improving governance in its accomplishment of the following objectives:
  o Promoting appropriate ethics and values within the organization.
  o Ensuring effective organizational performance management and accountability.
  o Effectively communicating risk and control information to appropriate areas of the organization.
  o Effectively coordinating the activities of and communicating information among the board, external and internal auditors, and management. (2110)
- Evaluating the design, implementation, and effectiveness of the organization's ethics-related objectives, programs, and activities. (2110.A1)
- Assessing whether the information technology governance of the organization sustains and supports the organization's strategies and objectives. (2110.A2)
- Help the organization manage risk by:
- Evaluating the effectiveness of risk management processes. (2120)
- Contributing to the improvement of risk management processes. (2120)
- Evaluating risk exposures relating to the organization. (2120.A1)
- Evaluating the potential for the occurrence of fraud and how the organization manages fraud risk. (2120.A2)
- Help the organization maintain effective controls by:
- Evaluating the adequacy, effectiveness, and efficiency of controls. (2130, 2130.A1)
- Promoting the continuous improvement of controls. (2130)

These three main areas of work are closely interconnected, and to evaluate and improve one area often evaluates and improves the other two at the same time. PA 2110-2 Governance: Relationship with Risk and Control further emphasizes this point. Each internal audit group has to determine how best to accomplish these activities given their existing roles, stakeholder expectations of internal auditing, and the corporate culture within their organizations. As a result, the particular internal audit practices for fulfilling these requirements will vary from organization to organization.

Internal Audit Coverage of Governance

Corporate governance means different things to different people, and its nature continues to evolve. PA 2110-1: Governance: Definition emphasizes this point, and notes that governance definitions vary depending on a variety of environmental, structural, and cultural circumstances. Thus, the *Standards'* mandate to *"assess and make appropriate recommendations for improving the governance process . . . "* (2110) has proven challenging for most internal auditors. At the same time, it is important to realize that internal auditing has had coverage in areas related to governance for years, such as coverage of executive travel and entertainment expenses and incentive payments.

Internal auditing's involvement in corporate governance is also evolving. Corporate governance is evolving in many parts of the world, and internal auditing's role is only one part of the evolution. Current guidance and the *Standards* offer a working explanation of governance, and they delineate the internal auditor's role in the process. In the Glossary the *Standards* define governance as *the combination of processes and structures implemented by the board to inform, direct, manage, and monitor the activities of the organization toward the achievement of its objectives.* By "board" the IPPF means *an organization's governing body, such as a board of directors, supervisory board, head of an agency or legislative body, board of governors or trustees of a nonprofit organization, or any other designated body of the organization, including the audit committee to whom the chief audit executive may functionally report.*

An organization uses various legal forms, structures, strategies, and procedures to ensure that it:

- Complies with society's legal and regulatory rules.

- Satisfies the generally accepted business norms, ethical precepts, and social expectations of society.

- Provides overall benefit to society and enhances the interests of the specific stakeholders in both the long- and short-term.

- Reports fully and truthfully to its owners, regulators, other stakeholders, and general public to ensure accountability for its decisions, actions, conduct, and performance.

The way in which the organization conducts its business so that these four obligations are met is commonly referred to as its governance process. Thus any internal auditing efforts to shore up activities that help fulfill these obligations are in effect improving the governance process.

Becoming familiar with the various models outlining effective governance principles, such as those promulgated by King III, CalPERS and TIAA-CREF (see the "Suggested Readings List" in Appendix E), can serve as a starting point for internal auditors seeking to help their organizations meet these responsibilities. In addition, the four governance obligations often reflect the risk concerns or internal control components of the internal audit activity.

You Must Assess and Make Appropriate Recommendations for Improving Governance (2110)

The *Standards* specify that internal auditors must help the organization fulfill its corporate governance obligations by *assessing and making appropriate recommendations for improving the governance process in its accomplishment of four particular objectives:*

- *Promoting appropriate ethics and values within the organization.*

- *Ensuring effective organizational performance management and accountability.*

- *Communicating risk and control information to appropriate areas of the organization.*

- *Coordinating the activities of and communicating information among the board, external and internal auditors, and management.* (2110)

Thus, to comply with the *Standards*, internal auditors must address these four areas.

Internal auditors who perform robust and thorough analyses of risk management and internal control systems will more than likely address many of these issues as a matter of course. For example, an evaluation of the organization's risk management processes should cover accountability issues, while controls assurance activities should consider how goals are established and communicated and how their accomplishment is monitored.

Additional work in the governance area may be necessary, however, to completely comply with the *Standards* and to meet the needs of the organization. Expectations of stakeholders related to internal auditing's role in assessing and making recommendations on governance are evolving. CAEs should be alert for ways to educate key stakeholders, understand key stakeholder expectations, and deliver value aligned with expectations related to governance. Organizations in various parts of the world are at different points in governance maturity and have different practices based on culture and regulation. Internal auditors should deliberately consider their organization's governance practices and needs, and define how internal auditing can best impact the organization in assuring good governance practices. For internal auditors to contribute in the governance area, it is critical that they:

- Define governance and the organization's governance processes.

- Determine what is in internal auditing's scope. For instance, should they go out and perform assessments throughout the organization, or assess certain corporate functions charged with performing the governance-related activities?

- Develop plans aligned with this understanding and start executing.

For internal audit teams seeking ways to add more value, opportunities abound in the governance arena (see Exhibit 9-2).

The Values Factor

Corporate values are generally understood to be the attitudes, beliefs, and principles that top management and the board expect everyone in the organization, from the CEO down, to exhibit in their work. Organizational values that are appropriately developed and communicated can be an extremely effective element of the control system. If they permeate the organization to the point that they are internalized by workers and are inherently considered in all business processes, corporate values essentially become the guiding force behind all decisions and activities. Most would agree that such a force from the top is essential to effective internal controls.

The *Standards* make it clear that internal auditors are to be living and promoting the organization's values. Implementation Standard 2110.C1 requires *all consulting engagement objectives to be consistent with the overall values and goals of the organization.* Internal auditors are thus prohibited from accepting assignments that work to undermine or oppose those values. For example, in an organization that places high priority on excellent customer service, it would be inappropriate for the internal audit staff to participate in an initiative that would cut costs at the expense of providing excellent customer service.

And as noted above, Standard 2110 requires that internal auditors include some type of coverage of organizational values in their audit work. Assessing how values are established, communicated, and preserved may be less commonly addressed in routine risk and control evaluations, but it certainly can be done.

Self-assessment exercises and questionnaires are excellent methods for measuring the comprehension and preservation of corporate values throughout the organization. Self-assessments measure how well employees understand corporate values, how well their goals and objectives are aligned with those values, whether they feel their work requirements compel them to compromise those values, and whether they see others in the organization exemplifying those values. To assess values, most find it important to ask employees in the organization beyond top leadership to ensure that the tone at the top truly is positive in practice, both in perception and reality.

Some organizations create audit programs to ensure that each specific value is understood and preserved. For example, an audit program addressing a corporate value like "We value and respect all individuals" might focus heavily on human resources policies and procedures, standards and behavior evidenced throughout the organization, and attitudes toward customers. In organizations where specific departments are assigned responsibility for a particular value, such as health and safety or ethics, internal auditing is still responsible for reviewing those programs and making a determination as to whether they operate effectively as control mechanisms.

Leading edge audit shops have gone so far as to examine whether or not their organizations' corporate values are reflected in the practices of joint venture, alliance, and business process outsourcing partners. Auditors can work with the mergers and acquisitions department as well as the legal team to ensure that all contracts and agreements clearly state that the partnering organization is expected to operate in alignment with the organization's core values.

Again, self-assessment questionnaires can be used to provide assurance that those partners are indeed following through with this requirement. Questionnaires could:

- Ask whether or not the partnering organization's board has adopted policies with regard to each of the core values, and require examples of board actions.

- Determine whether those policies are substantially similar to those of the parent organization, and require written descriptions of any differences.

- Ascertain whether or not the partnering organization's board conducts a review with its management regarding compliance with adopted board policies, and verify the date of the last review.

- Check for annual staff training programs on board policies and procedures involving the corporate values, and require descriptions of such programs.

- Verify that the staff of the partnering organization are required to confirm their compliance with board policies and procedures at least annually.

All of these initiatives are designed to ensure that corporate values do more than just hang on the wall. They should be the lifeblood of the organization, a continuous, renewing force that guides and directs all activities and decisions.

The Board Factor

Another governance initiative of leading edge audit staffs is the development of audit programs for evaluating the board and audit committee. Several publications effectively outline ways the board can best meet its responsibilities and improve its effectiveness (see "Suggested Readings List" in Appendix E). Effective audit programs can be built using the criteria suggested in these documents.

Two extremely useful resources are *Corporate Governance and the Board – What Works Best* and its companion document, *Audit Committee Effectiveness – What Works Best,* both of which are published by The IIA Research Foundation.

The Corporate Governance book also provides a checklist for evaluating the board. Sample questions are shown in Exhibit 9-3. The Audit Committee book includes insights and assessments that can be helpful to internal auditing in understanding the role of the key committee with which it has interaction and which, when working effectively, can be a key differentiator in embedding good governance in the organization.

Commonly Identified Governance Principles

As is evident from the previous discussions, governance is a broad concept with many variations in different areas of the world. However, as described in an IIA white paper on governance, the following principles are often included in defining effective governance processes:

1. Ensure a properly organized and functioning board that has the correct number of members; an appropriate board committee structure; established meeting protocols; sound, independent judgment about affairs of the organization; and periodically reaffirmed membership.

2. Ensure board members possess appropriate qualifications and experience, with a clear understanding of their role in the governance activities, a sound knowledge of the organization's operations, and an independent/objective mindset.

3. Ensure that the board has sufficient authority, funding, and resources to conduct independent inquiries.

4. Maintain an understanding by executive management and the board of the organization's operating structure, including structures that impede transparency.

5. Articulate an organizational strategy against which the success of the overall enterprise and the contributions of individuals are measured.

6. Create an organizational structure that supports the enterprise in achieving its strategy.

7. Establish a governing policy for the operation of key activities of the organization.

8. Set and enforce clear lines of responsibility and accountability throughout the organization.

9. Ensure effective interaction among the board, management, [independent outside] and internal auditors, and any other assurance providers.

10. Secure appropriate oversight by management, including establishment and maintenance of a strong set of internal controls.

11. Make sure that compensation policies and practices — especially related to senior management — are consistent with the organization's ethical values, objectives, strategy, and control environment, and encourage appropriate behavior.

12. Communicate and reinforce throughout the organization an ethical culture, organizational values, and appropriate tone at the top, which includes an environment that allows employees to raise concerns without fear of retaliation, as well as monitors and investigates potential conflicts of interest.

13. Effectively use internal auditors, ensuring the adequacy of their independence, resources, scope of activities, and effectiveness of operations.

14. Clearly define and implement risk management policies, processes, and accountabilities at the board level and throughout the organization.

15. Effectively use [independent outside] auditors, ensuring their independence, adequate resources, and scope of activities.

16. Provide appropriate disclosure of key information, in a transparent manner, to stakeholders.

17. Provide disclosure of the organization's governance processes, comparing those processes with recognized national codes or best practices.

18. Ensure appropriate oversight of related-party transactions and conflict of interest situations.[1]

In addition to assessing board effectiveness, internal auditing can help improve governance by serving as a valuable resource to board members. For example, internal auditors can:

- Help shape the information that flows to the board so that it is relevant, timely, accurate, complete, and forward-looking.

- Collect information that provides objective critiques of execution of past strategies.

- Advise the board on the company's measurement process, metrics used, and the degree of alignment to strategy.

- Prepare analyses of ethical or other value-based code violations and identify recurring issues and trends.

- Perform assessments of the effectiveness of communication channels.

- Provide benchmarks and peer comparisons for measuring performance against the marketplace.

- Add value to the "transformational transactions" process by ensuring relevant issues are brought to the board's attention.

- Assess post-deal integration plans and progress toward their execution.

- Analyze capital expenditures relative to strategy, plans, and budgets.[2]

Some CAEs find they also contribute to governance through asking management questions before board meetings on board materials that may not be clear, or by providing the audit committee with suggested questions on matters that arise in the CAE's review of the materials and topics for audit committee and board meetings.

You Must Evaluate the Design, Implementation, and Effectiveness of the Organization's Ethics-related Objectives, Programs, and Activities (2110.A1)

A more obvious and increasingly commonplace corporate governance initiative involves ethics. Organizations often name ethical integrity as one of their key corporate values. Even those who do not include it in the official list of values still recognize its importance in the governance process.

Standard 2110.A1 requires internal auditors to *evaluate the design, implementation, and effectiveness of the organization's ethics-related objectives, programs, and activities.* This is perhaps the most clear and focused requirement of the *Standards* related to governance. This may include periodically assessing the state of the ethical climate of the organization and the effectiveness of its strategies, tactics, communications, and other processes in achieving the desired level of legal and ethical compliance.

Components of an Ethical Culture

When conducting such reviews, internal auditors may determine the presence and effectiveness of the following elements of an enhanced ethical climate:

- A formal code of conduct, which is clear and understandable, and related statements, policies (including procedures covering fraud and corruption), and other expressions of aspiration.

- Frequent communications and demonstrations of expected ethical attitudes and behavior by the influential leaders of the organization.

- Explicit strategies to support and enhance the ethical culture with regular programs to update and renew the organization's commitment to an ethical culture.

- Several easily accessible ways for people to confidentially report alleged violations of the code, policies, and other acts of misconduct.

- Regular declarations by employees, suppliers, and customers that they are aware of the requirements for ethical behavior in transacting the organization's affairs.

- Clear delegation of responsibilities to ensure that ethical consequences are evaluated, confidential counseling is provided, allegations of misconduct are investigated, and case findings are properly reported.

- Easy access to learning opportunities that enable all employees to be ethics advocates.

- Positive personnel practices that encourage every employee to contribute to the ethical climate of the organization.

- Regular surveys of employees, suppliers, and customers to determine the state of the ethical climate in the organization.

- Regular reviews of the formal and informal processes within the organization that could potentially create pressures and biases that would undermine the ethical culture.

- Regular reference and background checks as part of hiring procedures, and of those promoted to senior positions in the organization, as well as integrity tests, drug screening, and similar measures.

Internal auditors in some organizations go so far as to serve as the primary driver behind all ethics-related initiatives.

You Must Assess Whether the Information Technology Governance of the Organization Sustains and Supports the Organization's Strategies and Objectives (2110.A2)

In nearly every organization, IT is core to the organization's processes. Further, it is frequently a major expenditure of organizations, such that decisions on investment in IT are part of the overall capital allocation processes of organizations. Unfortunately, these investments are not always successful or optimized.

In recent years, the governance over IT has received greater attention. As part of the enhancement to the *Standards* effective in 2009, a mandate was added that internal auditing place specific focus on IT governance. Information technology governance in the Glossary to the *Standards* is noted to consist of *leadership, organizational structures, and processes that ensure that the enterprise's information technology supports the organization's strategies and objectives*. The specific challenge that Standard 2110. A2 poses for internal auditing is in defining how to assess whether the IT governance of the organization supports the organization's strategies and objectives, and executing on this emerging role.

Auditing IT governance may include:

- Reviewing the IT strategic planning process, including ensuring there is a clear definition of IT mission and vision, the IT mission and vision are aligned with the business mission and vision, there is a strategic IT planning methodology in place, and that this plan identifies major IT initiatives and resources (appropriate people and financial) needed.

- Reviewing IT tactical planning, including the project management methodologies used, the project management controls applied and the project management tools used, the integration of IT and business staff along the various stages of the projects, change management methodologies used for large projects, clear definition of expected gains and benefits of the project, and the clarity of definition of scope of the project and measurable delivery metrics.

- Reviewing the delivery process, including operational controls in place, the development or modification process, the project management process, analysis of actual versus expected gains and benefits, analysis of delivery metrics stated versus achieved, and post-implementation review, feedback, and customer satisfaction.

- Reviewing the application development methodology, practices, and controls, including the quality of the application development methodology, development metrics used to estimate project size and progress, and techniques used for testing.

- Reviewing the processes used to administer the current systems portfolio, the overall coverage of the policies issued relating to the areas defined by the business strategic planning process, the process followed by top-level management to elaborate, communicate, enforce and monitor the policy compliance, the process and framework used by top-level management to identify, categorize, and prioritize risks associated with the current systems portfolio, and periodic review of risks.

- Reviewing the process used by management to assess whether resources devoted to IT are being used effectively and efficiently.

- There are a number of useful publications for the internal auditor on IT governance. They include *GTAG 15: Information Security Governance* issued in 2010 by The IIA as well as Implementing and Continually Improving IT Governance by the Information Systems Audit and Control Association (ISACA) in 2009.

Too Little, Too Late?

Many consider corporate governance to be the ultimate risk management and control process, due to its broad scope and high-level foundation. While internal auditors may be challenged to develop programs that meet the *Standards'* requirements in the governance arena, experts the world over agree that internal auditors' involvement in governance is crucial and long overdue.

Internal Audit Coverage of Risk Management

The Glossary to the *Standards* defines risk as *the possibility of an event occurring that will have an impact on the achievement of objectives. Risk is measured in terms of impact and likelihood.* Risk is not entirely bad, since risks often come along with the organization embracing areas of opportunity. Yet risks can and do prevent managers and organizations from achieving their business objectives, and, in extreme cases, they can even destroy the organization.

Recent surveys have shown that improving risk management practices is a priority for senior management and for boards. Further, boards in many organizations, including major global organizations, have been enhancing their focus on the organization's risk management as well as on the board's role in risk oversight.

Risk is more than just "bad things happening." There are also risks in potential missed business opportunities, which can be just as costly and life threatening for organizations. In effect, successful business requires putting the organization's assets and resources at risk to achieve strategic and operational objectives. The Glossary to the *Standards* defines risk management as *a process to identify, assess, manage, and control potential events or situations, to provide reasonable assurance regarding the achievement of the organization's objectives.* The role of effective risk management in the organization is, therefore, to help the organization understand and proactively respond to business risks so that the organization can best achieve its objectives. It also recognizes that there is at times a cost of control that must be compared to the benefits of control. Recognizing that there will always be some level of risks, risk management becomes a matter of taking proactive steps to limit risks to organizational objectives to an acceptable level. This level is referred to as the organization's risk appetite in the *Standards* and represents the level of risk the organization is willing to accept.

This idea that risk must be both embraced and managed by the organization runs contrary to old internal audit thought. In the past, internal audit practitioners have at times sought only to eliminate downside hazard risk. It is also widely understood that management, not internal auditing, owns risk management. Yet risk management has quickly become one of the driving factors of organizations and the internal audit profession, a fact reflected in the *Standards* requiring internal audit coverage of risk management activities. The *Standards* outline four specific actions all internal auditors must take to assist with the organization's risk management effort.

You Must Evaluate the Effectiveness of Risk Management Processes (2120)

Internal auditors' knowledge of and reputation in risk management frequently results in organizations seeking out internal auditing's involvement as the organization embarks on embedding a risk management culture and risk management practices into the organization. Internal auditing is often a catalyst for such discussions and improvements in the organization's risk management. With the *Standards* requiring coverage by internal auditing of the organization's risk management activities, it is natural that internal auditors are bringing to the organization and its audit committee issues to be addressed when the organization is not effectively embracing enterprise risk management.

Early in this new century, there was already wider recognition of the need for effective risk management in organizations. As a result, a number of standards, frameworks, and requirements have been issued, including Australia-New Zealand risk management standards and Turnbull requirements in the UK. One important development that included The IIA as one of its five sponsors is the COSO Enterprise Risk Management (ERM) Framework issued in 2004. It builds on the earlier COSO *Internal Controls – Integrated Framework* that in recent years has been widely adopted as part of internal control attestation requirements for publicly traded companies in some markets, including the United States. The COSO ERM framework recognizes that ERM is:

- A process, ongoing and flowing through an entity.

- Effected by people at every level of an organization.

- Applied in strategy setting.

- Applied across the enterprise, at every level and unit, and includes taking an entity-level portfolio view of risk.

- Designed to identify potential events that, if they occur, will affect the entity, and to manage risk within its risk appetite.

- Able to provide reasonable assurance to an entity's management and board of directors.

- Geared to achievement of objectives in one or more separate but overlapping categories.

It also recognizes that internal auditing does not own enterprise risk management, but is important in monitoring and recommending improvements in the organization's risk management practices. As noted earlier, internal auditing is often a catalyst for the organization embracing enterprise risk management. This has happened through internal auditing facilitating risk management sessions, educating the board and senior management on risk management, and promoting risk language and risk frameworks in its own work.

While over the past two decades this has been an area of significant innovation for the internal audit profession, the business and global economic challenges of 2008 and 2009 demonstrate there is still a great need for more effective risk management practices in organizations. Finding ways to assess risks, including the risks of what may seem like highly improbable events, and ensuring organizations plan for and manage the potential impacts of such events is important to business and societal success.

Since internal auditors are charged with assessing the effectiveness of risk management processes, it is clear that internal auditors have a major responsibility and a major opportunity to help their organizations plan for the future. Internal auditors can provide great value when they assess and recommend appropriate improvements in the organization's risk management practices.

Dynamic Management of Risk

Assessing risks in real time means that identifying, evaluating, and acting to manage risks is an ongoing process that is conducted as frequent as necessary to understand and address the risk which cannot be accomplished in a once-a-year, weeklong exercise. Few, if any, organizations today monitor and assess risk real time, but many are seeking to monitor and assess risk, particularly risks requiring such focus, more frequently and timely than in the past. Organizations, their markets, and the general business environment are constantly changing, and the risks affecting the organization change right along with them.

To stay on top of an entity's dynamic risk environment, internal auditing's processes for assessing risk must include mechanisms for continually acquiring new risk information. Organizations are turning to practices such as increasingly frequent management call programs, quarterly risk committee involvement, and automated tools to capture and understand risk indicators. The risk assessment process and the frequency of measures must reflect the frequency and velocity of changes in the organization's risk profile.

Scenario Planning

In the current environment, a number of organizations and regulators are seeking to bolster the risk management practices they use by looking at scenario planning — what is the impact and planned response if certain extreme events occur. Whether changes in availability of capital, commodity cost volatility, credit worthiness, global economic growth, terrorist or military upheaval, pandemic outbreaks or other factors, organizations are seeking value in having their risk management practices focus not just on managing the middle of a probability curve, but now also address potential actions at the far ends of the probability curves. Some now believe that applying probability curves that map past events to the future improperly minimizes future probabilities. Hence, having risk management practices include scenario planning and stress testing is becoming more common.

Organizationwide Assessments

Organizationwide risk assessment can be described as the identification and evaluation of exposures at the strategic or entity level of the organization. A thorough understanding of the business, its overall strategy, the changing external environment, the issues that are important to key stakeholders, and the primary risk concerns of the organization are prerequisite to a successful organizationwide risk assessment program. The goal of this macro assessment is to provide a top-down look at all of the key risks affecting the organization as a whole.

Internal auditing's involvement in management's entity-level assessment process will vary, depending on executive management's level of activity in this area. If management, perhaps through a separate risk management function, already has a process in place for assessing high-level risk as part of an overall ERM system, then internal auditing should participate as appropriate and utilize that assessment.

In many organizations, however, such a risk management process is lacking and the internal audit activity may need to facilitate the process. In such situations, internal auditing may serve as a catalyst, working to move the organization forward in embracing risk management. Where internal auditing serves in the catalyst role, it should be cognizant of the desired end state where management has embraced ownership for risk management and internal auditing does not own risk management processes. Standard 2120.C3 states that *when assisting management in establishing or improving risk management processes, internal auditors must refrain from assuming any management responsibility by actually managing risks.*

Assessing the Entity's Adoption of Risk Management

Key elements of moving an organization toward embracing risk management include: use by all of a common framework and language for risk; aligning understanding of risks with achievement of business objectives, overall and at the business unit level; gaining input from those engaged in the business; some type of ranking or prioritization of risk; and the ability to present clear, understandable representations of the organization's risk profile and resulting actions. Programs led by internal auditing often include some or all of the following steps:

- Inviting key players from throughout the organization to a daylong brainstorming session to identify and rank the greatest business risks companywide.

- Facilitating understanding and use of a common risk framework for the organization.

- Conducting a risk assessment exercise with senior management and the board, either through interviews, questionnaires, or a combination of the two, to pinpoint the most critical risks as seen from the perspective of successfully running the organization and meeting the demands of all stakeholders.

- Taking a look at the annual strategic plan to identify the key strategic risks to the organization.

- Facilitating management discussion of risk and risk responses as part of the strategic planning process.

- Capturing and communicating varying perspectives of risk prioritization between top executives and line management to provide early warnings of what field personnel see in the business as well as to seek to minimize the risk of groupthink in executive offices.

- Developing a risk universe that clearly links all business activities from the perspective of risk to shareholder value.

- Grouping risks together based on how they relate to one another. Within each group, for example, the impact of certain risks may grow or diminish as other risks rise or fall. It may be found that across the organization there are some natural offsets to risk, or that there are certain risks with a much bigger impact than any one business unit imagines because the risks impact a number of businesses. Or, as one risk is transferred or shared, another risk may emerge. This awareness of impacts and interdependencies offers increased understanding of which risks are critical and require more attention.

- Ensuring quarterly communication with management, from the executive level down, to determine what management perceives to be the upcoming strategic risks to the organization.

- Building in to audit committee communication, education and transparency on the organization's risk management.

- Using in its discussions and approach common language on the organization's risk management framework, risk profile, and risk tolerances.

- Benchmarking the organization with leading risk management frameworks and practices.

Useful questions to ask include:

- How is change affecting the risks we face and the risks we have chosen to take?

- What would we hate to see reported in the media?

- What problems or near misses have already happened to us or our competitors in recent years?

- What are the types of fraud and business impropriety issues to which the business could be particularly susceptible?

- What are the major regulatory and legal risks to which the business is exposed?

- What risks arise from the business processes?[3]

- What are the greatest risks to our business objectives?

A draft risk framework categorizing the various business risks commonly faced by organizations can be a useful brainstorming tool for this exercise. A variety of these models and processes exist, from those specific to a particular industry or product to those with more generally applicable categories of risk. Each internal audit department has to determine which risk framework, or adaptation thereof, is right for them. Several samples are shown in Exhibit 9-4.

Through identifying risks at the highest levels of the organization, a company-specific risk framework can be assembled. Such frameworks may categorize the identified risks into broad categories, which are then broken down into additional subcategories. As the risks change as strategy and the business environment change, the framework is updated to reflect the new risk environment. This framework is often used by the CAE to risk-rate the audit universe and develop the annual audit plan (see Chapter 8).

Again, in organizations with effective ERM programs, the framework is normally developed by the risk committees or executive management and the board, not internal auditing. Best practice for internal auditors working in environments without a comprehensive approach might be to encourage the adoption of ERM. Once ERM is in place, the audit activity is primarily responsible for evaluating the program's effectiveness, including how well the risk assessment process is designed and functioning. However, until such a program has been implemented, internal auditors may want to forge ahead and facilitate development and use of the framework themselves.

Standard 2120 makes it clear that internal auditors must review the risk management processes as part of their activities for the board and senior management. This represents newer territory for most internal audit shops. Exhibit 9-5 shows the continuum of potential internal auditor involvement in enterprise risk management, from core roles to roles that internal auditing should not undertake. Few organizations have established processes for assuring the adequacy and effectiveness of risk management procedures. A tool to help perform this measurement is illustrated in Exhibit 9-6. In addition, PA 2120-1 and other resources offer advice on accomplishing this objective.

Assessing the Risk Management Program

To assess the overall adequacy of the risk management program, internal auditors should satisfy themselves that the organization's risk management processes accomplish five key objectives:

- The risks arising from business strategies and activities are identified and prioritized.

- Management and the board have determined the level of risks tolerable to the organization, including the acceptance of risk to accomplish the organization's strategic plans.

- Risk mitigation activities have been designed and implemented to reduce or otherwise manage risk at levels acceptable to management and the board.

- Ongoing monitoring activities are performed to periodically reassess risk and the effectiveness of controls to manage risk.

- The results of risk management processes are periodically reported to the board and management.

Standard 2120 notes *the internal audit activity may gather the information to support this assessment during multiple engagements. The results of these engagements, when viewed together, provide an understanding of the organization's risk management processes and their effectiveness.* It may be more than one assessment that forms the basis for internal auditing's assessment of the organization's risk management processes.

Assessing Risk Management Processes[4]

In addition to the above five primary areas of concern, there are other issues that should be considered when evaluating the effectiveness of risk management activities:

- Are the risk management processes appropriate for the nature of the organization's activities? Depending on the nature, size, and complexity of the business activities, risk management processes can be formal or informal, quantitative or subjective, and embedded in the business units or centralized at a corporate level. Does the risk management process used by the organization fit its culture, management style, and business objectives?

- Is the risk management methodology comprehensive and is the organization aware of it and trained on it?

- Is the methodology understood by key groups or individuals involved in corporate governance, including the board and audit committee?

- Is risk management seen as everyone's responsibility, rather than the responsibility of one function, such as internal auditing or insurance?

- Is there a common risk management vocabulary in use throughout the organization?

- Is there appropriate awareness of the organization's key business objectives and significant risks?

- Are business objectives, risks, and controls aligned?

- Does the workforce have sufficient understanding of the risks relevant to the individual tasks they perform? Do employees understand the purpose of controls?

- Do employees and others working for the organization, such as in contractor roles, have sufficient knowledge, skills, and tools to support the achievement of the organization's objectives and manage risks effectively?

- Is operating staff involved in identifying and responding timely to change and in operating early warning mechanisms?

- Is there an effort to instill an attitude of "doing things right the first time" in employees, thereby reducing the likelihood of risk?

- Is there appropriate and clear accountability for fulfilling business objectives and managing related risks?

- Is there awareness of trigger events, or frequency of events, for each significant business risk that should alert management to a potentially significant issue?

- Are key risk indicators in place to provide early warning of a project or strategic initiative not succeeding?

- How quickly is the organization able to identify and respond to inside changes as well as changes in the external environment?

- Are necessary actions taken promptly to remedy significant failings or weaknesses in the organization?

- How well are best practices and ideas for improving the business shared throughout the organization?

- How reliable is the upward reporting of risk management issues?

- Does current management information give the board and senior management sufficient early warning of potential problems? For example, do they receive enough timely information on customer satisfaction and employee attitudes?

- Do senior management and the board receive sufficient information on emerging risks and rapidly changing risks?

- Are there channels of communication for people to report suspected breaches or other improprieties?

- Is the environment such that people are willing to report problems, rather than "sit on them"?

- Do remuneration policies and working practices encourage good risk management and actually discourage taking reckless or bad risks?

- Are the actions of different parts of the organization appropriately coordinated?

- To what extent do executive committees put risk management and significant risk management issues on their agendas?

- Are key financial, operational, and compliance controls current?

- Are full risk analyses performed as part of the due diligence of an acquisition?

- Do the risk management processes consider and embed the organization's risk management processes in areas of significant off-shoring or outsourcing?

- Do the findings of the risk management assessment indicate a need for more extensive monitoring of the risk management system?

- Is the risk management part of the strategic planning process?

- Do risk assessment activities result, where appropriate, in management actions linked?

- Is reporting by the chief risk officer relevant, accurate, timely, and transparent?

- Is frequency of risk measurement consistent with the frequency of potential changes in risk and what is needed for effective decision-making?

- Is the risk management process and culture robust enough to address risks of groupthink and ensure that varying objective points of view on risk are brought to the table?

- Are the audit committee and the board getting sufficient communications and discussion on risk?

To determine the adequacy of the system, internal auditors should take a look at the design of risk management processes to determine how efficient and effective they are. Efficiently designed processes accomplish goals in an accurate, timely, and economical fashion. Economically designed processes accomplish goals and objectives with minimal use of resources. To evaluate the effectiveness of the system, internal auditors consider the questions asked earlier, assessing how well management directs, or manages, risk management processes and how well the processes address risks.

Assessing the Adequacy of Risk Management Using ISO 31000[5]

Assessing the Adequacy of Risk Management Using ISO 31000, a Practice Guide issued in December 2010, provides many useful insights on assessing risk management practices of organizations. The guide uses the recently issued ISO 31000 as a basis for the risk management framework. It notes that other frameworks may be used to perform the risk assessment. This guidance does not imply implicit or explicit endorsement of any specific framework.

The Practice Guide uses the structure and some of the terminology of the ISO 31000 Risk Management standard. While ISO 31000 is not designed as a basis for certification, its concepts and structures form a basis for assessing any risk management process. It provides guidance for the framework of risk management applicable to organizations of any size. ISO 31000 defines a risk management framework as a "set of components that provide the foundations and organizational arrangements for designing, implementing, monitoring, reviewing, and continually improving risk management throughout the organization." ISO 31000's Framework for Managing Risk starts at the top with "Mandate and Commitment" and also includes "Design of Framework for Managing Risk," "Implementing Risk Management," "Monitoring and Review of the Framework," and "Continual Improvement of the Framework."

Three forms of assurance process that may be used in assessing a risk management process are:

1. Process elements approach.
2. Key principles approach.
3. Maturity model approach.

These approaches are taken from HB158:2010 Delivering Assurance Based on ISO 31000:2009 Risk Management — Principles and Guidelines, a joint publication of Standards Australia, IIA-Australia, and The IIA Research Foundation. HB158 provides a more extensive discussion of these and other issues.

While each approach is self-contained, each offers a different perspective on the effectiveness of a risk management process in an organization. Often, the adoption of more than one approach can yield the most informative and useful results. The risk management process should be appropriately tailored to the organization, its size, culture objectives, and risk profile. Therefore, the assurance process also needs to be tailored to the organization's needs.

The results of any desk-based review must be validated by examining whether the risk management framework is operating effectively in practice. This means that this type of assurance activity should not be conducted in isolation and should always accompany or involve normal control-based assurance that determines whether:

- Risks are being effectively identified and appropriately analyzed.

- There is adequate and appropriate risk treatment and control.

- There is effective monitoring and review by management to detect changes in risks and controls.

1. Process Element Approach

This approach checks whether each element of the risk management process is in place. It is essential to validate management's expressions of intent through sufficient audit evidence to substantiate that the element is being satisfied in practice. Management representation alone would rarely be sufficient. ISO 31000 identifies seven components of the risk management process:

- Element 1 – Communication: Sound risk management requires structured and ongoing communication and consultation with those who are affected by the operations of the organization or activity.

- Element 2 – Setting the Context: The external environment (political, social, etc.) and internal environment (objectives, strategies, structures, ethics, discipline, etc.) of the organization or activity must be understood before the full range of risks can be identified.

- Element 3 – Risk Identification: Identifying the risks should be a formal, structured process that considers sources of risk, areas of impact, and potential events and their causes and consequences.

- Element 4 – Risk Analysis: The organization should use a formal technique to consider the consequence and likelihood of each risk.

- Element 5 – Risk Evaluation: The organization should have a mechanism to rank the relative importance of each risk so that a treatment priority can be established.

- Element 6 – Risk Treatment: Sound risk management requires rational decisions about risk treatment. Classically, such treatment is to avoid the activity from which the risk arises, share the risk, manage the risk by the application of controls, or accept the risk and take no further action.

- Element 7 – Monitor and Review: Monitoring includes checking the progress of treatment plans, monitoring controls and their effectiveness, ensuring that proscribed activities are avoided, and checking that the environment has not changed in a way that affects the risks.

2. Key Principles Approach

This approach is based on the concept that to be fully effective, any risk management process must satisfy a minimum set of principles or characteristics. ISO 31000 includes a section (Clause 4) on these principles. An audit based on these principles would assess to what extent they are true for the risk management process in an organization:

- Risk management creates and protects value.

- Risk management is an integral part of organizational processes.

- Risk management is part of decision-making.

- Risk management explicitly addresses uncertainty.

- Risk management is systematic, structured, and timely.

- Risk management is based on the best available information.

- Risk management is tailored.

- Risk management takes human and cultural factors into account.

- Risk management is transparent and inclusive.

- Risk management is dynamic, iterative, and responsive to change.

- Risk management facilitates continual improvement and enhancement of the organization.

3. Maturity Model Approach

The maturity model approach builds on the assertion that the quality of an organization's risk management process should improve with time. Immature systems of risk management yield very little return for the investment that has been made and often operate as compliance overhead or an imposition, more concerned with the reporting of risks than with their effective treatment. Effective risk management processes are developed over time, with additional value being provided at each step in the maturation process.

This approach provides an assessment of where the organization's risk management process lies on the maturity curve, so that the board and management can assess whether it meets the current needs of the organization and is maturing as expected.

A key aspect of the Maturity Model approach is the linking of risk management performance and progress in the execution of a risk management plan to a performance measurement and management system. The outputs from such a system can be presented to senior management and the board as evidence of improvement in risk management.

The components for such a system normally consist of:

- A protocol of performance standards, considering current approaches to risk management and anticipating future strategic needs. Performance standards are normally supported by a list of more detailed performance requirements that enable measurement of any improvement in performance.

- A guide to how the standards and sub-requirements can be satisfied in practice.

- A means of measuring actual performance against each standard and sub-requirement.

- A means of recording and reporting performance and improvements in performance.

- The periodic independent verification of management's assessment.

Clause 4 of ISO 31000 contains a list of practical and important "principles" that should be the starting point for any maturity evaluation. These principles address not only "does the process element or system exist" but also "is it effective and relevant for your organization" and "does it add value." In fact, the first principle is that risk management must add value.

Actual performance against each performance standard is assessed using some system of maturity measurement that gives credit for intent, but full scores can only be obtained by the complete implementation and practical application of the standard. A possible system for measuring maturity (based on the original idea of capability maturity models developed by the Carnegie Mellon University) is found in HB158:2010 Delivering Assurance Based on ISO 31000-2009 Risk Management - Principles and Guidelines (a joint publication of Standards Australia, IIA-Australia, and The IIA Research Foundation).

Gathering Evidence

As with any other assurance engagement, auditors must obtain sufficient evidence before they can form an opinion on the adequacy and effectiveness of the risk management system.

The following types of audit procedures are suggested methods for gathering such evidence:

- Research and review reference materials and background information on risk management methodologies to determine whether or not the process used by the organization is appropriate and represents best practice for the industry.

- Research and review current development trends, industry information, and other appropriate sources of information to determine risks and exposures that may affect the organization and related control procedures used to address, monitor, and reassess those risks, including emerging risks.

- Review corporate policies and board and audit committee minutes to determine the organization's business strategies, risk management philosophy and methodology, appetite for risk, and acceptance of risks.

- Review previous risk evaluation reports by management, risk management functions, internal auditors, external auditors, and any other sources that may have issued such reports.

- Conduct interviews with line and executive management to determine business unit objectives, related risks, and management's risk mitigation, control, and monitoring activities.

- Assimilate information to independently evaluate the effectiveness of risk mitigation, monitoring, and communication of risks and associated control activities.

- Assess the appropriateness of reporting lines for risk monitoring activities.

- Review the adequacy and timeliness of reporting on risk management results.

- Review the adequacy of information provided to the board for its execution of its risk oversight responsibilities.

- Review the completeness of management's risk analysis as well as the actions taken to remedy issues raised by risk management processes, and suggest improvements.

- Determine the effectiveness of management's self-assessment processes through observations, direct tests of control and monitoring procedures, tests of the accuracy of information used in monitoring activities, and other appropriate techniques.

- Review risk-related issues that may indicate weakness in risk management practices and, as appropriate, discuss with management, the audit committee, and the board of directors. If the auditor believes that management has accepted a level of risk that is inconsistent with the organization's risk management strategy and policies, or that is deemed unacceptable to the organization, the auditor should refer to Standard 2600 and any related guidance for additional direction (see Chapter 13). (PA 2120-1)

Even in organizations without a defined risk management process, internal auditing can provide assurance that whatever risk management activities are in place are adequate and effective. For example, at one organization, a total of 17 different areas, including the treasury function, the controller, and the legal department, are responsible for risk management. The internal audit activity conducted a coordinated review of these processes to determine whether the various pieces fit together appropriately, their activities were properly coordinated, accountabilities were in place, and the reporting of these functions was suitable and effective. The end result was an overall assessment of the adequacy of the risk management processes, including recommendations for improvements.[6]

You Must Help Improve Risk Management Processes (2120)

A second element of the risk management standards requires audit initiatives that strive to improve the effectiveness of risk management processes. Specific suggestions that may help enhance the system of internal controls are provided later in this chapter. However, it is important for internal auditors to understand that shoring up the processes for managing risk is an integral and necessary part of any internal control improvement effort.

Further, the earlier discussion on how to assess risk management processes by its nature also serves as a road map for how to help organizations improve their risk management processes.

In addition, auditors who conduct timely risk assessments (as discussed later in this chapter) that identify and evaluate exposures at both the organizational and functional level are certainly on their way toward improving risk management. After all, one essential element of effective risk management is a thorough understanding of what the risks are.

Activities for Improving Risk Management Efforts

Internal auditors can do more, such as:

- Including detailed information about risk in all audit reports, not only by alerting management of areas that contain potential exposures, but also by providing evidence of the repercussions of exposures, such as analyses that quantify the cost of risk. Such additional information helps management prioritize actions in response to recommendations.

159

- Serving as risk educators for the entire enterprise, especially at levels where decisions on level of risk to accept and resource prioritization are made.

- Participating in risk management steering teams or activity groups. Auditors are ideal candidates for such activities as extracting, analyzing, and preparing historical data for external consultants hired to quantify exposures, because they possess the requisite knowledge of risk, systems knowledge, and skill sets. Other tasks well-suited to internal auditors include facilitating group sessions devoted to risk identification and problem-solving, or helping operating managers understand the relative importance of their activity to total enterprise exposure.

- Documenting established risk mitigation techniques by building a reference manual of risk management methods in each functional area.

- Advocating the establishment of and participating in risk management forums, whose participants often include line managers, business unit executives, and auditors, that continuously evaluate and monitor the risk profile of each business unit. Such forums instill risk management techniques and processes at the business unit level by identifying risks and mitigating controls, defining actionable items, monitoring the actions used to mitigate risk, submitting periodic reports, and designing and implementing risk mitigation plans. Auditors can effectively contribute by serving as group facilitators and by acting as consultants and substantiating the effectiveness of the overall risk management processes.[7]

- Bringing the need for appropriate risk management processes to management's attention and offering suggestions for establishing such a system in the vast number of organizations lacking formal risk management programs.

- Helping as the organization implements a risk management system, which may involve serving in a consulting role to improve fundamental processes. If such assistance exceeds normal assurance and consulting activities, independence could be impaired and appropriate disclosure should be made. Additional guidance can be found in PA 1130.A2-1: Internal Audit's Responsibility for Other (Non-audit) Functions (see Exhibit 5-5 in Chapter 5).

- Coordinating efforts with chief risk officers and others responsible for risk management, ensuring internal auditing leverages the information elsewhere on risk to provide enhanced coverage for the organization on areas of greater risk.

- Performing projects that dive down into areas of identified risk in the organization's enterprise risk management efforts to assess more fully higher priority areas of risk. Out of this work, where appropriate, issues and recommendations along with management action plans can result from a process similar to other internal audit engagements.

- Benchmarking risk management activities with other organizations or studies. In practice today, some industries such as elements of the financial services industry have more advanced risk management practices than some other industries.

Many of these activities fall under the consulting umbrella, and, as pointed out earlier, all types of consulting work generate valuable cues for improving the risk management system.

Ultimately, it is up to senior management and the board to determine what role, if any, the internal audit activity will play in the risk management process of the organization. Once decided, these responsibilities should be documented in the audit charter.

You Must Evaluate the Risk Exposures Relating to the Organization (2120.A1)

For most internal auditors, identifying and evaluating risk exposures has been routinely performed through risk assessments. Internal auditors are now expected to identify and evaluate significant risk exposures in the normal course of their duties to the organization.

With the evolution of internal auditing, organizations commonly rely upon entity-level risk assessments as the basis for deploying internal audit resources, as opposed to employing a rotational scheme or an internal control checklist approach. And as pointed out in Chapter 8, the *Standards* actually require the CAE to develop audit plans that are based on a risk assessment and aligned with organizational goals and objectives. To most effectively meet these risk assessment requirements, best practice suggests that the internal audit risk identification and evaluation activity be closer to a "real-time," collaborative process that includes both organizationwide risk assessments and the preliminary assessment of risk during the course of specific internal audit engagements. The organizationwide evaluation of risk is expected to translate to engagement-level preliminary assessment of risk.

Engagement-level Risk Assessments

Risk assessment during a specific audit engagement is designed to identify and evaluate exposures at the operations or micro level of the organization, for purposes of ensuring the risks relevant to the area under review are addressed. As noted in the following chapter, this is required by the *Standards* in 2210.A1. In addition to understanding the business products, services, markets, and other strategic issues, effective engagement-level assessments require the audit team to consider the business process risks, the quality of the local management team, and the various ways individuals might behave given differing situations.

The organizational risk framework developed at the entity level becomes one of the tools used to perform this engagement-level risk assessment. It is important that there be alignment between the entity-level risk assessment and the reasons at that level that the specific internal audit project was chosen with the later engagement-level preliminary risk assessment. During each audit assignment, the audit team may walk operating management through the framework to understand which specific risks apply to the area under review, along with the prioritization of risk and the risk responses, including controls that the organization uses to address risk. The categories thus help to generate ideas and make it unlikely that any significant risks will be overlooked.

Another approach relies on the business objectives of the function as its starting point. For each objective, management is asked to identify the risks, conditions, or events that would prevent the achievement of that objective. This list of impediments represents the risks faced by the function. Management is then asked about the risk responses, including controls, that management relies on to manage risk.

Other ways to identify and evaluate risks at the micro level, some of which take place externally to the actual audit engagement, include:

- Conducting risk assessment workshops with operating personnel, which adds another level of depth to the developing organizational risk profile.

- Implementing continuous auditing procedures, which search for potential problems in an area on an ongoing basis. Examples include monitoring unexpected cost increases in a given area, increases in staff turnover, and key performance indicators. Such real-time monitoring activities enable audit teams to inform process owners of risks more quickly, as well as to choose to conduct an otherwise unplanned audit based on the anomalies discovered.

- Participating on project teams devoted to high-risk projects or new process implementations. Such teams are usually formed before the work begins, allowing internal auditors to act as consultants and help identify risks and solutions on the front end. Risk information is thereby gathered and can be used later when planning an audit.

Once complete, the audit team uses the results of the functional risk assessment to perform its audit of the area. The findings of the assessment can help auditors determine what particular issues need to be looked at more closely, whether a different kind of audit would be more appropriate given the types of risks identified, and whether the engagement should be delayed or canceled altogether.

The entity-level and engagement-level risk assessments are interdependent and symbiotic, each leading to the more robust development and application of the other. All of the engagement-level assessments from the various processes can be compared to identify risk trends across the organization. In addition, the collective results of engagement-level assessments are usually rolled up into the organizational risk framework, presenting a comprehensive and continuously updated look at the risk environment of the organization.

Assessment in an Assurance Engagement

The *Standards* provide specific instructions regarding the focus of risk assessments performed for assurance work. *In assurance engagements, internal auditors are required to evaluate risk exposures related to governance, operations, and information systems (2120.A1). Specifically, auditors are expected to identify risks to the reliability and integrity of financial and operational information; the effectiveness and efficiency of operations; the safeguarding of assets; and the compliance with laws, regulations, and contracts (2120.A1).* To be in compliance with the *Standards*, any audit that is designed to provide overall assurance on the internal control system to senior management, the board, or other third parties must cover these crucial aspects. PA 2200-2: Using a Top-down, Risk-based Approach to Identify the Controls to be Assessed in an Internal Audit Engagement provides additional guidance on risk assessment in the assurance engagement.

Risk Assessment Pitfalls

Risk assessments that capture only traditional, financial hazards are increasingly limited in today's business environment. More often than not, it is the less tangible soft issues such as human resources, integrity, reputation, and information quality that prove truly detrimental or advantageous to the organization.

Blindly selecting risks from a generic risk framework is also a mistake. Such matrices should be used only as a brainstorming tool for identifying exposures that are specific to the industry and the circumstances of the organization.

Internal auditors will also find that developing a list of risks on their own without input from others and then proceeding to tell management and staff what their risks are is doomed to fail. The collaborative approaches described above are much more effective. The top-down entity-level and bottom-up engagement-level risk assessments must be linked together and aligned.

In addition, the audit staff should be careful not to identify too many risks, since doing so can prevent the real ship sinkers from receiving adequate attention. Some suggest that 15 to 25 significant risks is a good rule of thumb to follow. The previously mentioned COSO ERM Framework includes application guidance that provides a number of views of risk models and risk categories actually used by organizations.

While accuracy in assessing risk is important, often a precise, detailed quantification of risk can also be detrimental, since such measurement processes can complicate the assessment effort and slow down progress. Most often, organizations are quantifying and prioritizing risks based on their impact on the achievement of the organization's objectives and the likelihood that they will occur. At its simplest, identified risks may be assigned one of four ratings: high impact/high likelihood, high impact/low likelihood, low impact/high likelihood, and low impact/low likelihood. For other risks, such as those measuring exposures for organizations with complex financial or commodity instruments and positions, risk quantification may be very important in the organization's risk management process.

High impact/high likelihood risks receive top priority and usually immediate action, while exposures noted as low impact/low likelihood are relegated to the back burner and reviewed less frequently. Controls also may be reduced. By employing such simple prioritization schemes, audit teams can accomplish their goal of assigning auditors to appropriate areas in a way that makes the best use of time, money, and resources.

You Must Evaluate Fraud Risk and How It is Managed (2120.A2)

Fraud risk is singled out in the *Standards* on risk management coverage as an area for specific internal audit coverage. As part of the internal auditor's work, he or she should:

- Consider the practices the organization has to explicitly assess fraud risk. These practices may be conducted by an internal controls group in the organization, by the enterprise risk function, by compliance counsel, or by others or some combination of these activities.

- If the organization is not explicitly assessing fraud risk, consider explicitly conducting a fraud risk assessment. This is similar to other risk assessment activities, except that it is done not from a focus on the organization's objectives, but rather on the scenarios of fraud that fit the organization's environment.

- Be alert throughout internal auditing's work and engagements to the risk of fraud and the manner in which it is managed within the organization. Note that in Standard 1210.A2, internal auditors are expected to be proficient in this area.

- Consider monitoring and detection practices that highlight indicators that fraud may have been committed and decide whether any further action is necessary or whether an investigation should be recommended.

- Consider the risk responses and management controls in place to respond to fraud risks and make recommendations on how to improve the risk management processes that prevent and detect fraud. These processes may be entity-level controls embedded in the organization's ethics program, other monitoring controls, or detailed transaction-level controls embedded in processes.

- Notify the appropriate members of management and board if there are sufficient indicators of the commission of a fraud to recommend an investigation.

Exhibit 9-7 includes a fraud prevention scorecard and a fraud detection scorecard. These can be useful tools for the internal auditor in evaluating the risk of fraud and how it is managed. These, along with a list of cross-industry fraud risk scenarios that can be useful in fraud risk assessment, can be found in the publication *Managing the Business Risk of Fraud: A Practical Guide* developed collectively by The IIA, the AICPA, and the Association of Certified Fraud Examiners.

Further guidance on fraud risks identification and assessment for internal auditors can be found in the Practice Guide Internal Auditing and Fraud.

Risky Business

As the internal auditor's role in risk grows, it is important to keep in mind that organizational management still retains ownership of risk management, with the board having oversight responsibility. Internal auditors can serve as the catalyst that gets the process started and as risk advisers to the responsible decision makers. Internal auditors also have the responsibility to assess the effectiveness of the risk management program. But it is management, from the executive level down to the line managers, who ultimately are responsible for managing risk.

Internal Audit Coverage of Internal Control

The standards in the 2130 series make a well-defined connection between control and risk. Without the risk-focused approach to internal control, internal auditors may get into the practice of simply assuming that the procedures and rules — the controls — put in place by an organization were the right ones for the business. As a result, their control assessments were designed primarily to make sure that individuals within a particular function performed their jobs in the manner they were instructed.

The *Standards* make it clear, however, that compliance with procedures and processes is not the goal of the internal control system. Instead, internal control is more broadly described as a way to appropriately manage risk so that business objectives can be achieved at the lowest cost. For example, the Glossary to the *Standards* defines *control* as *any action taken by management, the board, and other parties to **manage risk** and increase the likelihood that established objectives and goals will be achieved. Management plans, organizes, and directs the performance of sufficient actions **to provide reasonable assurance** that objectives and goals will be achieved.* To consider the organization to have *adequate control*, there must be *reasonable assurance that the organization's **risks have been managed effectively** and that the organization's goals and objectives will be achieved efficiently and economically.* (emphasis added to all)

The experience with companies with publicly traded stock subject to United States Securities and Exchange Commission (SEC) regulations, including the Sarbanes-Oxley Act, provides an interesting perspective on what is needed to ensure effective internal controls. When that requirement was first put into effect, many (including those passing the law) assumed existing processes related to internal controls in organizations would result in relatively little work required to ensure adequate control. In actuality, organizations found it took a significant investment of time and effort to understand and assess the design of internal controls just over financial reporting, and as part of that process many organizations identified major needs for remediation of processes to improve controls. Despite the fact that the words "internal control" have been part of the internal auditing vocabulary for years, truly implementing effective internal controls consistent with models such as COSO can take significant effort. For many organizations, internal auditing played a key role in this process, due to its objectivity and competency in internal control.

It is clear that the *Standards* expect internal control evaluations to ensure that individuals throughout the organization are not just following orders, but are managing risks appropriately. This image of internal control affects how internal auditors fulfill the following control assessment requirements of the *Standards*.

According to the *Standards, the internal audit activity must assist the organization in maintaining effective controls by evaluating their effectiveness and efficiency and by promoting continuous improvement* (2130). Internal auditors should be "looking out," so to speak, for the well-being of the internal control system at all times. As they traverse the landscape of the organization performing their myriad services, internal auditors should be constantly aware of their role as the protector and promoter of internal control.

Internal auditors know how to assess control effectiveness and efficiency — it has been their bread and butter since the birth of the profession. But as alluded to earlier, it is impossible to competently evaluate the control system without considering risk. One of the most effective methods for assuring that control assessments are risk-based is the use of a risk/control matrix like that shown in Exhibit 9-8. Such matrices compel the audit team to look at control in terms of the risk to objectives, not just in terms of policies and procedures that should be followed.

Internal auditors who provide consulting services to their organizations are in a great position to help improve the overall control system. Information they gather in any type of consulting or problem-solving assignment can almost always be used to shore up controls throughout the organization.

In addition, increasing numbers of internal audit teams are advising management on the design of controls for new processes and systems.

As stated earlier, the *Standards* actually require internal auditors to use their consulting work to improve the control system. While allowing consulting clients to maintain their influence over the scope of the consulting engagement by calling for internal auditors to *address controls consistent with the engagement's objectives* (2130.C1), the *Standards* also require internal auditors to *be alert to significant control issues* (2130.C1) and to *incorporate knowledge of controls gained from consulting engagements into evaluation of the organization's control processes* (2130.C2). Internal auditors should be observant of the effectiveness of risk management and control processes during formal consulting engagements, and that substantial risk exposures or material control weaknesses should be brought to the attention of management and, if appropriate, of executive management and the board.

An effective control system requires everyone in the organization to understand their role in internal control and its importance. In this regard, the role of the internal auditor as a control educator and consultant is crucial. Many audit shops have introduced their organizations to highly effective control models like COSO and CoCo and have been instrumental in helping establish systems based upon their tenets. As noted earlier, experience from the implementation of Sarbanes-Oxley in the United States shows that this is a significant effort, and improvements in the organization's operations can result. Simple efforts such as rephrasing control concepts in terms relevant to the working population, as in the questionnaire shown in Exhibit 9-9, can move the organization forward in having an effectively operating internal control system.

Audit organizations that focus only on formal internal control assurance engagements and do not provide consulting services can promote continuous improvement as well by leveraging the results of those assessments. The control self-assessment exercises often used by auditors to gather assurance evidence are very effective tools for continuous improvement, since they engage process owners in awareness and discussion of controls, and are conducted throughout the year in various areas.

The power of these and other control evaluation exercises can be enhanced by identifying, often through the use of specialized computer software, trends in control weaknesses across the organization. Awareness of these systemic issues can be increased through e-mail or print newsletters or by maintaining a Web page devoted to control updates. The "continuous monitoring" procedures mentioned above in the section on risk are also effective methods for promoting continuous improvement of the control system, because they provide early warning of potential control problems. Many internal audit groups of major organizations are now looking for ways to embed the use of technology-enabled auditing into their internal audit risk assessment and internal audit projects to leverage for controls improvement the information that is embedded in the data sitting in the organization's systems.

You Must Evaluate the Adequacy, Effectiveness, and Efficiency of Controls (2130, 2130.A1)

Assuring senior management and the board that the system of internal control is operating effectively and efficiently has always been one of internal auditing's most important roles. Standard 2130.A1 goes on to say that *the internal audit activity must evaluate the adequacy and effectiveness of controls in responding to risks within an organization's governance, operations and information systems regarding the:*

- *Reliability and integrity of financial and operational information.*
- *Effectiveness and efficiency of operations and programs.*
- *Safeguarding of assets.*
- *Compliance with laws, regulations, policies, procedures, and contracts.*

The inclusion of governance, operations, and information systems in this standard basically covers everything management does to move the organization toward the achievement of its objectives. By specifically requiring control reviews of these three areas, the *Standards* underscore the point that internal control concerns are quite comprehensive and are not limited to manual transaction level controls.

PA 2130-1 presents three key questions to consider when evaluating the overall effectiveness of the organization's control processes:

- Were important discrepancies or weaknesses discovered from the audit work performed and other assessment information gathered?

- If so, were corrections or improvements made after the discoveries?

- Do the discoveries and their consequences lead to the conclusion that a pervasive condition exists resulting in an unacceptable level of business risk?

The Practice Advisory notes that the temporary existence of an important control discrepancy or weakness does not necessarily indicate that the problem is pervasive and poses an unacceptable residual risk. The pattern of discoveries, degree of intrusion, and level of consequences and exposures are factors that should be considered in determining whether the system is jeopardized and unacceptable risks exist.

In increasing numbers of organizations, providing assurance on the adequacy of the control system requires internal auditors to assess how well the system satisfies criteria outlined in various "control models," such as COSO, Cadbury, and CoCo. These models, which were designed to help management and oversight bodies achieve their strategic objectives, all define control in terms of managing risks to objectives. In doing so, they outline the specific elements that most effectively provide such protection. Organizations worldwide have incorporated and adopted various elements from these models into the design of their own control systems. An outline of several such models appears in Exhibit 9-1.

If the organization's existing practices are in line with the selected model's criteria, then the control system can be deemed adequate and effective. It is important to note that traditional audit techniques that focus only on "hard" control activities at the process level will result in an incomplete assessment. To assure management that the internal control system is adequate, it is especially important to evaluate softer controls, such as "tone at the top," management philosophy, incentives, and communication effectiveness. Almost all of the established control models include these softer aspects, elements of internal control that provide the foundation for strong internal controls.

As mentioned earlier, control self-assessment exercises involving those directly engaged in a business unit or process have proven extremely useful for "scoring" the control system and evaluating soft controls. For example, the various elements of a chosen control model can be presented in an auditor-facilitated group session where each individual "grades" the organization on how well it exhibits each particular control. Another approach is to distribute self-assessment questionnaires, either specifically targeted to members of a business unit or process soon to be reviewed, or randomly as part of a yearly, organizationwide exercise. A sample questionnaire is shown in Exhibit 9-9.

You Must Promote the Continuous Improvement of the Control Environment (2130)

A second element of the control standards requires audit initiatives that promote the continuous improvement of the control environment. As noted earlier, there is a direct link between risk identification, risk management, and effectiveness and efficiency of controls.

Additional Control Considerations

While the CAE is required to report periodically to the board and senior management on important control issues, PA 1230-1 recommends that the CAE report at least once a year on the state of the organization's control processes. Additional guidance on the types of information to include in such reports is covered in the Practice Advisory.

It is important for internal auditors to remember that a goal of their internal control evaluation and improvement efforts should be to sharpen up the system rather than to pile on unnecessary procedures. Internal control can be expensive, and it is important to uncover areas that are over-controlled.

Finally, as is the case with risk management, internal control is a management responsibility, and internal control design is a management function. As part of their assurance role, internal auditors should assess and evaluate the control systems in place. However, more integral assistance, such as internal control design and implementation, can be provided through internal auditors' consulting activities.

In the instance of consulting engagements, however, care must be taken to avoid violating the engagement client's trust. The engagement client must be aware that controls evaluation is an objective of the consulting engagement, albeit a secondary one. Clients should be advised that the internal auditor's foremost responsibility is always adequate control of risk. Therefore, the identification of any significant governance, risk management, or control issues relevant to the organization as a whole will be considered in modifying risk assessments and may be communicated to senior management and the board, if necessary.

A Systematic and Disciplined Approach

Standard 2100 notes that internal auditors must use a *systematic and disciplined approach*. This has been one of the differentiating attributes of internal auditing for years. It is one of the reasons that organizations turn to and respect internal auditing for its ability to look at nearly any process in the organization and assess risk management, controls, and governance. Consistently having a systematic and disciplined approach to the process of internal auditing is a key attribute that helps ensure internal auditing is delivering the quality service that the *Standards* require.

Valuable Work

The profession of internal auditing is founded on the trust placed in its objective assurance regarding internal control, and today that assurance extends to the risk management and governance arenas as well. The standards describing the nature of internal audit work lay out a framework for not only meeting this fiduciary responsibility, but also for exponentially increasing the activity's value to the organization. The rise and fall of any organization is directly related to the effectiveness of its governance, risk management, and control systems. Because it is now required to serve more proactively the very structure holding the organization together, internal auditing has never been more valuable.

Exhibit 9-1
Internal Control Models

Increasingly, internal auditors are basing their control assurance opinions on the degree to which the organization's control system conforms with criteria outlined in established control models. Numerous models exist, including those shown here: COSO, CoCo, and Cadbury/Turnbull.

The COSO Model, from *Internal Control – Integrated Framework,* published in 1992 by the AICPA. Reprinted with permission.

COSO defines internal control as a process, effected by an entity's board of directors, management, and other personnel, designated to provide reasonable assurance regarding the achievement of objectives in the following categories:

- Effectiveness and efficiency of operations.

- Reliability of financial reporting.

- Compliance with applicable laws and regulations.

COSO names five elements of control, shown below. Internal auditors seeking to measure their systems against the criteria defined in COSO must assess the extent to which these components are in place and operating as intended.

The control environment component provides an atmosphere in which people conduct their activities and carry out their control responsibilities. It serves as the foundation for the other components. Within this environment, management assesses risks to the achievement of specified objectives. Control activities are implemented to help ensure that management directives to address risks are carried out. Meanwhile, relevant information is captured and communicated throughout the organization. The entire process is monitored and modified as conditions warrant.

The sub-points noted under each category heading are derived from the narrative accompanying the framework. COSO does not attempt to list specific sub-elements in the framework, but does provide detailed criteria for each category posed as questions.

Note: COSO announced in late 2010 a project to review and update this framework initially released in 1992 to make the existing framework and related evaluation tools more relevant in the increasingly complex business environment so that organizations worldwide can better design, implement, and assess internal control. The target publication date for the project is 2012.

Exhibit 9-1 (continued)
Internal Control Models

---

1. **CONTROL ENVIRONMENT**
   1.1 Integrity and Ethical Values
   1.2 Commitment to Competence
   1.3 Board of Directors/Audit Committee
   1.4 Management Philosophy and Operating Style
   1.5 Organization Structure
   1.6 Assignment of Authority and Responsibility
   1.7 Human Resource Policies and Practices

2. **RISK ASSESSMENT**
   2.1 Entity-wide Objectives
   2.2 Activity-level Objectives
   2.3 Risk Identification
   2.4 Change Management

3. **CONTROL ACTIVITIES**
   3.1 Top-level Reviews
   3.2 Direct Functional or Activity Management
   3.3 Information Processing
   3.4 Physical Controls
   3.5 Performance Indicators
   3.6 Segregation of Duties
   3.7 Controls Over Information Systems
   - Data Center
   - Application Development and Maintenance
   - System Software
   - Access Security
   - Application Controls

4. **INFORMATION AND COMMUNICATION**
   4.1 Information
   4.2 Communication

5. **MONITORING**
   5.1 Ongoing Monitoring
   5.2 Separate Evaluations
   5.3 Reporting Deficiencies

Exhibit 9-1 (continued)
Internal Control Models

The Cadbury Model, from *Internal Control and Financial Reporting: Guidance For Directors Of Listed Companies Registered In The U.K.*; and the Turnbull Model, from *Internal Control: Guidance for the Directors on the Combined Code,* both published by The Institute of Chartered Accountants in England and Wales in December 1994 and September 1999, respectively. Reprinted with permission.

The Cadbury model is comprised of five elements and represents a slightly modified version of COSO. The more detailed framework that supports the structure shown below was included in the October 1993 exposure draft. This detailed guidance was deleted in the final December 1994 report.

1. **Control environment.**
   - A commitment by directors, management, and employees to competence and integrity (e.g., leadership by example, employment criteria).
   - Communication of ethical values and control consciousness to managers and employees (e.g., through written codes of conduct, formal standards of discipline, performance appraisal).
   - An appropriate organizational structure within which business can be planned, executed, controlled, and monitored to achieve the company's/group's objectives.
   - Appropriate delegation of authority with accountability which has regard to acceptable levels of risk.
   - A professional approach to financial reporting which complies with generally accepted accounting practice.

2. **Identification and evaluation of risks and control objectives.**
   - Identification of key business risks in a timely manner.
   - Consideration of the likelihood of risks crystallizing and the significance of the consequent financial impact on the business.
   - Establishment of priorities for the allocation of resources available for control and the setting and communicating of clear control objectives.

3. **Information and communication.**
   - Performance indicators, which allow management to monitor the key business and financial activities and risks and the progress towards financial objectives, and to identify developments which require intervention (e.g., forecasts and budgets).
   - Information systems, which provide ongoing identification and capture of relevant, reliable, and up-to-date financial and other information from internal and external sources (e.g., monthly management accounts, including earnings, cash flow, and balance sheet reporting).
   - Systems, which communicate relevant information to the right people at the right frequency and time in a format that exposes significant variances from the budgets and forecasts and allows prompt response.

Exhibit 9-1 (continued)
Internal Control Models

4. **Control procedures.**

   - Procedures to ensure complete and accurate accounting for financial transactions.
   - Appropriate authorization limits for transactions that reasonably limit the company's/group's exposures.
   - Procedures to ensure the reliability of data processing and information reports generated.
   - Controls that limit exposure to loss of assets/records or to fraud (e.g., physical controls, segregation of duties).
   - Routine and surprise checks which provide effective supervision of the control activities.
   - Procedures to ensure compliance with laws and regulations that have significant financial implications.

5. **Monitoring and corrective action.**

   - A monitoring process which provides reasonable assurance to the board that there are appropriate control procedures in place for all the company's/group's financially significant business activities and that these procedures are being followed (e.g., consideration by the board or board committee of reports from management, from an internal audit function or from independent accountants.
   - Identification of change in the business and its environment which may require changes to the system of internal financial control.
   - Formal procedures for reporting weaknesses and for ensuring appropriate corrective action.
   - The provision of adequate support for public statements by the directors on internal control or internal financial control.

Exhibit 9-1 (continued)
Internal Control Models

In 1999, the Institute of Chartered Accountants in England & Wales (ICAEW) issued a report on internal control, which expanded the concept beyond financial controls to include those of an operational and compliance nature as well. This Turnbull model more solidly links internal control to the management of risk by describing internal control as responsible for facilitating the effectiveness and efficiency of operations, helping ensure the reliability of internal and external reporting, and assisting compliance with laws and regulations. In the Turnbull model, an effective internal control system includes the following four elements.

1. Risk assessment.

- Does the company have clear objectives and have they been communicated so as to provide effective direction to employees on risk assessment and control issues? For example, do objectives and related plans include measurable performance targets and indicators?

- Are the significant internal and external operational, financial, compliance, and other risks identified and assessed on an ongoing basis? (Significant risks may, for example, include those related to market, credit, liquidity, technological, legal, health, safety and environmental, reputation, and business probity issues.)

- Is there a clear understanding by management and others within the company of what risks are acceptable to the board?

2. Control environment and control activities.

- Does the board have clear strategies for dealing with the significant risks that have been identified? Is there a policy on how to manage these risks?

- Do the company's culture, code of conduct, human resource policies, and performance reward systems support the business objectives and risk management and internal control system?

- Does senior management demonstrate, through its actions as well as its policies, the necessary commitment to competence, integrity, and fostering a climate of trust within the company?

- Are authority, responsibility, and accountability defined clearly such that decisions are made and actions taken by the appropriate people? Are the decisions and actions of different parts of the company appropriately coordinated?

- Does the company communicate to its employees what is expected of them and the scope of their freedom to act? This may apply to areas such as customer relations; service levels for both internal and outsourced activities; health, safety, and environmental protection; security of tangible and intangible assets; business continuity issues; expenditure matters; accounting; and financial and other reporting.

- Do people in the company (and in its providers of outsourced services) have the knowledge, skills, and tools to support the achievement of the company's objectives and to manage effectively risks to their achievement?

- How are processes/controls adjusted to reflect new or changing risks or operational deficiencies?

Exhibit 9-1 (continued)
Internal Control Models

3. **Information and communication.**

   - Do management and the board receive timely, relevant, and reliable reports on progress against business objectives and the related risks that provide them with the information, from inside and outside the company, needed for decision-making and management review purposes? This could include performance reports and indicators of change, together with qualitative information such as on customer satisfaction, employee attitudes, etc.

   - Are information needs and related information systems reassessed as objectives and related risks change or as reporting deficiencies are identified?

   - Are periodic reporting procedures, including semi-annual and annual reporting, effective in communicating a balanced and understandable account of the company's position and prospects?

   - Are there established channels of communication for individuals to report suspected breaches of laws or regulations or other improprieties?

4. **Monitoring.**

   - Are there ongoing processes embedded within the company's overall business operations, and addressed by senior management, which monitor the effective application of the policies, processes, and activities related to internal control and risk management? (Such processes may include control self-assessment, confirmation by personnel of compliance with policies and codes of conduct, internal audit reviews, or other management reviews.)

   - Do these processes monitor the company's ability to reevaluate risks and adjust controls effectively in response to changes in its objectives, its business, and its external environment?

   - Are there effective follow-up procedures to ensure that appropriate change or action occurs in response to changes in risk and control assessments?

   - Is there appropriate communication to the board (or board committees) on the effectiveness of the ongoing monitoring processes on risk and control matters? This should include reporting any significant failings or weaknesses on a timely basis.

   - Are there specific arrangements for management monitoring and reporting to the board on risk and control matters of particular importance? These could include, for example, actual or suspected fraud and other illegal or irregular acts, or matters that could adversely affect the company's reputation or financial position.

Exhibit 9-1 (continued)
Internal Control Models

The CoCo Model, published by the Canadian Institute of Chartered Accountants in 1995. Reprinted with permission.

CoCo defines control as those elements of an organization (including its resources, systems, processes, culture, structure, and tasks) that, taken together, support people in the achievement of the organization's objectives. The CoCo model presents four components of control and outlines criteria for each.

Purpose

A1   Objectives should be established and communicated.

A2   The significant internal and external risks faced by an organization in the achievement of its objectives should be identified and assessed.

A3   Policies designed to support the achievement of an organization's objectives and the management of its risks should be established, communicated, and practiced so that people understand what is expected of them and the scope of their freedom to act.

A4   Plans to guide efforts in achieving the organization's objectives should be established and communicated.

A5   Objectives and related plans should include measurable performance targets and indicators.

Commitment

B1   Shared ethical values, including integrity, should be established, communicated, and practiced throughout the organization.

B2   Human resource policies and practices should be consistent with an organization's ethical values and with achievement of its objectives.

B3   Authority, responsibility, and accountability should be clearly defined and consistent with an organization's objectives so that decisions and actions are taken by the appropriate people.

B4   An atmosphere of mutual trust should be fostered to support the flow of information between people and their effective performance toward achieving the organization's objectives.

Capability

C1   People should have the necessary knowledge, skills, and tools to support the achievement of the organization's objectives.

C2   Communication processes should support the organization's values and the achievement of its objectives.

C3   Sufficient and relevant information should be identified and communicated in a timely manner to enable people to perform their assigned responsibilities.

C4   The decisions and actions of different parts of the organization should be coordinated.

Exhibit 9-1 (continued)
Internal Control Models

C5 Control activities should be designed as an integral part of the organization, taking into consideration its objectives, the risks to their achievement, and the inter-relatedness of control elements.

Monitoring and Learning

D1 External and internal environments should be monitored to obtain information that may signal a need to reevaluate the organization's objectives or controls.

D2 Performance should be monitored against the targets and indicators identified in the organization's objectives and plans.

D3 The assumptions behind an organization's objectives and systems should be periodically challenged.

D4 Information needs and related information systems should be reassessed as objectives change or as reporting deficiencies are identified.

D5 Follow-up procedures should be established and performed to ensure appropriate change or action occurs.

D6 Management should periodically assess the effectiveness of control in its organization and communicate the results to those to whom it is accountable.

Exhibit 9-2
Strengthening Internal Auditing's Role in Governance

The following are 14 practical strategies for internal audit functions to consider as they regard their involvement in governance and oversight processes. Although best practices in the governance area are still in their relative infancy, they will continue to evolve, spurred primarily by business demands rather than regulatory edict, reflecting what is good for governance is also good for business. Yet it is also clear that boards of directors and audit committees at leading companies are eager for progress on corporate governance issues. It is with this sense of immediacy in mind that the following set of coordinated strategies is presented for internal audit functions and their constituents to consider in repositioning the governance activities.

Governance Environment: The Culture, Structure, and Policies Providing the Foundation for Good Governance

Strategy 1:   Assess Overall Governance Structure and Policies

Strategy 2:   Assess Governance Environment and Ethics

Strategy 3:   Assess Specific Audit Committee Activities

Strategy 4:   Assess Risk Management Structure and Activities

Strategy 5:   Assess Internal Audit's Structure and Organization

Governance Processes: Specific Activities That Support the Governance Environment

Strategy 6:   Assess Fraud Control and Communications Processes

Strategy 7:   Assess Compensation Policies and Related Processes

Strategy 8:   Assess Financial Governance Processes

Strategy 9:   Assess Governance Activities for Strategic Planning and Decision Making

Strategy 10:   Assess Governance Performance Measures

Governance Procedures: Specific Procedures and Practices Critical to the Implementation and Operation of Governance Activities

Strategy 11:   Assess Internal and External Governance Reporting Procedures

Strategy 12:   Assess Procedures to Escalate and Track Governance Issues

Strategy 13:   Assess Governance Change and Learning Procedures

Strategy 14:   Assess Governance Support Software and Technology

Source: From *Strengthening Internal Audit's Performance in Corporate Governance* by PricewaterhouseCoopers LLP, 2004.

Exhibit 9-3
Evaluating the Board

The following checklist can be an effective tool for evaluating the board aspect of the organization's corporate governance process.

Strategy and Planning — Does the Board:

- Insist on enough time and the right atmosphere for full, frank discussions on strategy?

- Have aggressive but constructive debates based on the directors' skills, knowledge, and insights?

- Get the right information on risks, interdependencies, resources, and competitors?

- Apply lessons learned from past successful— and unsuccessful — strategies?

- Agree on planned extent of change, whether it is incremental, substantial, or transformational?

- Achieve satisfaction that tactical plans will result in successful strategic implementation?

Risk Management — Does the Board:

- Understand significant risks and feel comfortable with how management addresses them?

- Ensure that the corporate culture rewards appropriate risk management and assigns responsibility for it?

- Receive in a timely manner alerts regarding serious risk considerations and assurance that the right actions are being taken to manage the risks?

- Ensure that the organization has an effective, ongoing process to identify risk, measure its potential impact against a varied set of assumptions, and do what is necessary to manage it proactively?

Tone at the Top — Does the Board:

- Recognize that the mindset and actions of the CEO and senior management team must convey the organization's values, mission, and direction for the future?

- Have mechanisms for assessing the values that are actually instilled in the organizational culture, including querying employees, customers, suppliers, and business partners?

Measuring and Monitoring of Performance — Does the Board:

- Ensure that measures are linked to strategy, tactics, and the real value drivers?

- Ensure that measures balance financial with nonfinancial information; balance forward-looking with retrospective information; enable benchmarking against competitors, peers, and best practices; and balance key scorecard categories, including operations, customers, and employees?

- Ensure it is satisfied with targets set for the measures?

- Ensure that information systems provide reliable, timely information?

Exhibit 9-3 (continued)
Evaluating the Board

- Ensure that measures are linked to rewards throughout the company, so everyone is pulling toward common, approved goals?

- Ensure there is rigorous follow-up and discussion of reasons for missed targets, including results that both underperform and greatly over-perform?

Transformational Transactions — Does the Board:

- Make sure they are completely comfortable with the business reasons for the proposed transaction, including how it links to current strategy?

- Critically evaluate management's information, transaction assumptions, and ability to integrate the target successfully?

- Apply lessons learned from past successful and unsuccessful transactions?

- Have the courage to walk away from a bad deal?

- Obtain the counsel of objective advisers, rather than only those with a direct interest in making the deal happen?

- Recognize that there will undoubtedly be a change in allegiance and differing objectives of management in to-be-divested units?

- Ensure the company has the right partners, reliable due diligence, and a properly structured deal before entering strategic joint ventures or alliances?

- Critically review proposed capital expenditures, and make sure they're linked to current corporate strategy?

Management Evaluation, Compensation, and Succession Planning — Does the Board:

- Evaluate the chief executive's performance relative to corporate strategy and short and long-term company and personal goals?

- Evaluate the CEO's progress in meeting both quantitative and qualitative objectives, including developing competent, motivated leadership throughout the organization and setting the right ethical values and tone at the top?

- Ensure that evaluation/compensation decisions are made objectively by board members who are not beholden to management?

- Give sufficient attention to evaluating management below the chief executive level by ensuring the development and retention of essential talent and getting to know those who may someday lead the company?

- Feel comfortable with succession plans and processes for finding a new chief executive should it become necessary?

- Have in place the right evaluative mechanisms that afford decision-making confidence and the courage to make touch choices, such as replacing an underperforming CEO?

179

Exhibit 9-3 (continued)
Evaluating the Board

External Communication — Does the Board:

- Recognize the threat posed by earnings management and other misrepresentations of information?

- Recognize the relevance of operating information and help ensure its integrity by probing controls over and the verification of to-be-reported information?

- Make sure it is comfortable that communication processes represent best practice?

- Ensure stakeholders are treated equally by making sure that information is disseminated to all interested parties at the same time?

- Scrutinize the processes surrounding confidential or unannounced deals or developments?

- Make sure it is comfortable that confidentiality is ensured for unannounced deals?

Effective Dynamics — Does the Board:

- Have an independent voice that is in no way beholden to the chief executive and is ready to constructively challenge the management team?

- Possess the requisite individual characteristics, including integrity, judgment, credibility, trustworthiness, strategic thinking, intuition, vision, industry knowledge, communication skills, decision-making ability, interpersonal skills, willingness to actively participate, and ability to constructively handle conflict?

- Operate in an atmosphere of openness and trust that enables directors to speak their minds and pursue issues to their conclusion?

- Ensure meetings are effective by achieving advance buy-in on the agenda, distributing the right amount of advance material in a timely manner, discussing tough issues first, and minimizing bureaucracy?

- Devote time for outside meetings that enable the development of trust among members and with management?

Source: Steinberg, Richard M., and Deborah Pojunis, "Corporate Governance: The New Frontier," *Internal Auditor* (December 2000), pp. 34–39; and Steinberg, Richard M., and Catherine L. Bromilow, *Corporate Governance and the Board – What Works Best* (Altamonte Springs, FL: The Institute of Internal Auditors Research Foundation, 2000), pp. 77–94.

Exhibit 9-4
Risk Frameworks

The following models list several potential risks categorized by type. While no one-size-fits-all approach exists, internal auditors, as well as the senior management officials and boards they serve, may find these models useful as they identify risks in their own environments.

FRAMEWORK #1 — BUSINESS RISK FRAMEWORK
By David McNamee

Business risk can be divided into three primary areas: ownership, process, and behavioral.

Ownership Risks are associated with acquiring, maintaining, and disposing of all assets except human assets. Since many ownership risks are insurable, the primary approaches to managing them are risk transfer or risk sharing through insurance.

- External threats are forces outside the control of the organization that can affect the organization's business processes and goals. Examples include customer or constituent demands; labor, financial, and product markets; suppliers, including unions; competitors; government regulation; economic and political forces; technology; and physical and environmental forces.

- Custodial risks are associated with owning and safeguarding assets. Examples of custodial risks include obsolescence, damage in handling or storing the assets, and theft from storage.

- Hazards, which are also a type of process risk, are related to loss or impairment through fire and other natural or manmade disasters and accidental loss.

- Opportunity costs, which are also a type of behavioral risk, represent the cost of making less-than-optimum decisions about asset acquisition and disposition. Examples include purchasing the wrong asset, paying too much, selling the asset too soon or too late, selling the asset too cheaply, and disposing of the wrong asset.

Process Risks are associated with putting assets to work to achieve objectives and are managed primarily through an active system of internal controls in the processes, including active management oversight.

- Hazards, which are also a type of ownership risk, are associated with loss or impairment through fire and natural or manmade disasters and accidental loss.

- Errors, omissions, and delays represent the risks to processes arising from random differences in human or machine activity in the process. Poor judgment in plans or operations, inappropriate or outdated control mechanisms, and machine malfunction are examples of these risks.

- Frauds can arise from intentional misrepresentation of suppliers, employees, and customers. Examples of these risks to the process include theft, bid rigging, bribery, kickback schemes, and customer abuse.

Exhibit 9-4 (continued)
Risk Frameworks

- Productivity loss, which is also a type of behavioral risk, can result from poor design of the process or its control system. Examples include scheduling conflicts, inappropriate work rules, missing controls, lack of monitoring control systems, underutilizing assets in the process, and goal conflicts.

Behavioral Risks are associated with acquiring, maintaining, and disposing of human assets and are perhaps the most varied and difficult risks to manage. Primary mitigation techniques for behavioral risks include avoidance — redesigning the workplace to reduce the level of risk — and risk transfer through workers' compensation and liability insurance.

- Productivity loss, which is also a type of process risk, arises from poor management practices or poor worker commitment. Underutilization of human assets, poor leadership, favoritism, lack of work structure and discipline, inconsistent management decisions, and personal and work goal conflicts are examples of these risks.

- Dysfunctional workplaces can represent risks to employees who work in a dysfunctional environment and risks to the organization because employees are working in such an environment. Examples of these risks are gender or racial harassment, excessive pressure to meet objectives without compensating relief valves, employee theft and sabotage, workplace injuries, employee lawsuits, and workplace violence.

- Opportunity costs, which are also a type of ownership risk, are associated with the cost of making less-than-optimum decisions about the acquisition and disposition of human assets — people, knowledge, and skills. Hiring the wrong people, a poor compensation system, and letting the wrong people or skills leave the organization are examples.

Source: Reprinted with permission from "Targeting Business Risk" by David McNamee, *Internal Auditor* (October 2000).

FRAMEWORK #2 — IDENTIFYING AND ASSESSING RISK FROM AN ERM PERSPECTIVE
By KPMG

Strategic Risk

- Are the crucial strategies appropriate to enable the organization to meet its business objectives?

- What are the risks inherent in those strategies, and how might the organization identify, quantify, and manage these risks?

- How much risk is the organization willing to take?

- What risks result from e-business developments?

Exhibit 9-4 (continued)
Risk Frameworks

FRAMEWORK #2 — IDENTIFYING AND ASSESSING RISK FROM AN ERM PERSPECTIVE (continued) **By KPMG**

Operational Risk

- What are the risks inherent in the processes that have been chosen to implement the strategies?

- How does the organization identify, quantify, and manage these risks given its appetite for risk? How does it adapt its activities as strategies and processes change?

Reputation Risk

- What risks to brand and reputation are inherent in the way the organization executes its strategies?

Regulatory or Contractual Risk

- What risks are related to compliance with regulations or contractual arrangements — not just those that are financially based?

Financial Risk

- Have operating processes put financial resources at undue risk?

- Has the organization incurred unreasonable liabilities to support operating processes?

- Has the organization succeeded in meeting measurable business objectives?

Information Risk

- Is our data/information/knowledge reliable, relevant, and timely?

- Are our information systems reliable?

- Do our security systems reflect our e-business strategy?

New Risks

- What risks have yet to develop? (These might include risks from new competitors or emerging business models, recession risks, relationship risks, outsourcing risks, political or criminal risks, financial risk disasters [rogue traders], and other crisis and disaster risks.)

Source: Reprinted with permission from KPMG LLP, the U.S. member firm of KPMG International, a Swiss association.

Exhibit 9-4 (continued)
Risk Frameworks

FRAMEWORK #3 — RISK MATRIX
By The Institute of Chartered Accountants in England and Wales

Business

Wrong business strategy

Competitive pressure on price/market share

General economic problems

Political risks

Obsolescence of technology

Substitute products

Adverse government policy

Industry sector in decline

Takeover target

Inability to obtain further capital

Bad acquisition

Too slow to innovate

Financial

Liquidity risk

Market risk

Going concern problems

Overtrading

Credit risk

Interest risk

Currency risk

High cost of capital

Treasury risk

Misuse of financial resources

Occurrence of types of fraud to which the business is susceptible

Misstatement risk related to published financial information

Breakdown of accounting system

Unrecorded liabilities

Unreliable accounting records

Penetration and attack of IT systems by hackers

Decisions based on incomplete or faulty information

Too much data and not enough analysis

Unfulfilled promises to investors

Exhibit 9-4 (continued)
Risk Frameworks

FRAMEWORK #3 — RISK MATRIX
By The Institute of Chartered Accountants in England and Wales

Compliance

Breach of listing rules

Breach of financial regulations

Breach of federal regulations

Litigation risk

Breach of competition laws

VAT problems

Breach of other regulations and laws

Tax penalties

Health and safety risks

Environmental problems

Operational and Other

Business processes not aligned to strategic goals

Failure of major change initiative

Loss of entrepreneurial spirit

Stock-out of raw materials

Skills shortage

Physical disasters (including fire and explosion)

Failure to create and exploit intangible assets

Loss of intangible assets

Breach of confidentiality

Loss of physical assets

Lack of business continuity

Succession problems

Loss of key people

Inability to reduce cost base

Major customers impose tough contract obligations

Overreliance on key suppliers or customers

Failure of new products or services

Poor service levels

Failure to satisfy customers

Quality problems

Lack of orders

Failure of major project

Loss of key contacts

Exhibit 9-4 (continued)
Risk Frameworks
FRAMEWORK #3 — RISK MATRIX (continued) **By The Institute of Chartered Accountants in England and Wales**

Inability to make use of the Internet

Failure of outsource provider to deliver

Industrial action

Failure of big technology related project

Lack of employee motivation or efficiency

Inability to implement change

Inefficient/ineffective processing of documents

Poor brand management

Product liability

Inefficient/ineffective management process

Problems arising from exploiting employees in developing countries

Other business probity issues

Other issues giving rise to reputation problems

Missed business opportunities

Source: Reproduced from "Implementing Turnbull: A Boardroom Briefing" (http://www.icaew.com/en/technical/corporate-governance) with permission of the Institute of Chartered Accountants in England & Wales.

FRAMEWORK #4 — Basel II

Basel II is a framework for banks that links capital requirements to the risks faced by banks. These risks are credit risk, operational risk and market risk. The Framework can be found in the Bank for International Settlement publication *International Convergence of Capital Measurement and Capital Standards, A revised Framework* (June 2006).

Credit Risk — The risk that counterparties to loans or other financial contract will fail to discharge an obligation and thus cause the bank to incur a financial loss.

Operational Risk — The risk of loss resulting from inadequate or failed internal processes, people and systems or from external events. This definition includes legal risk (i.e., fines, penalties, or punitive damages), but excludes strategic and reputational risk.

Market Risk — The risk of losses in on and off-balance-sheet positions arising from movements in market prices. The risks subject to this requirement are:
- The risks pertaining to interest rate related instruments and equities in the trading book;
- Foreign exchange risk and commodities risk throughout the bank.

Exhibit 9-4 (continued)
Risk Frameworks

FRAMEWORK #5 — ILLUSTRATIVE EXAMPLES OF EMERGING RISKS

Increasing natural resource constraints (e.g., loss of freshwater reserves, depletion of oil reserves, loss of biodiversity) that could raise the cost of raw materials and increase food prices, human suffering, and the pressure to identify alternate energy sources.

Natural or manmade disasters (e.g., floods, terrorism, cyberterrorism, viruses, spyware) that could cause business disruption and human catastrophes.

Increased industrial pollution and rising global carbon emissions leading to climate change that could cause a decrease in biodiversity, a shift in locations of production and consumption, and regional resource shortages.

Rapidly shifting demographic patterns (e.g., aging population) that could cause talent shortages in certain labor markets or within certain capabilities, lack of adequate skills, or shifts in customer demands and/or loyalties.

Rising labor costs driven, in part, by expanding benefits (pension, workers' compensation, and other non-salary expenses), which could result in lower profitability and loss of competitive advantage.

Increased volatility in asset prices and commodity markets (e.g., oil price shock, asset price collapse) that could cause fluctuations in cost structures that cannot readily be passed on to the consumer or otherwise absorbed.

Decline in global economic growth (e.g., caused by slowed Chinese economic growth, global recession, unsustainable deficit levels) that could negatively impact demand and put downward pressure on prices.

Political crises (e.g., failed and failing states, war, Middle East instability, failure of democratic institutions, regime change), which could result in nationalization of assets, increased regulation, protectionist tendencies, or other loss of control.

Pandemics and other health crises (e.g., fast-traveling pathogens such as avian flu, developing world disease such as HIV/AIDS, tuberculosis, malaria), which could jeopardize supply chain, consumers, employees, and others.

Economic inequality, which could exacerbate poverty and suffering and increase pressure on business to engage in humanitarian efforts.

Rise in nuclear capabilities, which could endanger global political stability and physical security.

A global liquidity crunch (e.g., resulting from subprime mortgage lending practices) that could raise the cost of capital for financing transactions (e.g., nanotechnology) that could evolve in unforeseen ways in an emerging market — for example, leapfrogging existing technologies as new applications arise.

Exhibit 9-4 (continued)
Risk Frameworks

FRAMEWORK #5 — ILLUSTRATIVE EXAMPLES OF EMERGING RISKS (continued)

Technology and communication disruptions (e.g., Internet blackout) or system failures, which could lead to business disruptions and economic loss.

Changes in laws and regulations (e.g., spread of liability regimes impacting foreign investment, or industry-specific laws such as prohibition impacting the alcoholic beverage industry) that could cause an overhaul in the manner by which businesses are run, or affect the sources of their profits.

A realignment of power in the capital markets of a country (e.g., increased governmental control of companies, foreign investment) that could lead to classes of activist investors who could pressure for different industry approaches to capital structure, profit allocation, or strategic goals.

Terrorist threats, which could reduce economic confidence or cause direct economic losses as well as loss of life, property, and security.

Increased competition from emerging markets and/or within the home market, which could cause downward pressure on prices.

Rise in anti-globalization sentiment and protectionism (e.g., fiscal policies, trade embargos, heightened tariffs, or other anticompetitive practices), which could cause retrenchment from global trade and investment.

Increase in corruption (e.g., bribery in procurement or sales), which could create anti- competitive business practices and lead to regulatory fines and sanctions and reputational damage for perpetrators.

Decline in recognition or enforcement of intellectual property rights (e.g., patents, licenses), which could cause unlicensed commercial activity or loss of proprietary information.

Source: PricewaterhouseCoopers, *Exploring Emerging Risks, 2009.*

For additional risk frameworks and a risk assessment questionnaire, see *Adding Value: Seven Roads to Success* by James Roth, published by The Institute of Internal Auditors Research Foundation.

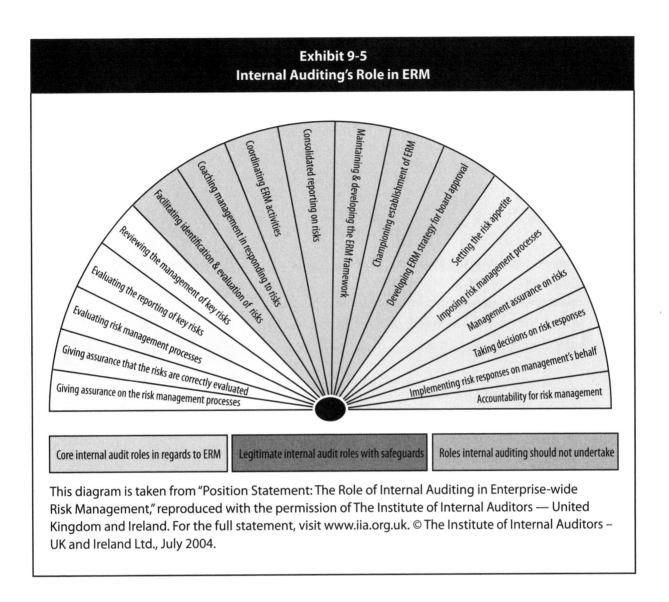

Exhibit 9-5
Internal Auditing's Role in ERM

Consolidated reporting on risks
Coordinating ERM activities
Coaching management in responding to risks
Facilitating identification & evaluation of risks
Reviewing the management of key risks
Evaluating the reporting of key risks
Evaluating risk management processes
Giving assurance that the risks are correctly evaluated
Giving assurance on the risk management processes

Maintaining & developing the ERM framework
Championing establishment of ERM
Developing ERM strategy for board approval
Setting the risk appetite
Imposing risk management processes
Management assurance on risks
Taking decisions on risk responses
Implementing risk responses on management's behalf
Accountability for risk management

| Core internal audit roles in regards to ERM | Legitimate internal audit roles with safeguards | Roles internal auditing should not undertake |

This diagram is taken from "Position Statement: The Role of Internal Auditing in Enterprise-wide Risk Management," reproduced with the permission of The Institute of Internal Auditors — United Kingdom and Ireland. For the full statement, visit www.iia.org.uk. © The Institute of Internal Auditors – UK and Ireland Ltd., July 2004.

Exhibit 9-6
Benchmarking the Risk Management Program

The effectiveness of risk management processes can be measured by verifying the presence of the following features of minimally successful, moderately successful, and leading-edge risk management programs.

Minimal

- Minimalistic disclosure.
- Loose linkage to business objectives.
- Limited discussion by the board.
- Relevant regulations or standards regarding risk, control, and governance viewed mainly as a compliance exercise.
- Board review just sufficient to comply with regulations.
- Monitoring heavily dependent on directors themselves.
- Little employee involvement.

Moderate

- Link to what drives the business.
- Reasonable involvement of employees.
- Risk awareness training.
- Positive acceptance of internal auditing.
- Buy-in obtained from different levels of management.
- Some use of workshop techniques.
- Application of the fundamentals of good risk management and internal control.
- Simple and straightforward early warning mechanisms.

Leading Edge

- Awareness of business objectives throughout the company.
- Focus risk management to "acceptable" level.
- Internal audit activity is source of advice on aspects of risk and control.
- Other independent monitoring activities.
- Regulations and standards regarding risk, control, and governance are used to improve the business.
- Risk management and internal control are part of the vocabulary throughout the business.
- Consultation throughout the company.

Source: Reproduced from "Implementing Turnbull: A Boardroom Briefing" (http://www.icaew.com/en/technical/corporate-governance) with the kind permission of the Institute of Chartered Accountants in England & Wales.

Exhibit 9-7	
Fraud Risk Tools for the Internal Auditor	

FRAUD PREVENTION SCORECARD

To assess the strength of the organization's fraud prevention system, carefully assess each area below and score the area, factor, or consideration as:

Red: indicating that the area, factor, or consideration needs substantial strengthening and improvement to bring fraud risk down to an acceptable level.

Yellow: indicating that the area, factor, or consideration needs some strengthening and improvement to bring fraud risk down to an acceptable level.

Green: indicating that the area, factor, or consideration is strong and fraud risk has been reduced — at least — to a minimally acceptable level.

Each area, factor, or consideration scored either red or yellow should have a note associated with it that describes the action plan for bringing it to green on the next scorecard.

Fraud Prevention Area, Factor, or Consideration Score Notes	Score	Notes
Our organizational culture — tone at the top — is as strong as it can possibly be and establishes a zero-tolerance environment with respect to fraud.		
Our organization's top management consistently displays the appropriate attitude regarding fraud prevention and encourages free and open communication regarding ethical behavior.		
Our Code of Organizational Conduct has specific provisions that address and prohibit inappropriate relationships whereby members of our board or members of management could use their positions for personal gain or other inappropriate purposes.		
We have done a rigorous fraud risk assessment using the COSO *Enterprise Risk Management – Integrated Framework* and have taken specific actions to strengthen our prevention mechanisms as necessary.		

Exhibit 9-7 (continued) Fraud Risk Tools for the Internal Auditor		
FRAUD PREVENTION SCORECARD (continued)		
Fraud Prevention Area, Factor, or Consideration Score Notes	**Score**	**Notes**
We have assessed fraud risk for our organization adequately based on evaluations of similar organizations in our industry, known frauds that have occurred in similar organizations, in-house fraud brainstorming, and periodic reassessments of risk.		
We have addressed the strengths and weaknesses of our internal control environment adequately and have taken specific steps to strengthen the internal control structure to help prevent the occurrences of fraud.		
Our organizational structure contains no unnecessary entities that might be used for inappropriate purposes or that might enable less-than-arms-length transactions or relationships.		
We have assessed all overseas and decentralized operations carefully and have taken proactive steps to ensure that they have fraud preventive controls in place to conform with the strictest legal standards and highest ethical principles.		
We have divested our organization of all unnecessary third-party and related-party relationships.		
For any remaining third-party and related-party relationships, we have taken positive measures to ensure that such relationships do not allow opportunities for frauds to occur without detection.		
We have assessed the alignment of authorities and responsibilities at all levels of organization management and are not aware of any misalignments that might represent vulnerabilities to fraud.		

Exhibit 9-7 (continued) Fraud Risk Tools for the Internal Auditor		
FRAUD PREVENTION SCORECARD (continued)		
Fraud Prevention Area, Factor, or Consideration Score Notes	**Score**	**Notes**
Our audit committee has taken a very proactive posture with respect to fraud prevention.		
Our audit committee is composed only of independent directors and includes persons with financial accounting and reporting expertise.		
Our audit committee meets at least quarterly and devotes substantial time to assessing fraud risk and proactively implementing fraud preventive mechanisms.		
We have a strong internal audit department (if applicable) that functions independently of management. The charter of our internal audit department expressly states that the internal audit team will help prevent and detect fraud and misconduct.		
We have designated an individual with the authority and responsibility for overseeing and maintaining our fraud prevention programs, and have given this individual the resources needed to manage our fraud prevention programs effectively. This individual has direct access to the audit committee.		
Our human resources department conducts background investigations with the specific objective of assuring that persons with inappropriate records or characters inconsistent with our corporate culture and ethics are identified and eliminated from the hiring process.		
Our human resources department conducts background investigations with respect to promotions or transfers into positions of responsibility.		

Exhibit 9-7 (continued) Fraud Risk Tools for the Internal Auditor		
FRAUD PREVENTION SCORECARD (continued)		
Fraud Prevention Area, Factor, or Consideration Score Notes	**Score**	**Notes**
Personnel involved in the financial reporting process have been assessed with regard to their competencies and integrity and have been found to be of the highest caliber.		
All of our employees, vendors, contractors, and business partners have been made aware of our zero-tolerance policies related to fraud and are aware of the appropriate steps to take in the event that any evidence of possible fraud comes to their attention.		
We have a rigorous program for communicating our fraud prevention policies and procedures to all employees, vendors, contractors, and business partners.		
We have policies and procedures in place for authorization and approvals of certain types of transactions and for certain values of transactions to help prevent and detect the occurrences of fraud.		
Our performance measurement and evaluation process includes an element specifically addressing ethics and integrity as well as adherence to the Code of Organizational Conduct.		
All new hires must undergo rigorous ethics and fraud awareness and fraud prevention training.		
All employees must attend periodic (at least annual) ethics and fraud awareness and fraud prevention training, and the effectiveness of this training is affirmed through testing.		

Exhibit 9-7 (continued) Fraud Risk Tools for the Internal Auditor		
FRAUD PREVENTION SCORECARD (continued)		
Fraud Prevention Area, Factor, or Consideration Score Notes	**Score**	**Notes**
Terminated, resigning, or retiring employees participate in an exit interview process designed to identify potential fraud and vulnerabilities to fraud that may be taking place in our organization. A specific focus of these interviews is an assessment of management's integrity and adherence to the Code of Organizational Conduct. All concerns resulting from these interviews are communicated to our audit committee.		
We have an effective whistleblower protection program and fraud hotline in place, and its existence and procedures are known to all employees, vendors, contractors, and business partners.		
We review the above fraud preventive mechanisms on an ongoing basis and document these reviews as well as the communication with the audit committee regarding areas that need improvement.		
We have a fraud response plan in place and know how to respond if a fraud allegation is made. The fraud response plan considers: • Who should perform the investigation. • How the investigation should be performed. • When a voluntary disclosure to the government should be made. • How to determine the remedial action. • How to remedy control deficiencies identified. • How to administer disciplinary action.		

Source: *Managing the Business Risk of Fraud: A Practical Guide*, The IIA, the AICPA and the ACFE, 2008.

Exhibit 9-7 (continued)
Fraud Risk Tools for the Internal Auditor

FRAUD DETECTION SCORECARD

To assess the strength of the organization's fraud detection system, carefully assess each area below and score the area, factor, or consideration as:

Red: indicating that the area, factor, or consideration needs substantial strengthening and improvement to bring fraud risk down to an acceptable level.

Yellow: indicating that the area, factor, or consideration needs some strengthening and improvement to bring fraud risk down to an acceptable level.

Green: indicating that the area, factor, or consideration is strong and fraud risk has been reduced — at least — to a minimally acceptable level.

Each area, factor, or consideration that scores either red or yellow should have a note associated with it that describes the action plan for bringing it to green on the next scorecard.

Fraud Prevention Area, Factor, or Consideration Score Notes	Score	Notes
We have integrated our fraud detection system with our fraud prevention system in a cost-effective manner.		
Our fraud detection processes and techniques pervade all levels of responsibility within our organization, from the board of directors and audit committee, to managers at all levels, to employees in all areas of operation.		
Our fraud detection policies include communicating to employees, vendors, and stakeholders that a strong fraud detection system is in place, but certain critical aspects of these systems are not disclosed to maintain the effectiveness of hidden controls.		
We use mandatory vacation periods or job rotation assignments for employees in key finance and accounting control positions.		
We periodically reassess our risk assessment criteria as our organization grows and changes to make sure we are aware of all possible types of fraud that may occur.		

Exhibit 9-7 (continued) Fraud Risk Tools for the Internal Auditor		
FRAUD DETECTION SCORECARD (continued)		
Fraud Prevention Area, Factor, or Consideration Score Notes	**Score**	**Notes**
Our fraud detection mechanisms place increased focus on areas in which we have concluded that preventive controls are weak or are not cost-effective.		
We focus our data analysis and continuous auditing efforts based on our assessment of the types of fraud schemes to which organizations like ours (in our industry, or with our lines of business) are susceptible.		
We take steps to ensure that our detection processes, procedures, and techniques remain confidential so that ordinary employees — and potential fraud perpetrators — do not become aware of their existence.		
We have comprehensive documentation of our fraud detection processes, procedures, and techniques so that we maintain our fraud detection vigilance over time and as our fraud detection team changes.		
Our detective controls include a well-publicized and well-managed fraud hotline.		
Our fraud hotline program provides anonymity to individuals who report suspected wrongdoing.		
Our fraud hotline program includes assurances that employees who report suspected wrongdoing will not face retaliation. We monitor for retaliation after an issue has been reported.		
Our fraud hotline has a multilingual capability and provides access to a trained interviewer 24 hours a day, 365 days a year.		

Exhibit 9-7 (continued) Fraud Risk Tools for the Internal Auditor		
FRAUD DETECTION SCORECARD (continued)		
Fraud Prevention Area, Factor, or Consideration Score Notes	**Score**	**Notes**
Our fraud hotline uses a case management system to log all calls and their follow-up to resolution, is tested periodically by our internal auditors, and is overseen by the audit committee.		
Our fraud hotline program analyzes data received and compares results to norms for similar organizations.		
Our fraud hotline program is independently evaluated periodically for effectiveness and compliance with established protocols.		
We use a rigorous system of data analysis and continuous auditing to detect fraudulent activity.		
Our information systems/IT process controls include controls specifically designed to detect fraudulent activity, as well as errors, and include reconciliations, independent reviews, physical inspections/counts, analyses, audits, and investigations.		
Our internal audit department's charter includes emphasis on conducting activities designed to detect fraud.		
Our internal auditors participate in the fraud risk assessment process and plan fraud detection activities based on the results of this risk assessment.		
Our internal auditors report to the audit committee and focus appropriate resources on assessing management's commitment to fraud detection.		

Exhibit 9-7 (continued) Fraud Risk Tools for the Internal Auditor		
FRAUD DETECTION SCORECARD (continued)		
Fraud Prevention Area, Factor, or Consideration Score Notes	**Score**	**Notes**
Our internal audit department is adequately funded, staffed, and trained to follow professional standards, and our internal audit personnel possess the appropriate competencies to support the group's objectives.		
Our internal audit department performs risk-based assessments to understand motivation and where potential manipulation may take place.		
Our internal audit personnel are aware of, and are trained in, the tools and techniques of fraud detection, response, and investigation as part of their continuing education program.		
Our data analysis programs focus on journal entries and unusual transactions, and transactions occurring at the end of a period or those that were made in one period and reversed in the next period.		
Our data analysis programs identify journal entries posted to revenue or expense accounts that improve net income or otherwise serve to meet analysts' expectations or incentive compensation targets.		
We have systems designed to monitor journal entries for evidence of possible management override efforts intended to misstate financial information.		
We use data analysis, data mining, and digital analysis tools to: (a) identify hidden relationships among people, organizations, and events; (b) identify suspicious transactions; (c) assess the effectiveness of internal controls; (d) monitor fraud threats and vulnerabilities; and (e) consider and analyze large volumes of transactions on a real-time basis.		

Exhibit 9-7 (continued) Fraud Risk Tools for the Internal Auditor		
FRAUD DETECTION SCORECARD (continued)		
Fraud Prevention Area, Factor, or Consideration Score Notes	**Score**	**Notes**
We use continuous auditing techniques to identify and report fraudulent activity more rapidly, including Benford's Law analysis to examine expense reports, general ledger accounts, and payroll accounts for unusual transactions, amounts, or patterns of activity that may require further analysis.		
We have systems in place to monitor employee e-mail for evidence of potential fraud.		
Our fraud detection documentation identifies the individuals and departments responsible for: • Designing and planning the overall fraud detection process. • Designing specific fraud detective controls. • Implementing specific fraud detective controls. • Monitoring specific fraud detective controls and the overall system of these controls for realization of the process objectives. • Receiving and responding to complaints related to possible fraudulent activity. • Investigating reports of fraudulent activity. • Communicating information about suspected and confirmed fraud to appropriate parties. • Periodically assessing and updating the plan for changes in technology, processes, and organization.		

Exhibit 9-7 (continued) Fraud Risk Tools for the Internal Auditor		
FRAUD DETECTION SCORECARD (continued)		
Fraud Prevention Area, Factor, or Consideration Score Notes	**Score**	**Notes**
We have established measurement criteria to monitor and improve compliance with fraud detective controls, including: • Number of, and loss amounts from, known fraud schemes committed against the organization. • Number and status of fraud allegations received by the organization that required investigation. • Number of fraud investigations resolved. • Number of employees who have signed the corporate ethics statement. • Number of employees who have completed ethics training sponsored by the organization. • Number of whistleblower allegations received via the organization's hotline. • Number of messages supporting ethical behavior delivered to employees by executives. • Number of vendors who have signed the organization's ethical behavior policy. • Number of customers who have signed the organization's ethical behavior policy. • Number of fraud audits performed by internal auditors.		
We periodically assess the effectiveness of our fraud detection processes, procedures, and techniques; document these assessments; and revise our processes, procedures, and techniques as appropriate.		

Source: *Managing the Business Risk of Fraud: A Practical Guide*, The IIA, the AICPA and the ACFE, 2008.

			Exhibit 9-8			
			Risk/Control Matrix Most Common Features			
(1) Business Objective	(2) Risks	(3) L/S	(4) Controls/ Risk Management Techniques	(5) Evaluation of Adequacy	(6) Tests of Effectiveness	(7) Final Evaluation

Many experts consider that some type of risk/control matrix should be the central audit tool of internal auditors. In fact, more and more best practice audit shops are using such matrices. While no two matrices in use are exactly alike, the one shown above includes the most common features.

Step 1: Identify the business objectives. The key to this step is to begin with the business objectives of the business unit or process, not the control objectives. The best way to accomplish this is to sit down with management and ask them to discuss their goals for the activity being reviewed. If business objectives are not in place, then the audit team should work with management to develop appropriate ones.

Step 2: Identify risks to business objectives. Ask management what events or circumstances could prevent them from achieving their goals. These impediments represent the risks that need to be controlled or mitigated. Another approach to identifying risk is to walk management through the list of organizational risks identified at the macro level and ask whether or not each one could impact the achievement of business objectives.

Step 3: Rate each risk in terms of likelihood and significance. Risks are usually rated as high, medium, and low, depending on how likely it is that the risk will occur and how significant the impact of its occurrence would be. Some organizations rate likelihood and significance separately and provide a hybrid rating, such as high likelihood-high significance or low likelihood-low significance.

Step 4: Identify the controls. The controls identified should be understood in terms of managing the risk. In fact, risk management techniques may be a more appropriate title for this column. Common techniques include transferring or sharing the risk with another party; eliminating the risk altogether (e.g., by redesigning the process); insuring against some or all of the risk; controlling the risk; or accepting the risk.

Step 5: Evaluate the adequacy of controls. This step asks the question, "Are the control processes for managing this risk well-designed?" The auditor arrives at the answer by employing his or her hard, analytical skills and professional judgment. The audit team should first identify and document the controls management says are in place. Then they should evaluate how well designed the controls are by considering how effective, efficient, and economical they are and if they are working the way they are designed to work. Auditors spend up to half of their time in this analytical phase of the audit, which generates most of the value-added recommendations for improvement.

Exhibit 9-8 (continued)
Risk/Control Matrix Most Common Features

Step 6: Test the effectiveness of controls. Once the controls have been deemed adequate, or well-designed, then tests must be conducted to determine whether the controls are in fact operating as intended. For examples, tests should assess whether employees have internalized the organization's values and behave accordingly, whether personnel are complying with procedures, and whether computer systems are functioning as intended. Only 25 to 35 percent of time is usually devoted to testing. This reduction in testing is justified for two reasons. First, the detailed analysis in Step 5 gives auditors firm knowledge of which controls are critical, allowing the team to test "smarter." Second, although auditors might miss the ineffectiveness of some secondary controls, the net audit risk is lower because the design weaknesses, which would have likely been overlooked without the detailed analysis of Step 5, have been uncovered.

Step 7: Arrive at final opinion on adequacy and effectiveness of controls. Here again, the result may be a hybrid response. The design may be deemed adequate, but tests may show ineffectiveness due to lack of compliance with procedures. Or, the design may be flawed due to over-control on insignificant risks, leading to an opinion of inadequacy.

*© James Roth, AuditTrends. Reprinted with permission.

**Exhibit 9-9
Risk Assessment Survey and Cover Letter**

The survey instrument shown below can be used to assess how well the various elements of a chosen control model are exhibited throughout the organization. In this example, notice how the COSO control components have been renamed using what some will see as more relevant terminology: Control Environment has been renamed "Company Culture," Risk Assessment is instead called "Obstacles," Control Activities are referred to as "Policies and Procedures," and Monitoring is presented as "Evaluations and Feedback." The cover letter also works hard to educate the recipient about the meaning and importance of internal control and the participant's assessment of the system. The presentation of control concepts in such user-friendly terms is intended to increase the control literacy of the workforce.

Cover Letter

The Audit Committee of the Board of Directors has requested that management annually assess the internal control system of ABC Company. They have asked Internal Audit Services to facilitate this process.

As an associate at ABC Company, you have many opportunities to observe and perform activities that help to shape and manage the internal control structure. Thus, I am soliciting your personal assessment of the effectiveness of ABC Company's internal control system. Please complete and forward the attached survey to Research Inc. on or before *(insert date)*. *All responses will be kept confidential.*

Your response will be used to draw conclusions concerning the internal control system in your business unit/entity and ABC Company overall. The results will then be discussed with business unit and corporate officers who will develop action plans to address key concerns noted from the surveys. This information will also be shared with the Board of Directors Audit Committee. Since a limited number of employees were randomly selected to complete a survey, your response is very important to us and to ABC Company. Your perceptions are an integral part of our assessment of ABC Company's internal control system.

The internal control system is defined as a process designed to provide reasonable assurance regarding the achievement of the organization's objectives in the following categories: "Effectiveness and Efficiency of Operations; Reliability and Integrity of Financial and Operational Information; Safeguarding of Assets; and Compliance with Applicable Laws, Regulations, and Contracts." A good internal control environment keeps ABC Company on course toward its vision and profitability goals and minimizes surprises along the way. Everyone in an organization contributes to an effective internal control structure.

As you work through the survey, please use the following definitions in your considerations:

Exhibit 9-9 (continued) **Risk Assessment Survey and Cover Letter**	
Business Unit	For example, Business Services, Corporate, Consumer Services.
Organization	Your vice president's overall area of responsibility (Finance, Human Resources, Engineering).
Senior Management	Executives who run your particular business unit/organization.
Department	Your functional area within your organization.
Work Unit	The group of employees who report to your manager.
Customer	The person who pays for ABC Company's products/services OR an internal recipient of your work unit's products/services.

Your complete honesty is requested. *Please be assured that your individual responses will be held in confidence and remain anonymous.* The responses will be sent to an independent market research firm who will not share the source questionnaires with us. However, if you would like to openly discuss any part of this survey beyond your written comments, please call me at 555-123-4567, send me an e-mail, or contact anyone else in the Internal Audit Services Organization.

Thank you for your help in assessing the internal control system of ABC Company.

Sincerely,

(CAE Signature)

Survey Instrument

PLEASE CHECK THE RESPONSE THAT BEST DESCRIBES YOUR REACTION TO EACH STATEMENT

SECTION 1: Company Culture

The company culture sets the tone of an organization, influencing the control consciousness of its people. It is the foundation for all other components of internal control.

	SA = Strongly Agree	A = Agree	D = Disagree	SD = Strongly Disagree	DK = Don't Know
1. Senior management of my business unit demonstrates high ethical standards.					
2. Senior management of my business unit complies with what I believe to be the laws/ regulations affecting the company.					
3. My supervisor complies with what I believe to be the laws/regulations affecting the company.					
4. Co-workers in my work unit comply with what I believe to be the laws/regulations affecting the company.					

		SA = Strongly Agree	A = Agree	D = Disagree	SD = Strongly Disagree	DK = Don't Know
5.	My work unit employs individuals with the necessary knowledge, skill, and training to perform their jobs adequately.					
6.	My business unit learns from its mistakes.					
7.	Satisfying the customer is more important in my business unit than meeting sales or cost objectives.					
8.	Reporting actual performance takes priority over reporting more favorable results.					
9.	Associates in my work unit are treated fairly and justly.					
10.	In my business unit, we do not just try to satisfy customers, we try to delight them.					
11.	In my business unit, we do not "shoot the messenger" who delivers unfavorable information.					
12.	If you marked Disagree/Strongly Disagree with any of the above questions on Company Culture, why do you feel this way? (Please indicate the specific question you are responding to.)					

SECTION II: Goals and Obstacles

Organizations identify and analyze potential obstacles to the achievement of their goals in order to determine how to manage these obstacles.

13.	The performance targets in my work unit are realistic and obtainable.					
14.	For the coming year I am accountable for specific, measurable objectives.					
15.	My business unit adequately takes into account customer impacts in its decisions and actions.					
16.	I have sufficient resources, tools, and time to accomplish my objectives.					

	SA = Strongly Agree	A = Agree	D = Disagree	SD = Strongly Disagree	DK = Don't Know
Exhibit 9-9 (continued) **Risk Assessment Survey and Cover Letter**					
17. In my department, we are proactive in identifying obstacles that could impact the achievement of our objectives.					
If you answered "SA" or "A" to question 17, please answer question 18. Otherwise, proceed to question 19.					
18. My department works successfully to resolve obstacles once they are identified.					
19. My department adequately manages the processes supporting new products, services, technology, and other significant changes.					
20. My department's goals and objectives are consistent with my business unit's goals and objectives.					
21. Associates in my work unit know what actions to take when they find mistakes or gaps in performance.					
22. Personnel turnover in my work unit is adequately managed to minimize performance inefficiencies.					
23. If you marked Disagree/Strongly Disagree with any of the above questions on Goals and Obstacles, why do you feel this way? (Please indicate the specific questions you are responding to.)					
24. In your opinion, what are the primary business/financial risks facing your business unit?)					
SECTION III: Policies and Procedures *Policies, procedures, and other safeguards help ensure that objectives are accomplished.*					
25. The policies and procedures in my work unit allow me to do my job effectively.					
26. Unethical behavior in my work unit is not tolerated.					

	SA = Strongly Agree	A = Agree	D = Disagree	SD = Strongly Disagree	DK = Don't Know
Exhibit 9-9 (continued) **Risk Assessment Survey and Cover Letter**					
27. Associates who steal from the company (physical property, money, information, time) will be discovered.					
28. When discovered, associates who steal from the company are subject to the appropriate discipline.					
29. Associates who break laws and regulations affecting the company will be discovered.					
30. When discovered, associates who break laws and regulations affecting the company are subject to the appropriate discipline.					
31. In my department, policies and procedures are appropriately updated.					
32. I believe sales practices in my business unit are ethical.					
33. If you marked Disagree/Strongly Disagree with any of the above questions on Policies and Procedures, why do you feel this way? (Please indicate the specific questions you are responding to.)					
34. Please identify the process(es) in your business unit/department you feel are the most inefficient and/or need improvement.					
SECTION IV: Information and Communication *Pertinent information must be identified, captured, and communicated in a form and time frame that enables people to carry out their responsibilities.*					
35. Management has accurate, relevant, and timely information to effectively manage my business unit's performance.					
36. Senior management in my business unit interacts with and supports my work unit in achieving our business unit goals and objectives.					

		SA = Strongly Agree	A = Agree	D = Disagree	SD = Strongly Disagree	DK = Don't Know
	Exhibit 9-9 (continued) **Risk Assessment Survey and Cover Letter**					
37.	I have the right information to effectively attend to customer needs.					
38.	Management encourages and rewards process improvement recommendations.					
39.	The communication across departmental boundaries within my business unit enables us to perform our jobs effectively.					
40.	I am aware of the appropriate communication channel to report suspected wrongdoing.					
41.	Persons who report suspected wrongdoings are protected from reprisal.					
42.	If I report wrongdoing to my supervisor, I am confident that the wrongdoing will stop.					
43.	If you marked Disagree/Strongly Disagree with any of the above questions on Information and Communication, why do you feel this way? (Please indicate the specific questions you are responding to.)					

SECTION V: Evaluation and Feedback

Through evaluation and feedback processes, an organization assesses, tracks, and monitors its performance over time.

44.	Senior management in my business unit monitors my work unit using relevant key performance indicators.					
45.	I have enough information to monitor vendor performance.					
46.	Customer feedback and complaints are followed up in a timely and effective manner.					
47.	My business unit appropriately monitors customer satisfaction (using internal or external information).					
48.	The quality of my work is measured.					

	SA = Strongly Agree	A = Agree	D = Disagree	SD = Strongly Disagree	DK = Don't Know
Exhibit 9-9 (continued) **Risk Assessment Survey and Cover Letter**					
49. My supervisor provides developmental feedback to me at appropriate intervals.					
50. Management will follow-up on reported fraudulent activity and take appropriate action.					
51. If you marked Disagree/Strongly Disagree with any of the above questions on Evaluation and Feedback, why do you feel this way? (Please indicate the specific questions you are responding to.)					
52. I suspect/know that fraudulent activity is occurring in my workplace. Yes No					
If question 52 is answered "Yes," please complete the following:					
53. What is the activity referred to in question 52?					
54. Did you report it? Yes No					
55. If "Yes," to the best of your knowledge, what action was taken? If "No," why not?					

Source: Used with permission from Bruce Adamec at CreativeAssurance.

References

[1] Reding, K., Sobel, U. Anderson, M. Head, S. Ramamoorti, M. Salamasick, and C. Shreve, *Internal Auditing: Assurance and Consulting Services, 2nd Edition* (Altamonte Springs, FL: The Institute of Internal Auditors, 2009), pp. 3–15, 3–16.

[2] This description of suggested activities is taken from "Corporate Governance: The New Frontier," by Richard M. Steinberg and Deborah Pojunis, *Internal Auditor* (December 2000), pp. 34–39.

[3] These six questions appear in *Implementing Turnbull — A Boardroom Briefing,* by Martyn E. Jones and Gillian Sutherland, published by The Centre for Business Leadership of the Institute of Chartered Accountants in England and Wales, September 1999, p. 14.

[4] Questions were compiled from various sources, including suppressed PA 2110-1: Assessing the Adequacy of Risk Management Processes; *Implementing Turnbull — A Boardroom Briefing,* by Martyn E. Jones and Gillian Sutherland (The Centre for Business Leadership of the Institute of Chartered Accountants in England and Wales, September 1999); and *Risk Management and the Value Added by Internal Audit* (The Audit and Assurance Faculty of the Institute of Chartered Accountants in England and Wales, June 2000).

[5] The material in these sections is adapted from PG - *Assess the Adequacy of Risk Management Using ISO 31000* and HB158:2010 Delivering Assurance Based on ISO 31000-2009 Risk Management - Principles and Guidelines (a joint publication of Standards Australia, IIA-Australia, and The IIA Research Foundation).

[6] Roth, James, *Adding Value: Seven Roads to Success* (Altamonte Springs, FL: The Institute of Internal Auditors Research Foundation, 2002).

[7] Ideas compiled from "Managing Risks Company-wide" and "Shifting Risk," two articles appearing in the March 2001 and May 2001 issues of The IIA newsletter *Auditwire.*

Chapter 10

YOU MUST PLAN THE ENGAGEMENT (2200-2240)

Good engagement planning is essential in ensuring consistently successful internal audit engagements. *For each engagement, the internal audit team must develop and document a plan (2200).* The Glossary to the *Standards* defines an engagement as a *specific audit assignment, task, or review activity.* Examples include a traditional internal audit, a control self-assessment review, a fraud examination, or a consulting or problem-solving project. Thus, to comply with the *Standards,* all types of internal audit services must begin with sufficient planning.

When putting together the actual plan, the *Standards* require four elements to be included:

1. *The objectives of the engagement. (2210)*
2. *The scope of the engagement. (2220)*
3. *The allocation of resources for the engagement. (2230)*
4. *The engagement work program. (2240)*

These four areas must be addressed in plans for all types of internal audit work.

Engagement Objectives

The Glossary to the *Standards* defines engagement objectives as *broad statements developed by internal auditors that define intended engagement accomplishments.* According to the *Standards,* these statements of intended engagement accomplishments, or objectives, must be developed for each engagement (2210).

The *Standards* emphasize the role of the internal auditor in assessing governance and risk as well as internal controls. Audit objectives should be phrased in terms of contributing to the organization properly managing the activity's risks through effective governance, risk management, and control practices.

If internal auditing is to be successful in adding value and improving the organization's operations (a key focus in the very Definition of Internal Auditing), then in the planning phase internal auditors must be thinking about how they expect that the individual engagement will contribute to adding value and improving the organization's operations.

In engagements designed to provide assurance to senior management and the board, the *Standards* require that, as part of establishing engagement objectives, *a preliminary assessment be conducted of the risks relevant to the activity under review. Engagement objectives must reflect the results of this assessment* (2210.A1). Building the foundation of the engagement on assessment of risk further emphasizes the fundamental focus of the internal audit profession on a risk-based approach in all assurance activity that is undertaken. Engagements are selected based on an entity-level risk assessment discussed in Chapter 9. It is important that high risks be covered by the internal audit plan, and that there be alignment between the entity-level risk assessment and the internal audit plan.

However, that overall risk assessment is not enough. The engagement planning must be aligned with and leverage the information from that overall level risk assessment. It must also go further, and this preliminary assessment of risks at the engagement level ensures the engagement is targeted on risk. That understanding of risk is the basis for the engagement objectives, scope, resource allocation, and work program. According to PA 2210-1, the purpose of risk assessment during the planning phase of the engagement is to define the initial objectives and identify other significant areas of concern. After identifying the risks, the auditor determines the procedures and scope (nature, timing, and extent) of those procedures.

Reliance on the overall risk assessment for planning purposes is further discussed in Standards 2010 and 2010.A1 (see Chapter 8), in Standard 2120.A1 (see Chapter 9), and in related Practice Advisories.

Engagement objectives are not necessarily limited to the risks identified in the overall risk assessment, however. In fact, the *Standards* caution internal auditors to also *consider the probability of significant errors, fraud, noncompliance, and other exposures when developing the engagement objectives* (2210.A2). Overall risk assessments discussed in Standard 2010 and in Chapter 8 are not expected to identify every risk or weakness that needs to be considered at an engagement level. Even beyond the planning stage of the engagement, internal auditors are always responsible for being alert for signs of issues in reliability and integrity of financial information, the effectiveness and efficiency of operations and programs, the safeguarding of assets, and compliance with laws, regulations, policies, procedures, and contracts.

Standard 2210.A3 notes that *adequate criteria are needed to evaluate controls. If internal auditors' assessments determine that management criteria are adequate, then such criteria should be used in evaluations. If they are found inadequate, internal auditors must work with management to develop appropriate evaluation criteria.* As part of its role in the control system, management must establish operating targets and expectations related to goals and objectives. Management is also responsible for determining whether those standards are appropriate and being met. In other words, management must have performance measures related to goals and objectives in place, and they must monitor the effectiveness of those measurements themselves. Internal auditors must consider control criteria in performing control engagements.

Engagement Scope

The established scope must be sufficient to satisfy the objectives of the engagement (2220). The scope generally serves to delineate the boundaries of the engagement by identifying the activities being reviewed as well as any related activities that are not. Scope statements may also describe the nature and extent of audit work and may provide additional supportive information, such as the time period reviewed (PA 2410-1).

The *Standards* do not require any specific areas to be included in the scope of all types of engagements, thereby giving audit staffs the flexibility to design their services so that they best meet the needs of their engagement customers. For example, one increasingly important aspect of scope development in consulting exercises is management input. Reluctance to base the scope on customer input due to fears of compromising audit independence should be allayed by the *Standards'* emphasis on auditor objectivity. The objective mindset of the internal auditor should protect against any management bias or attempts to mislead the auditor (see Chapter 5).

The *Standards* are more specific when it comes to developing the scope of an assurance engagement. *The scope of an assurance engagement must include consideration of relevant systems, records, personnel, and physical properties, including those under the control of third parties* (2220.A1).

PA 2200-2: Using a Top Down Risk-based Approach to Identify the Controls to Be Assessed in an Internal Audit Engagement, provides guidance to apply such an approach to scoping. "Top down" refers to basing the scope on the more significant risks to the organization. A top down approach ensures that internal auditing is focused on providing assurance on management of significant risks. A system of internal controls includes both manual and automated controls, and to manage risk both types of controls need to be assessed. The internal audit scope needs to include all controls required to provide reasonable assurance that risks are effectively managed. The GAIT-R Practice Guide provides guidance on recommended processes for identifying key general information technology controls.

Standard 1110.A1 requires that in any assurance engagement, *the internal audit activity must be free from interference in determining the scope of internal auditing, performing work, and communicating results* (see Chapter 5). In some of these types of engagements, therefore, it may be inappropriate or undesirable to acquire management input. While internal auditors may obtain input, their objective judgment takes precedence over management's opinions on assurance engagement scope.

Occasionally, a restriction may be placed upon the internal audit activity that precludes it from accomplishing its objectives and plans for a particular engagement. This situation is usually referred to as a "scope limitation." Among other things, a scope limitation may restrict:

- The scope defined in the charter.
- Internal audit activity's access to records, personnel, and physical properties relevant to the performance of an engagement.
- The approved work schedule or level of effort.
- The performance of necessary engagement procedures.
- The approved staffing plan and financial budget of the audit function (PA 1130-1).

A scope limitation and its potential effect should be communicated, preferably in writing, to the board, audit committee, or other appropriate governing authority (PA 1130-1). Certain situations, such as changes to the board or senior management or other organizational modifications, may make it necessary to recommunicate scope limitations from time to time.

Engagement Resource Allocation

Internal auditors must determine appropriate and sufficient resources to achieve engagement objectives based upon three elements: an evaluation of the nature and complexity of each engagement, time constraints, and available resources (2230). Evaluating the nature and complexity of the engagement usually involves the results of the overall risk assessment and the preliminary risk assessment of the activity under review. Appropriate internal audit skills must be deployed to address the identified risks.

Upon evaluating these three factors, it may be decided that additional knowledge, skills, and other competencies are needed and should be acquired through external resources. PA 1210.A1-1 offers guidance on obtaining services to support or complement the audit activity. Coverage of risk by internal auditing should be based on the needs of the organization, not the constraints of existing internal audit knowledge.

Engagement Work Program

The Glossary to the *Standards* defines an engagement work program as *a document that lists the procedures to be followed during an engagement* . . . Standard 2240 states that *internal auditors must develop and document work programs that achieve the engagement objectives* (2240). It is notable that this is one of the few areas of the *Standards* that require a document to be created. This reflects the systematic and disciplined approach that the Definition of Internal Auditing highlights as characteristic of internal auditing.

Work programs for assurance engagements *must include the procedures for identifying, analyzing, evaluating, and documenting information during the engagement* (2240.A1). In addition, the *Standards* require that the assurance *work program be approved prior to its implementation, and any adjustments be approved promptly* (2240.A1).

In most situations, the audit team will not be absolutely certain of the extent of testing required or of the types of tests necessary to acquire sufficient information until the engagement is 30 to 40 percent complete. Thus, the work program should remain a fairly dynamic document through the first part of the engagement, with any major alterations receiving appropriate approval.

Planning the Consulting Engagement

Although it is necessary to develop a plan for consulting assignments, the *Standards* recognize that the form of these plans will vary depending on the type of work involved and the needs of the client. In fact, internal auditors are required to work with the client to develop a consulting engagement plan. Standard 2201.C1 states that the audit team must *establish an understanding with consulting engagement clients about objectives, scope, respective responsibilities, and other client expectations*. This fluid, highly responsive nature of consulting work makes adequate planning that much more important; and to avoid misunderstandings and unmet expectations, the *Standards* require *this understanding to be documented when the engagement is significant* (2201.C1). For instance, a short training session provided by the internal audit activity may not require a work program; however, a significant project targeted at providing counsel and advice to help an area improve its operations more likely requires a work program.

The *Standards* and related guidance present several additional planning considerations regarding objectives, scope, and work programs for consulting engagements. These elements should be periodically reassessed and adjusted during the course of work as appropriate.

Engagement Objectives

Internal auditors should design objectives to meet the appropriate needs of management receiving consulting services. However, a couple of caveats are in order. Internal auditors should not agree to conduct consulting engagements simply to circumvent, or allow others to circumvent, requirements that would normally apply to an assurance engagement if the service in question is more appropriately conducted as an assurance engagement. It is allowable, however, to make adjustments to methodologies where services once conducted as assurance engagements are deemed more suitable to being performed as consulting engagements.

In addition, situations may arise where the audit team believes that objectives should be pursued beyond those requested by management. For example, the *Standards* state that *consulting engagement objectives must address governance, risk management, and control processes to the extent agreed upon with the client* (2210.C1). However, the audit team may uncover control weaknesses or risk exposures that they feel can and should be addressed in the course of the consulting engagement. In such instances, auditors may take one of two approaches:

- Persuade management to include the additional objectives in the consulting engagement; or

- Document the fact that the objectives were not pursued, disclose that observation in the final communication of consulting engagement results, and include the objectives in a separate and subsequent assurance engagement.

If the latter option is chosen, it is important to avoid as much as possible the appearance of betraying the client. Chapter 8 discusses considerations for the CAE in handling such communications from consulting engagements. PA 1000.C1-2 states that internal auditors should be observant of the effectiveness of risk management and control processes during formal consulting engagements, regardless of the specified objectives. In addition, the Practice Advisory calls for substantial risk exposures or material control weaknesses to be brought to the attention of management. Therefore, consulting clients should be advised up front that any information acquired as a result of consulting work may be used to assess risk and plan future audits. After all, the primary responsibility of the audit team is to provide assurance to senior management and the board, and knowledge that is relevant to fulfilling that duty cannot be ignored or forgotten. Standard 2600, discussed in Chapter 13, further emphasizes this primary responsibility.

Engagement Scope

Internal auditors must ensure that the scope of the consulting engagement is sufficient to address the agreed-upon objectives (2220.C1). Although the scope of work should be acceptable to and developed in conjunction with the client, it should be designed to ensure that the professionalism, integrity, credibility, and reputation of the internal audit activity are maintained. In addition, the scope must be thorough enough to enable the audit team to perform sufficient work to draw conclusions and provide a report. According to the *Standards, if internal auditors develop reservations about the scope during the engagement, these reservations must be discussed with the client to determine whether to continue with the engagement* (2220.C1). For example, the scope may indicate that internal auditors will use certain information to perform an analysis for management, but once work begins, they may find that the data is insufficient to draw appropriate conclusions. The client must be made aware of such problems before continuing with the assignment. In addition, it is recommended that reservations regarding the value, benefit, or possible negative implications of the engagement also be communicated to those receiving the service.

Engagement Work Program

Work programs for consulting engagements may vary in form and content depending upon the nature of the engagement (2240.C1). Internal auditors should, however, be sure to document the objectives and scope of the engagement as well as the methodology to be used in satisfying the objectives.

Additional Considerations

Other recommended, but not required, considerations to be covered during the planning stage include:

- How, when, and to whom engagement results will be communicated.
- The engagement period to be covered and estimated completion dates.
- Meetings with management responsible for the activity being examined.

Additional guidance on planning is provided in PA 2200-1.

Planning Focused on Risk, Considering Risk Management and Governance Processes and Considering Ways to Add Value

Standard 2200 on planning, along with 2300 on performing the engagement (see Chapter 11) and 2400 on communicating engagement results (see Chapter 12), outline the basic requirements of the audit process. Much of the wording in the *Standards* is generalized so as to apply to the full range of services that might be provided and practices that may be appropriately used by the internal audit activity. For example, instead of requiring a written report, the *Standards* describe a method that allows results to be communicated in whatever format is appropriate to the situation.

It is important to remember that the *Standards* emphasize the importance of today's internal audit activity adding value based on the value drivers applicable to that internal audit activity's key stakeholders and evaluating risk management and governance, not just internal control.

When planning an engagement, the *Standards* call for internal auditors to consider:

1. *The objectives of the activity being reviewed.*
2. *The means by which the activity controls its performance in relation to its objectives.*
3. *The significant risks to the activity, its objectives, its resources, and its operations.*
4. *The means by which the potential impact of risk is kept to an acceptable level.*
5. *The adequacy and effectiveness of the activity's risk management and control processes compared to a relevant control framework or model.*
6. *The opportunities for making significant improvements to the activity's risk management and control processes.* (2201)

These planning considerations contribute to ensuring that engagement plans are in line with the nature of audit work as proscribed by the *Standards* (see Chapter 9) and the definition (see Chapter 2). A risk/ control matrix like that shown in Exhibit 9-8 (see Chapter 9) can be a useful tool for making sure all six areas are considered in the plan. Other tools and techniques discussed in Chapter 9 should also be helpful in meeting this requirement.

It should be noted that the fifth consideration in the list requires internal auditors to employ a relevant control framework or model when planning an engagement. Such models may be based on established frameworks, such as COSO or CoCo (see Exhibit 9-1 of Chapter 9), or they may contain criteria unique to the organization. Regardless of its basis, the model should offer an organizationwide definition of internal control, outline the goals of the internal control system, and provide a common language for communicating about control. Using the organization's broad-based internal control framework to plan an engagement helps internal auditors ensure their work is not too narrowly focused on the policies and procedures of the reviewed activity, but instead reflects the "big picture" concerns of the organization as a whole.

Planning a Consulting Engagement that Arises During an Assurance Engagement

The *Standards* anticipate that at times opportunities for consulting engagements arise during assurance engagements. When this occurs, *a specific written understanding as to the objectives, scope, respective responsibilities, and other expectations should be reached and the results of the consulting engagement communicated in accordance with consulting standards* (2220.A2).

Planning for a Blended Engagement that Includes Assurance and Consulting

When an engagement includes both assurance and consulting elements, the whole engagement should comply with the more prescriptive assurance standards. The consulting portion can always be broken off as a separate engagement and then conducted under the consulting standards. In practice, to increase clarity, blended engagements often are planned with both the assurance and consulting elements being planned and documented in a consistent format. Exhibit 3-4 provides a framework useful for planning these blended engagements.

Planning Internal Audit Engagements for Parties Outside the Organization

When internal auditors are performing engagements for parties outside the organization, the *Standards* require that *internal auditors establish a written understanding during the planning stage with these parties outside the organization*. This understanding must *include objectives, scope, respective responsibilities, and other expectations* (2201.A1). This is particularly important because the third parties typically are further removed from the internal audit work while it is being done as compared to those inside the organization. To help ensure engagements for parties outside the organization are successful, it is particularly important that when providing services to third parties, the front end understanding of objectives, scope, responsibilities, and expectations be documented in writing during the planning phase of the engagement and agreed to by the third party and internal auditing.

Examples of this third-party use of internal auditing include where internal auditing provides services to provide assurance where the organization's costs are shared or reimbursed by a third party. Another example is where internal auditing is used to provide assurance on areas similar to the assurance independent auditors may provide through Statement on Auditing Standards No. 70 reports.

During planning, internal auditors must also document understandings on *restrictions on distribution of the results and access to engagement records* (2201.A1). This written understanding with the outside users is uniquely important where internal auditors are performing services that will be used by third parties. Use of information within an organization is generally consistently understood.

However, providing results of internal audit work outside the organization creates a new information outflow that must be proactively controlled. A core principle in The IIA's Code of Ethics is confidentiality. An important part of this principle for internal auditors is ensuring they are prudent in the use and protection of information acquired in the course of their duties and ensuring that information is not used in any manner that would be detrimental to the legitimate and ethical objectives of the organization. Having a good understanding in the planning phase of the engagement between internal auditing and the third party of what uses can and cannot be made of the results and what access to records will be allowed reduces the risk of misunderstandings or misuse of information later. When providing assurance and deliverables to a third party that plans to rely on the internal audit work, internal auditors should consider the need to consult with legal counsel to address any potential liability that may be created if work is done for the third party.

The Importance of Engagement Planning

This chapter covered elements of the *Standards* and Practice Advisories that can help your internal audit activity execute an effective planning process. Planning is the road map that guides the internal audit activity in its execution of engagements. Key points in planning include:

- Perform a preliminary assessment of risk to ensure that the objectives of the engagement are focused on the right areas.

- In the planning phase, plan for how the engagement is expected to add value and contribute to improving the organization's operations.

- Align engagement scope with the objectives for the engagement.

- Ensure the extent and skills of the internal audit resources align with the scope and objectives to be achieved.

- Document in a work program a plan sufficient to achieve the engagement objectives.

The *Standards* emphasize planning because having a strong planning process is essential to high-quality internal auditing.

Chapter 11

YOU MUST PERFORM THE ENGAGEMENT WITH SUFFICIENT INFORMATION AND ADEQUATE SUPERVISION (2300-2340)

The 2300 series of the *Standards* outlines the systematic, disciplined approach to internal audits that is one of the hallmarks of the profession. *To conduct any type of engagement, internal auditors must (1) identify, (2) analyze and evaluate, and (3) document sufficient information to achieve the engagement's objectives* (2300). *In addition, the engagement must be properly supervised* (2340).

Identifying Information

Internal auditors must identify information that is sufficient, reliable, relevant, and useful for the accomplishment of engagement objectives (2310). The Interpretation to Standard 2310 provides descriptions of each of these information attributes:

- *Sufficient information is factual, adequate, and convincing so that a prudent, informed person would reach the same conclusions as the auditor.*

- *Reliable information is the best attainable information through the use of appropriate engagement techniques.*

- *Relevant information supports engagement observations and recommendations and is consistent with the objectives for the engagement.*

- *Useful information helps the organization meet its goals.*

Today, auditors have at their disposal abilities to use more data and analyze it more thoroughly than ever before. Through the electronic capturing and storage of data, both within the organization as well as from beyond the organization's physical borders, internal auditors now have access to greater amounts of information that should be considered in identifying information for the engagement. Besides the use of technology, internal auditors are harnessing the power of knowledge in the individuals in the organization in the internal audit work. One way this is done is through surveys or facilitated meetings, including control self-assessment, to utilize the knowledge of those involved daily in the processes under review to assess and improve the process. Internal auditors can also reach beyond the organization to service providers and industry groups in order to access benchmarking and best practices information relevant to the engagement objectives.

PA 2300-1 emphasizes that internal auditors need to consider concerns relating to the protection of personally identifiable information gathered during audit engagements as advances in information technology and communications continue to present privacy risks and threats. Privacy controls are legal requirements in many jurisdictions. Personal information includes:

- Name, address, identification numbers, income, blood type.
- Evaluations, social status, disciplinary actions.
- Employee files and credit and loan records.
- Employee health and medical data.

Internal auditors need to understand and comply with all laws regarding the use of personal information in their jurisdiction and in those jurisdictions where their organizations conduct business. The internal auditor may seek advice from legal counsel before beginning audit work if there are questions or concerns about access to personal information.

It is important to recognize that information identification starts in the planning phases of engagements. A critical part of planning the engagement is that the internal auditor should be considering what information should be used and how it will be captured as early as possible.

Analyzing and Evaluating Information

Internal auditors must base conclusions and engagement results on appropriate analyses and evaluations (2320). These "tests" should be appropriate to the materiality and likelihood of risks perceived in the activity, as well as to the established audit objectives.

It is possible to overanalyze an activity or situation, which can be costly in terms of time, staff resources, and money. "Stop and go" auditing is a practice used by some audit shops to avoid such scenarios. At the end of the planning phase for an engagement, the auditor may have achieved a high level of comfort regarding the adequacy and effectiveness of governance, risk management, and control processes. Audit management may therefore decide that a full-blown review of the area is inappropriate given the low level of risk in this area and the higher degree of risk lurking in other areas of the business. If the decision is made to proceed with the engagement, the audit team may achieve the desired comfort level after looking in detail at the design of control processes and sub-processes identified in the scope, and getting comfort at a high level with the operating effectiveness of the controls. They may determine that any further detailed testing of operating effectiveness is not necessary.

As they progress through the various phases of an engagement, the internal audit staff should adopt a way of thinking that compels them to ask whether it is actually necessary to continue with the next step, or whether enough information has been acquired to make an informed opinion with little chance of a problem being overlooked. Such approaches allow the engagement to stop midstream as evidence dictates.

At least as important is to realize when the information gathered is not yet appropriate to deliver on addressing the planned risks, or on delivering the value expected of the internal audit review. In such instances, the internal auditor should consider whether other information can be analyzed and evaluated that would allow the engagement objectives to be achieved. Analyzing and evaluating information is core to the ultimate results of the internal audit project, and therefore directly impacts whether the expectations of stakeholders will be realized on the internal audit project.

Documenting Information

Internal auditors must document relevant information to support the conclusions and engagement results (2330). This documentation is usually referred to as the engagement "workpapers."

PA 2330-1 recommends that workpapers document all aspects of the engagement process from planning through communicating results. Engagement workpapers have a number of uses, including:

- Aiding in the planning, performance, and review of engagements.
- Providing the principal support for engagement results.
- Documenting whether engagement objectives were achieved.
- Supporting the accuracy and completeness of the work performed.
- Providing a basis for the internal audit activity's quality assurance and improvement program.
- Facilitating third-party reviews. (PA 2330-1)

Workpapers may include:

- Planning documents and engagement programs.
- Control questionnaires, flowcharts, checklists, and narratives.
- Notes and memoranda from interviews.
- Organizational data, such as organization charts and job descriptions.
- Copies of important contracts and agreements.
- Information about operating and financial policies.
- Results of control evaluations.
- Letters of confirmation and representation.
- Analysis and tests of transactions, processes, and account balances.
- Results of analytical auditing procedures.
- The engagement's final communications and management's responses.
- Engagement correspondence if it documents the conclusions reached.

Many of these items are traditional documentation requirements applicable to assurance engagements and do not necessarily apply to consulting engagements. For example, documentation needs for a control self-assessment exercise may differ from those associated with consulting or problem-solving work. As a result, it is important that the CAE establish workpaper policies for the various types of engagements performed.

As mentioned in Chapter 8, *the CAE is responsible for controlling access to and developing retention requirements for engagement records associated with assurance work, regardless of the medium in which each record is stored (2330.A1 and 2330.A2). He or she must also obtain the approval of senior management and/or legal counsel prior to releasing such records to external parties, as appropriate (2330.A1).* Similarly, the CAE is required to *develop policies governing the custody and retention of consulting engagement records, as well as their release to internal and external parties (2330.C1). All such policies must be consistent with the organization's guidelines and any pertinent regulatory or other requirements (2330.A2, 2330.C1).* PAs 2330.A1-1 and 2330.A2-1 discuss control and retention of engagement records. See Chapter 8 for further discussion of record access and retention.

Documentation is important not only because it allows coordination and sharing of information among audit team members, but also because it gives structure and organization to the acquired evidence. As part of the systematic and disciplined audit process, effective documentation allows the internal auditor to review the entire body of work at the end of the engagement and arrive at objective, unbiased conclusions regardless of who performed the work or when it was completed. In addition, workpapers serve as useful tools for building in and later evaluating the internal audit activity's quality program; demonstrating compliance with the *Standards*; aiding in the professional development of the internal audit staff; and providing support in circumstances such as insurance cases and lawsuits.

Through the use of automated workpapers commonly available in the internal audit marketplace, internal auditors can leverage internal audit automated platforms to document their work. Some such tools facilitate clear linkage of overall risk assessments to individual projects, linkage of electronic workpapers to work program steps, documentation of supervision and linkage of internal audit communications, and reporting to underlying work. Many see the use of such automated internal audit workpaper platforms as an important part of their internal audit quality assurance and improvement process.

Supervising the Engagement

The *Standards* specifically state that *engagements must be properly supervised to ensure objectives are achieved, quality is assured, and staff is developed* (2340). The Interpretation to Standard 2340 notes that *the extent of supervision required will depend on the proficiency and experience of internal auditors and the complexity of the engagement. The CAE has overall responsibility for supervising the engagement, whether performed by or for the internal audit activity, but may designate appropriately experienced members of the internal audit activity to perform the review. Appropriate evidence of supervision is documented and retained.*

While the *Standards* do not proscribe any specific supervisory activities, PA 2340-1 and insights from practice provide several suggestions for what "proper supervision" might include:

- Ensuring that designated auditors collectively possess the required knowledge, skills, and other competencies to perform the engagement (see Chapter 6).

- Providing appropriate instructions during the planning of the engagement and approving the engagement program.

- Ensuring that the approved engagement program is competed unless changes are both justified and authorized.

- Determining that engagement workpapers adequately support the engagement observations, conclusions, and recommendations.

- Ensuring that engagement communications are accurate, objective, clear, concise, constructive, complete, and timely.

- Ensuring that engagement objectives are met.

- Providing opportunities for developing internal auditors' knowledge, skills, and other competencies.

- Ensuring staff training and development.

- Evaluating employee performance.

- Controlling resources, such as time and expenses.

Supervision of all internal audit assignments, whether performed by an in-house audit team or an outside source, remains the responsibility of the CAE (see Chapter 8). As such, the CAE is responsible for all significant supervisory judgments made during the engagement, including planning, examination, evaluation, reporting, and follow-up.

Supervision helps ensure all elements of the internal audit process are executed properly. It helps ensure proper focus on risks, stakeholder expectations, and adding value. Supervision helps ensure that there is appropriate communication of the right things communicated in the right way in engagement results. Supervision also is a core tool used to develop the hard and soft skills of internal audit team members. Supervision is also one of the most effective quality assurance measures available to audit staffs. Thus, adequate supervision is a key part of any internal audit activity.

Chapter 12

YOU MUST COMMUNICATE THE ENGAGEMENT RESULTS EFFECTIVELY (2400-2440)

The communication of audit results is one of the most important aspects of the internal auditor's job. The effectiveness of management decision-making is directly related to the quality and timeliness of management reporting, of which internal audit communications are a significant part. Also, an auditor's greatest idea or discovery is only as effective as his or her ability to express the concept to others and elicit the appropriate response. The *Standards* outline several requirements regarding content of communications, criteria for ensuring quality communications, procedures for communicating instances of nonconformance with the *Standards and criteria for opinions, conclusions, and ratings to ensure they are supported and accurate.*

Communication Content

While their format and content may vary depending on the type of service provided, all engagement *communications must include the engagement objectives and scope as well as applicable conclusions, recommendations, and action plans* (2410). Any final engagement communication that warrants coverage of these items yet fails to do so is not in conformance with the *Standards*. PA 2410-1 offers additional suggestions on what types of information might also be included in final communications.

According to the *Standards, communication of the progress and results of consulting engagements will vary in form and content depending upon the nature of the engagement and the needs of the client* (2410. C1). In some instances, such as when providing training as a service to management or serving on a committee, the reporting needs may be minimal. On the other hand, special analyses or self-assessment exercises may necessitate a more involved report, although the specifics are likely to vary greatly. Reporting requirements are generally determined by those requesting the service and should meet the objectives as determined by and agreed to with management. However, the format for communicating the results should clearly describe the nature of the engagement and any limitations, restrictions, or other factors about which users of the information should be made aware.

Acknowledging Satisfactory Performance

Assurance engagement communications are also *encouraged to acknowledge satisfactory performance* observed in the area that was reviewed (2410.A2). Note that this is the only place in the *Standards* where the word "encouraged" is used. In most of the *Standards* the word "must" is used, which reflects their mandatory nature. Several places in the *Standards* make use of the word "should" where conformance is expected unless, when applying professional judgment, circumstances justify deviation or where conformance is not under the control of the internal audit function. In 2410.A2, acknowledging satisfactory performance is not required, but is so important that there is a specific assurance standard encouraging acknowledgement of satisfactory performance. Whether and how this should be used frequently correlates with expectations of users of the communications, as well as how notable is the performance.

Communication Quality

According to Standard 2420, *quality engagement communications must be:*

- *Accurate.*
- *Objective.*
- *Clear.*
- *Concise.*
- *Constructive.*
- *Complete.*
- *Timely.*

The Interpretation to Standard 2420 describes each of these characteristics:

- *Accurate communications are free from errors and distortions and are faithful to the underlying facts.*

- *Objective communications are fair, impartial, and unbiased and are the result of a fair-minded and balanced assessment of all relevant facts and circumstances.*

- *Clear communications are easily understood and logical, avoiding unnecessary technical language and providing all significant and relevant information.*

- *Concise communications are to the point and avoid unnecessary elaboration, superfluous detail, redundancy, and wordiness.*

- *Constructive communications are helpful to the engagement client and the organization and lead to improvements where needed.*

- *Complete communications lack nothing that is essential to the target audience and include all significant and relevant information and observations to support recommendations and conclusions.*

- *Timely communications are opportune and expedient, depending on the significance of the issue, allowing management to take appropriate corrective action.*

PA 2420-1 provides further descriptions of each characteristic.

Each internal audit department must implement the elements based upon the needs of their organizations and the expectations of their stakeholders. Some audit groups may even require additional quality elements in their engagement communications, such as being:

- **Positive** — In most organizations, it is important that audit messages avoid needlessly overemphasizing the negative. Words with pejorative connotations, such as "mistakes," "wrong," "incompetent," and "delinquent," can cause the receiver to become defensive and stop listening to the auditor's message. And although the *Standards* only "encourage" satisfactory performance to be acknowledged in assurance communications (2410.A2), it is good practice in any engagement to comment on exceptionally good governance, risk management, or control activities or other best practices resulting from innovation and hard work. That does not change the fact that objective, clear communication is always important. In instances of fraud, clear communication likely will not be positively perceived by the perpetrator yet is still appropriate. However, in most other situations, communications can be constructive and facilitate positive improvements in the organization without using unnecessarily negative words.

- **Collaborative** — While it is the auditor's responsibility to objectively and truthfully convey the results of the engagement without interference from others, effective engagement communications often demonstrate that the audit team has taken the interests of the people involved into account. For example, documentation of cooperation between the audit team and the audit customer in the identification of risks, assistance in information gathering, and the development of action plans may be included. Presenting the customers' views regarding conclusions or recommendations may also be appropriate. Finally, credit should be given to the audit customer for proactive self-disclosure of problems to the internal audit team.

- **Strategic** — Best practice engagement communications convey that the engagement was performed for strategic reasons, such as:

  – The area is a major risk area requiring review.
  – The area is critical in executing on the organization's strategic plan.
  – There is a potential for significant cost savings.
  – There is a legal/regulatory compliance requirement.
  – The area is under change with a rising risk profile.
  – There is potential for operational improvement.

- **Prioritized** — The issues and actions discussed in the report most often should be prioritized and aligned with a view to the strategic priority of the risk. The *Standards* focus the internal audit activity's efforts on adding organizational value and providing assurance in high-risk areas. Engagement communications should reflect the achievement of those overall goals.

- **Helpful** — Engagement communications offer an excellent opportunity to provide something of value to the audit customer. Simply indicating how the engagement will benefit the audit customer can be an effective practice. For example, when explaining the reasons for conducting the engagement, it is important to emphasize internal auditing's goal of helping the customer and the organization, rather than presenting the rationale for the review in terms of criticizing the activity. In addition, in describing issues and recommendations, many internal audit departments incorporate a description of the benefits to the organization of addressing the issue.

Many organizations have further enhanced their engagement communications by shortening them considerably, highlighting key information. Often, a series of brief reports will be assembled, fitted to the needs of each different audience and therefore contain different levels of content. For example, an executive summary of engagement results, including any significant items requiring high-level attention, may be sent to the board and senior management. A more detailed, but still value-adding and risk-focused communication with added details that helps users more fully understand and act on issues is sent to operating management. Such minimalist but appropriately informative communications are much more likely to serve the needs of and receive the necessary attention from management and the board.

While in nearly all cases the final communication should be accurate and complete, consistent with Standard 2420, there may be instances where the communication has a significant error or omission. Whenever a final communication has contained *a significant error or omission, the CAE must communicate corrected information to all parties who received the original communication* (2421).

Effective Communication Strategies Go Beyond the Written Report

Internal audit communications go beyond the formal engagement communication. Leading internal audit activities earn the right to open, strong communication channels with operating management, senior management, and the board. These channels should be used to ensure appropriate focus on key issues and necessary actions, whether related to governance, risk management, or control. Standards 2060 (see Chapter 8) and 2600 (see Chapter 13) both address this.

Communicating Opinions, Conclusions, and Ratings

In the case of assurance engagements, it is important to consider the form and level of assurance expected by stakeholders. There are differences in what stakeholders may want:

- Some expect internal auditing to provide perspectives on areas under review, but do not require any conclusion or rating.

- Some want internal audit engagement communications rated for importance, so that the reader knows how to prioritize their efforts.

- Some want internal auditing to go on record with its assessment of what was found. This may consist of:

  - Overall opinions, conclusions, or ratings. These address overall effectiveness of governance, risk management, and/or internal controls. These may address a business unit, program, business process, or major category of control objective.
  - Engagement level opinions, conclusions, or ratings.

In providing this assurance, auditors may provide positive assurance or negative assurance.

Recent Changes to Standards on Reporting Opinions and Conclusions

Standards changes effective in 2011 in 2010.A2, 2410.A1, and 2450 focus on opinions, conclusions, and ratings. Because the practices vary by organization in this area, the *Standards* note that it is important to understand and tailor work to stakeholder expectations for opinions. This tailoring must happen during planning. Opinions, conclusions, and ratings may be given at the engagement level and/ or at the overall organizational level. The *Standards* do not require opinions, conclusions, or ratings. However, if opinions, conclusions, or ratings are issued, then they must be supported by sufficient work, and the reporting must meet the requirements of the *Standards*.

Understanding Stakeholder Expectations for Levels of Assurance

The *Standards* require that the CAE identify and consider the expectations of senior management, the board, and other stakeholders for internal audit opinions and other conclusions (2010.A2). This means that the level of assurance and the type of reporting must be aligned with stakeholder expectations.

Note that this is one of the few times that there is reference to other stakeholders beyond senior management and the board. Other stakeholders may include regulators or other users of internal audit reports.

Identifying these expectations over level of assurance during overall planning allows the CAE to also ensure that the level of resources committed by the organization and the skill levels delivered will be sufficient to allow the internal audit activity to provide the expected level of assurance. The CAE must not commit to a level of assurance beyond what the resources allowed can provide.

Aligning assurance levels with expectations of users is an element of 2010.A2, 2410.A1, and 2450. This alignment does mean that internal auditing must strive to provide the level of reporting desired. However, it certainly does not mean that internal auditors should modify their communication simply because process owners want a favorable assessment in an area with unacceptable audit findings. The considering of expectations is meant to plan the work and tailor the communications to be of value to stakeholders, delivering the expected assurance, insight, and objectivity.

Considering Opinions, Conclusions, or Ratings in Engagement Level Communications

For assurance engagements, the *Standards* require the internal auditor to provide an opinion and/or conclusions, where appropriate (2410.A1). The Interpretation to this standard notes that *opinions at the engagement level may be ratings, conclusions, or other descriptions of the results. Such an engagement may be in relation to controls around a specific process, risk, or business unit. The formulation of such opinions requires consideration of the engagement results and their significance.*

Further, the *Standards* require that, when issued, opinions, conclusions, or ratings must be supported by sufficient, reliable, relevant, and useful information. The appropriateness of statements offering an opinion depends on the depth and purpose of the engagement, the culture of the organization, and whether the phrasing of the opinion or conclusion does not give undue comfort. When the engagement is narrowly focused and fails either intentionally or unintentionally to produce enough evidence to issue an overall opinion or rating, then it would be inappropriate to do so. On the other hand, if the board and senior management request an opinion on each engagement instead of a list of detailed findings, then the auditor should strive to design and carry out appropriate procedures so that an overall opinion can be provided (see Chapter 8 discussion of CAE reporting requirements).

Some internal audit activities avoid opinions, conclusions, or ratings because discussion with process owners of what rating an engagement should receive can create negative relationships and can distract from focus on addressing the identified issues and the opportunities for positive change. Other internal audit activities find opinions, conclusions, or ratings to be very important in their efforts to help stakeholders and users of the communications quickly prioritize their focus on the most important engagement results.

Considering Communicating Overall Opinions

Beyond the individual engagement reports, some internal audit stakeholders in organizations may have expectations for overall opinions on the entity's internal controls, risk management, or governance.

Some find this to be a dangerous area for internal auditing, moving the audit activity into an area of providing undue comfort when a purpose of internal auditing is often to do the opposite — to highlight topics where the organization should be concerned and remind the organization that risks are important and need to be addressed.

It should be noted that where opinions are expressed in reports on controls, certain other audit regulatory bodies require significant caveats and disclosures in the auditors' report related to the inherent limitations in systems of internal controls and the level of coverage provided by the audit. These requirements also include detailed quality control requirements over the auditor's work. The external audit profession has been challenged over the years between expressing assurance on work done on internal controls and later expectation gaps that occur when undue reliance is placed by users on opinions that were incorrectly read as giving 100 percent comfort that nothing would go wrong in the organization's internal control system. Internal auditors should be sensitive to the responsibility they may be accepting, particularly if expressing an overall positive assurance opinion.

On the other hand, some organizations see nothing wrong and want internal auditing to be expressing some form of assurance.

- Some organizations with responsibility to report on their internal controls over financial reporting under the U.S. Sarbanes-Oxley Act seek similar assurance each year from their internal audit activity on the topic.

- Government entities in the United Kingdom are required by HM Treasury to issue a positive reasonable opinion over risk management, control, and governance.

- The King Code of Governance for South Africa 2009 (King III) notes that internal auditors should furnish an assessment to the board generally on the system of internal controls and to the audit committee specifically on the effectiveness of internal financial controls.

The key standard in this area, 2450, states, *when an overall opinion is issued, it must take into account the expectations of senior management, the board, and other stakeholders and must be supported by sufficient, reliable, relevant, and useful information.* There are three important parts of that sentence:

expectations, sufficiency of information and internal audit scope, and the quality of information obtained (reliable, relevant, and useful).

The Interpretation to 2450 requires the communication of an overall opinion to identify:

- The scope, including the time period to which the opinion pertains.

- Scope limitations.

- Consideration of all related projects, including the reliance on other assurance providers.

- The risk or control framework or other criteria used as a basis for the overall opinion.

- The overall opinion, judgment, or conclusion reached.

Also, the interpretation notes that the reasons for an unfavorable overall opinion must be stated. This last point has a somewhat subtle importance. By emphasizing that reasons for unfavorable opinions must be stated, it is noting that just because some overall opinion is being issued, that does not mean it will be a positive opinion. The results of work, and therefore the communication, may be an adverse or negative opinion. That is, the opinion may state, if necessary, that things are broken.

Overall opinions have been less common than engagement level ratings.

Even if an overall opinion is not requested or an expectation, note that there is a requirement in Standard 2600 for CAEs to speak up when the organization has accepted unacceptable residual risk (see Chapter 13).

An example of an overall opinion is found in Exhibit 12-1.

The Practice Guide Formulating and Expressing Internal Audit Opinions

The Practice Guide Formulating and Expressing Internal Audit Opinions recognizes two levels of internal audit opinions: micro-level opinions, corresponding to engagement level opinions, conclusions, and ratings in the *Standards;* and macro-level opinions, corresponding to overall opinions and conclusions in the *Standards.*

The Practice Guide also sets out two types of opinions — a positive (reasonable) assurance opinion and a negative (limited) assurance opinion. A positive assurance opinion provides the highest level of assurance and one of the strongest types of audit opinions. In providing positive assurance, the auditor takes a definite position, which may be binary in nature; for example, that internal controls are or are not effective in the situation or that risks are or are not being effectively managed. A negative assurance opinion is a statement that nothing came to the internal auditor's attention about a particular objective, such as the effectiveness of a system of internal control, adequacy of a risk management process, or any other specific matter. The internal auditor takes no responsibility for the sufficiency of the audit scope and procedures to find all significant concerns or issues. Such opinions generally are considered less valuable than positive assurance opinions, thus auditors consider their value before rendering them.

The internal auditor can also decline to give an opinion, in which case no rating is given or opinion statement made in the report. This is usually because the scope of the audit engagement is not sufficient to provide a basis for an opinion.

Often management or the board will ask the internal auditor for an informal verbal opinion. In such cases, it is acceptable for the auditor to respond that more work would be necessary to express an opinion.

In issuing these opinions, there will be matters that need to be addressed, including assuring the scope is truly sufficient to express the opinion, determining how to handle exceptions where the opinion of a sub-area would not be positive, and the need to keep the awareness that management, not internal auditing, is responsible for adequate governance, risk management, and internal controls.

With the advent of reports on internal controls that have come from Section 404 of Sarbanes-Oxley and similar laws in other countries, certain phrases such as "material weakness" or "significant deficiency" should be avoided in communicating issues, unless the use of the words is aligned with the use in the Section 404 work and has been carefully considered. Internal auditors should review their selection of wording to describe ratings of issues and reports to ensure that words that have specific definitions for another purpose, such as for Section 404 work, are not misused or misunderstood when used for internal audit reporting.

Clarity — Communicating the Level of Attention a Report Needs

An area that has received much discussion in the internal audit world is how to communicate to key stakeholders the relative severity of reports or issues. There is some indication that what audit committees seek is more focused on clear communication of the level of attention required, rather than an overall "rating" of the controls or management. An example of a rating framework is shown in Exhibit 12-2.

An example of format for an internal audit report is provided in Exhibit 12-3.

Communicating that Engagements are in Conformance with the *Standards*

As noted in Standard 2430, *internal auditors may report that their engagements are "conducted in conformance with the* International Standards for the Professional Practice of Internal Auditing" *only if the results of the quality assurance and improvement program support the statement.* See Chapter 7 for further discussion of internal audit quality assurance and improvement programs.

Note that this standard uses the word "may" and does not require reference to conformance with the *Standards*. While not all internal audit departments currently proactively report that they conform with the *Standards*, as the *Standards* grow further in awareness by key stakeholders and internal auditors, and as more internal audit activities mature to fully conforming with the *Standards*, it is more likely that what is perceived to be a leading practice today will become a more accepted practice in the future.

Communication of Nonconformance with the *Standards*

One additional required element of engagement communications is disclosure of nonconformance with the Definition of Internal Auditing, the Code of Ethics, or the *Standards*. *When nonconformance impacts a specific engagement, the communication conveying the results of the engagement must also describe the:*

- *Principle or rule of conduct of the Code of Ethics or Standard(s) with which full conformance was not achieved.*

- *The reason(s) for nonconformance.*

- *The impact of nonconformance on the engagement and the communicated engagement results* (2431).

A common example of an incident requiring disclosure is an audit team member's participation in an assurance review of an area where the auditor previously worked. The disclosure statement in such an instance might read as follows:

"Auditor X, who participated in this review, worked as (*insert previous job title*) in Area ABC for the previous five years, with her last day of work being (*month-date-year*). Due to the pressing need for subject matter expertise and operating management's expressed confidence in Auditor X's ability to maintain her objectivity, the decision was made to include Auditor X on the review team. Because less than one year has passed since Auditor X worked in the area, her participation in the engagement violates Standard 1130.A1 of The IIA's *International Standards for the Professional Practice of Internal Auditing*. However, because of the extra care taken to supervise the auditor's work and operating management's lack of concern regarding the auditor's objectivity, Auditor X's participation is not believed to have affected the objectivity of the results of the engagement."

Internal auditors who disclose isolated instances of nonconformance in this manner can state that the internal audit activity performed its duties in conformance with the *Standards*, as long as assessments under the quality assurance and improvement program demonstrate the audit activity's overall conformance (see Chapter 7).

Disseminating Results

Standard 2440 addresses requirements regarding disseminating engagement results. Basically, *the CAE is responsible for disseminating results to the appropriate parties* (2440). In the case of assurance engagements, *results are to be communicated to parties who can ensure that the results are given due consideration* (2440.A1). For consulting engagements, *the CAE is responsible for communicating final results to clients* (2440.C1). As noted in the Interpretation to Standard 2440, *the CAE or designee reviews and approves the final engagement communication before issuance and decides to whom and how it will be disseminated.*

If significant governance, risk management, and control issues are identified as part of consulting engagements, they should be communicated to senior management and the board (2440.C2). These *Standards* on communication dissemination are discussed in more detail with other CAE requirements in Chapter 8.

Communicating Internal Audit Results Outside the Organization

The *Standards* require that, *when releasing engagement results to parties outside the organization, the communication must include limitations on distribution and use of the results (2410.A3).* Planning for internal audit work being performed for parties outside the organization is discussed in Chapter 10. As noted in that chapter, there should be a documented understanding obtained during the planning of the engagement of restrictions on distribution of the result. This sensitivity to distribution of the report is tied to both the internal auditor's responsibilities of confidentiality, an important principle in The IIA's Code of Ethics, as well as protections ensuring that the internal audit engagement results are not misused by those without an understanding of the scope or other elements of the work. The *Standards* further require that, *if not otherwise mandated by legal, statutory, or regulatory requirements, prior to releasing results to parties outside the organization, the CAE must:*

- *Assess the potential risk to the organization.*
- *Consult with senior management and/or legal counsel as appropriate.*
- *Control dissemination by restricting the use of the results (2440.A2).*

When disseminating information externally, internal auditors should consider the following:

- The need for a written agreement concerning the information to be disseminated.

- The identification of information providers, sources, report signers, information recipients, and related persons to the report or information disseminated.

- The identification of objectives, scope, and procedures to be performed in generating applicable information.

- The nature of the report or other communication, including opinions, inclusion or exclusion of recommendations, disclaimers, limitations, and type of assurance or assertions to be provided.

- Copyright issues and limitations on further distribution or sharing of the information.

Internal auditors also should consider the risk of creating potential liability by communicating outside the organization, and whether third-party indemnifications should be required.

Other Communications Issues

Communicating Sensitive Information Outside the Chain of Command

When an internal auditor discovers information about exposures, threats, uncertainties, fraud, waste and mismanagement, illegal activities, abuse of power, misconduct that endangers public health or safety, or other wrongdoings, thorough consideration of the proper communication channel may be important. Once the internal auditor has decided that the information is substantial and credible, the auditor would normally communicate the information, on a timely basis, to those in management who can act on it. In most instances, those communications will resolve the matter from an internal auditing perspective, so long as management takes the appropriate action to manage the associated risks. If the communications result in a conclusion that management, by its inadequate or lack of actions, is exposing the organization to an unacceptable level of risk, the CAE should consider other options to achieve a satisfactory resolution, including the requirements for board communication in Standard 2600. In some countries, certain actions may be prescribed by local laws or regulations. PA 2440-2 discusses in further detail communicating sensitive information within and outside the chain of command. Internal auditors should seek legal counsel when the situation is sensitive and has significant consequences.

Legal Issues

When it comes to communicating results and issuing opinions regarding legal and regulatory violations, internal auditors must exercise caution. PA 2400-1 addresses this topic. In matters involving legal matters, internal auditors should consult with legal counsel. Where such situations are expected to arise, it is appropriate to establish appropriate policies and procedures and a close working relationship with relevant areas, such as legal counsel and compliance groups. The internal auditor's need to document engagement records may conflict with legal counsel's desire not to leave discoverable evidence that could harm a defense. Adequate planning, policy-making, consultation, and relationship development ahead of time are essential to prevent corporate counsel and internal auditing from being at odds with one another during a sudden crisis situation.

While internal auditing can articulate relevant facts, findings, and recommendations, it should not usually conclude on legal matters. Deciding whether or not a conclusion on legal compliance is appropriate is most often a matter more appropriately considered by legal department personnel.

There has been discussion over time of two court-recognized privileges or doctrines that can be invoked to protect engagement communications. These include attorney-client privilege and critical self-analysis privilege.

> Attorney-client privilege is used primarily to protect communications with attorneys, although it also can apply to communications with third parties, like internal auditors, who are working with the attorney. Certain elements and practices are necessary to protect the attorney-client privilege. It is advised that internal auditors discuss such elements and practices with attorneys early in the engagement planning to ensure the internal auditors and their related communications qualify and comply.

Some courts have recognized a "critical self-analysis" privilege that shields in some situations self-critical materials, such as audit engagement workpapers and other communications, from discovery. Such protection allows, even encourages, individuals or businesses to candidly evaluate compliance with regulatory and legal requirements without fear of creating evidence that can be used against them in future litigation. Such critical self-evaluation is seen by the court as "fostering the compelling public interest in observance of the law."

This critical self-analysis privilege may apply to organizations that have been required by relevant regulatory bodies to implement a self-regulatory program designed to ensure compliance with applicable laws and regulations. Regulatory agencies whose policies require self-regulation may be prohibited from using the results of related compliance efforts to discover the organization's weak areas or make a case against the organization. As with attorney-client privilege, internal auditors should discuss such elements and practices with attorneys early in the engagement planning to ensure the internal auditors and their related communications qualify and comply.

Timely, upfront communication with attorneys is critical in such situations. Documents prepared before the attorney-client relationship comes into existence may not be protected by the doctrine, even if they are delivered to the attorney. In addition, documents may not be protected if a substantial need for the information exists and the information is not otherwise available without undue hardship. This publication does not provide legal advice. Internal auditors are also encouraged to consult legal counsel in all matters involving legal issues as requirements may vary significantly in different jurisdictions.

The Final Word

Successful delivery of the audit product depends largely on how well the audit team communicates final engagement results. By fulfilling the requirements discussed in this chapter, internal auditors will not only achieve conformance with the *Standards,* but will also help ensure that their internal audit communications are as effective as possible. Communication is critical to the organization receiving the assurance, added value and contributions to improving the organization's operations that it values from internal auditing.

**Exhibit 12-1
Sample Macro-level Opinion**

To: Chair, Audit Committee

From: Executive VP – Internal Audit

Subject: Internal audit of internal control for the period ended December 31, 2011

We have completed the internal audit plan of internal control for the company. The objectives of this engagement were to assess the adequacy of internal controls to address strategic risks, operational risks, financial reporting risks, and compliance risks.

The plan was prepared considering the results of the risk assessment completed as a part of the company's enterprise risk management process and the risk assessments completed by internal auditing and the organizations' external auditors. Our work was conducted in accordance with the *International Standards for the Professional Practice of Internal Auditing*.

The internal audit examined (describe what has been examined; e.g., the management control framework, governance considerations, the risk management strategy, policies and practices, information used for decision-making, reporting as applicable to the entity examined, etc.).

The scope of the audit included (scope inclusions). Furthermore, the examination covered activities that have occurred during the period January 1, 20XX to December 31, 20XX.

The criteria used to assess the company were the company's internal control framework, which is based on the COSO internal control framework. The criteria were discussed and agreed with management in each area before the conduct of detailed audit procedures.

Internal auditing's overall opinion is that during the period January 1, 20XX to December 31, 20XX, internal controls over strategic risks, operations risks, financial reporting risks, and compliance risks are satisfactory in design and in operation.

In my professional judgment as Executive Vice President – Internal Audit, sufficient and appropriate audit procedures have been conducted and evidence gathered to support the accuracy of the conclusions reached and contained in this report. The conclusions were based on a comparison of the situations as they existed at the time against the audit criteria. The conclusions are only applicable for the entity examined. The evidence gathered meets professional audit standards and is sufficient to provide senior management with proof of the conclusions derived from the internal audit.

Source: Adapted from Standard 2450 and Appendix C, Practice Guide, Formulating and Expressing Internal Audit Opinions.

Exhibit 12-2
Audit Ratings Examples

Audit Ratings Example – Attention Directing

An overall rating will be included in the audit report for each business unit or function audited. The purpose of the rating is to categorize as accurately as possible the adequacy and effectiveness of internal controls. The rating system is useful as a means of summarizing the auditor's general level of concern relative to an individual unit, but it is no substitute for specific audit findings that are identified and communicated to management.

Audit reports will reflect one of the three ratings identified below. Auditors and management must realize that assigning ratings is a judgmental exercise informed by audit findings. As a practical matter, the definitions for any rating scheme cannot do more than create broad categories that reflect differing levels of concern. Although the overall rating is useful as a shorthand way of expressing the auditor's level of concern, *the focus of attention for auditors and management should be on the specific audit findings and the actions that will address them.*

The audit rating categories are:

"Adequate" or "Satisfactory." This rating indicates that, overall, conditions do not rise to a level of significant concern. The problems identified, while warranting correction, were not serious. Previously reported problems have been resolved or are being resolved in a timely manner.

"Requires Management Attention." This rating indicates an elevated level of concern relative to the conditions disclosed by the audit. Overall, controls are not what they should be and prompt management attention is necessary. A significant number of audit findings or inappropriate delays in resolving previously cited deficiencies suggest a "Requires Management Attention" rating.

"Requires Immediate Management Attention." This rating indicates control deficiencies that warrant significant and immediate corrective action. Major operational, accounting, or compliance problems were identified by the audit. Control weaknesses were noted that expose the company to meaningful financial or reputational risk. A repeat significant audit finding or a failure to sustain previously implemented corrective measures is also a basis for the assignment of this rating.

Audit Ratings Example – Tier Grading	
Effective	Controls evaluated are adequate, appropriate, and effective to provide reasonable assurance that risks are being managed and objectives should be met.
Some Improvement Needed	A few specific control weaknesses were noted; generally, however, controls evaluated are adequate, appropriate, and effective to provide reasonable assurance that risks are being managed and objectives should be met.

Exhibit 12-2 (continued) **Audit Ratings Examples**				

Major Improvement Needed	Numerous specific control weaknesses were noted. Controls evaluated are unlikely to provide reasonable assurance that risks are being managed and objectives should be met.
Unsatisfactory	Controls evaluated are not adequate, appropriate, or effective to provide reasonable assurance that risks are being managed and objectives should be met.

Source: From Appendix C, Practice Guide, Formulating and Expressing Internal Audit Opinions.

Audit Ratings Example – Tier Grading with Scale

Evaluation and Grading Matrix

Scope of Work Determinants	Well-controlled (A)	Satisfactory — High (B)	Satisfactory — Low (C)	Material Opportunities for Improvement (F)
Operating Effectiveness and Efficiency	Effective	Adequate	Serious Problems but Not Material	Disclosure
Reliability of Financial Reporting	Effective	Adequate	Serious Problems but Not Material	Disclosure
Compliance With Applicable Laws and Regulations	Effective	Adequate	Serious Problems but Not Material	Disclosure
Safeguarding of Assets	Effective	Adequate	Serious Problems but Not Material	Disclosure

Source: From Appendix C, Practice Guide, Formulating and Expressing Internal Audit Opinions.

Exhibit 12-3
Example Internal Audit Report Format

Internal Audit Report
(TITLE)
Executive Summary
DATE

Background:

- One paragraph with key information on operations, objectives, risks, and information on the area.

Internal Audit Objectives and Scope:

- Three to eight bullet points, each starting with a verb, describing the objectives and scope of the internal audit project.

Observations and Recommendations:

- Include one to four items, each numbered. Each title should start with a verb. The observation and recommendation should be fit into one or two paragraphs, with a maximum of three to four sentences in each paragraph. Management's action plan, or agreement with the recommendation, should be indicated.

1. **xxxxxx xxxxxxxxxx xxxxxxxxxxxx**

    xxxxxxxxxxxxxxxxxxxxxxxxxxxxxxxxxxxxxxxxxxxxxxxxxxxxxxxxxxxxxxxxxxxxxxxxxxxxxxxx
    xxxxxxxxxxxxxxxxxxxxxxxxxxxxxxxxxxxxxxxxxxxxxxxxxxxxxxxxxxxxxxxxxxxxxxxxxxxxxxxx
    xxxxxxxxxxxxxxxxxxxxxxxxxxxxxxxxxxxxxxxxxxxxxxxxxxxxxxxxxxxxxxxxxxxxxxxxxxxxxxxx
    xxxxxxxxxxxxxxxxxxxxxxxxxxxxxxxxxxxxxxxxxxxxxxxxxxxxxxxxxxxxxxxxxxxxxxxxxxx.

As a result of the audit, the following steps are recommended and have been agreed upon with the company's management:

- Management's action plan, or agreement with the recommendation, should be indicated.

Overall, the Executive Summary should be one to two pages. The Executive Summary should stand on its own and be separable from the detailed report.

Exhibit 12-3 (continued)
Example Internal Audit Report Format

Internal Audit Report
(TITLE)
Detailed Section of the Report

The detailed report may have up to 10 issues, if appropriate. The detailed report titles, observations, and recommendations should be consistent in wording and substance with any similar write-ups in the Executive Summary. Each issue can follow the following format:

1. **(Insert Title - with verb starting the title, and the title reflecting the issue to be taken)**

Risk Priority: (Fill in: rankings generally can consist of four categories of importance)

Observation:	Recommendation:
Provide facts, issues, and implications. Show why the issue is important. Restrict the writing generally to no more than three paragraphs of three to four sentences each.	Provide action-oriented recommendations that address the observation. Management Action Plan Owner: (provide a specific name and title) Action Plan Completion Date: (date)

2. **(Insert Title - with verb starting the title, and the title reflecting the issue to be taken)**

Risk Priority: (Fill in: rankings generally can consist of four categories of importance)

Observation:	Recommendation:
Provide facts, issues, and implications. Show why the issue is important. Restrict the writing generally to no more than three paragraphs of three to four sentences each.	Provide action-oriented recommendations that address the observation. Management Action Plan Owner: (provide a specific name and title) Action Plan Completion Date: (date)

Other issues follow similarly.

Appendices that provide focused analysis, benchmarking, and examples that can help implement recommendations can follow the observations. Each appendix should be referred to somewhere in the detailed report. Consider whether visually appealing content such as graphs or color ratings can be useful in conveying the message.

Chapter 13

YOU MUST HAVE A FOLLOW-UP PROCESS ON ASSURANCE ENGAGEMENTS AND YOU MUST COMMUNICATE UNACCEPTABLE RESIDUAL RISK (2500-2600)

The *Standards* assign the internal audit activity responsibilities beyond the planning and execution of internal audit engagements. Two key areas of responsibility are to ensure adequate follow-up on assurance engagement responses and to communicate when the CAE perceives management is taking on an unacceptable level of risk. These two areas are key because, when done effectively, they result in positive change and better governance as a result of the internal audit process.

Monitor Results

Responsibility for follow-up is the responsibility of internal auditing. Follow-up is usually defined as a process by which internal auditors determine the adequacy, effectiveness, and timeliness of actions taken by management on reported engagement observations and recommendations, including those made by external auditors and others. The process also includes determining whether senior management and/or the board have assumed the risk of not taking action on reported observations (PA 2500. A1-1).

The *Standards require the CAE to establish and maintain a system to monitor the disposition of results communicated to management* (2500). Such a system might include:

- A time frame within which management's response to the engagement observations and recommendations is required.

- An evaluation of management's response.

- A verification of the response (if appropriate).

- A follow-up engagement (if appropriate).

- A communications procedure that escalates unsatisfactory responses or actions, including the assumption of risk, to the appropriate levels of senior management or the board (PA 2500-1).

Certain reported observations and recommendations may be so significant that they require immediate action by management. It is recommended that these conditions be monitored by the internal audit activity until corrected because of the effect they may have on the organization (PA 2500-1).

The *Standards* for following up on an assurance engagement are more demanding than the monitoring requirements that apply to consulting engagements. In a consulting engagement, *the CAE is responsible for follow-up only to the extent agreed upon with the client* (2500.C1). However, the *Standards* require a follow-up process for assurance engagements that *monitors and ensures that management actions have been effectively implemented or that senior management has accepted the risk of not taking action* (2500.A1). Findings and recommendations from assurance work must be tracked until either the problem is solved or the appropriate level of management has accepted the risk.

The nature, timing, and extent of follow-up must be determined by the CAE. Factors that might be considered when determining appropriate follow-up procedures are:

- The significance of the reported observation or recommendation.
- The degree of effort and cost needed to correct the reported condition.
- The impacts that may result should the corrective action fail.
- The complexity of the corrective action.
- The time period involved (PA 2500.A1-1).

It is recommended that the CAE schedule follow-up activities as part of the development of engagement work schedules. Such scheduling should be based on the risk and exposure involved, as well as the degree of difficulty associated with the corrective action and the importance of timing in its implementation. The CAE may in some instances decide that, based on management's oral or written response, the action already taken is sufficient when weighed against the relative importance of the engagement observation or recommendation. On such occasions, follow-up may be performed as part of the next engagement (PA 2500.A1-1).

Repeat important findings that are not resolved often result in escalated action as mandated by board or senior management action. The action may include inviting the management responsible for the area to attend the audit committee meeting; special communications between the CEO and management responsible to emphasize the importance of the issue and to determine why the issue has not yet been resolved; and impact on performance evaluations of the management responsible.

Some audit shops have developed charts to track management action on significant issues. These reports, which are often updated quarterly and shared with senior management and the board, offer a high-level snapshot of what corrective activity is occurring and which individual or group is responsible. For example, one such report lists the issue; the long-term solution with its expected date of completion and responsible party; the short-term solution with its expected date of completion and responsible party; and the status of the initiative at the time of the report's creation. Such tracking mechanisms prove especially useful to senior management, because major initiatives often cross organizational boundaries and involve several groups of people. In addition, knowing that such reports are going to be seen by senior management and the board compels those involved to follow through on their commitments to action.

Monitoring follow-up is an important management and internal auditing responsibility performed on behalf of the board. Boards frequently assume, and need comfort, that actions discussed at their level are then executed as intended. That need, along with boards not being involved daily in management, as well as change in board composition over time, all create undue risk that the board may be surprised by an unresolved issue. An issue discussed at one time, if not adequately addressed, may later become a catastrophic problem if management action is not taken and internal audit follow-up does not detect the unresolved issue. Further, audit committees frequently look at management's responsiveness to addressing internal audit issues as a key indicator of control tone across the organization. A best practice is to have management report to the audit committee on actions on key issues identified by internal auditing.

Communicate Unacceptable Residual Risk

When the CAE believes that senior management has accepted a level of residual risk that may be unacceptable to the organization, the CAE must discuss the matter with senior management. If the decision regarding residual risk is not resolved, the CAE must report the matter to the board for resolution (2600). Residual risk is defined in the Glossary to the *Standards* as *the risk remaining after management takes action to reduce the impact and likelihood of an adverse event, including control activities in responding to a risk.* This standard is one of the most powerful and significant standards. It is core to the responsibilities the CAE has to the board and the organization.

For instance, it is not acceptable for the CAE and the audit team to overlook a certain risk just because senior management, and possibly even the board, has accepted the risk in the past. It is also not acceptable for the CAE to avoid responsibility for considering what the CAE believes to be unacceptable risk in an area of the organization simply because it is not a part of the internal audit plan. The CAE is required to bring areas of perceived unacceptable risk to the attention of senior management and the board repeatedly, if necessary.

This element of the *Standards* brings to life the phrase "Internal Auditing is the eyes and ears of the audit committee." To effectively carry out the intent of Standard 2600, the CAE must:

- Have access to senior management and the board to communicate and discuss timely the CAE's point of view.

- Identify whether there are areas of unacceptable residual risk.

- Demonstrate strong management and communication skills to professionally and effectively navigate these communications with senior management and the board.

It is not expected that it is common that the CAE will be frequently communicating unacceptable residual risks being taken by senior management. Most such situations likely will be resolved when senior management and the CAE communicate effectively with the common goals of the organization in mind. However, it is critical to the effectiveness of internal auditing in serving stakeholders that, when necessary, the CAE communicates to the board what he or she views as unacceptable residual risk.

By explicitly requiring the CAE to report on unacceptable residual risk, whether emerging risk, risk in areas not under internal audit engagements, or risk that may be left over from previous years' issues that were not adequately addressed, the *Standards* emphasize how important it is to escalate these issues, keep the board informed, and proactively act to ensure awareness of risk in order to protect the organization. This standard reflects the internal auditor's shift in focus toward good governance, risk management, and risk reporting.

Communicate, Communicate, Communicate

Some of the most important aspects of the CAE's job, as defined in the *Standards,* are communicating with senior management and the board on unresolved or unacceptably high risks, including the status of management actions to address risks identified through internal audit engagements. CAEs who excel in these areas provide great value to their most important stakeholders and help to ensure the effectiveness of governance processes and that the organization's operations improve.

Chapter 14

THE ROAD AHEAD

A purpose of this chapter is to applaud the success of the *Standards* and the IPPF. Another purpose is to provide direction to internal auditors on key points as they implement the *Standards* and the IPPF. The future of internal auditing demands that the profession anticipate and respond to the changing needs of organizations we serve.

The Definition

> Internal auditing is an independent, objective assurance and consulting activity designed to add value and improve an organization's operations. It helps an organization accomplish its objectives by bringing a systematic, disciplined approach to evaluate and improve the effectiveness of risk management, control, and governance processes.

The experience of the past decade has shown that the Definition of Internal Auditing, adopted in 1999, was remarkably visionary and continues to remain on point. Some of its strengths include that it:

- Grounds internal auditing in a systematic and disciplined approach.

- Foresaw the organization's need for internal auditing to cover risk management and governance as well as its core expertise in control.

- Recognizes the Internal Audit Value Proposition includes providing assurance and consulting services.

- Emphasizes internal auditing's unique role in being independent and objective in its work.

- Recognizes the importance of adding value and improving the organization's operations, linking internal auditing back into the overall organization and key stakeholders..

The *Standards*

The *Standards* align with the overall framework suggested by the 1997 Guidance Task Force and its Vision for the Future in many ways.

- The *Standards* fully align with the Definition of Internal Auditing.

- The *Standards* have received relatively wide acceptance, and feedback from surveys seems to show that the *Standards* generally are covering the right areas with the right level of details.[1]

- Not content to let the issuance of the complete rewrite of the *Standards* in January 2002 sit, the Internal Audit Standards Board continues to drive enhancements to the *Standards*, as again shown in the *Standards* revisions effective in 2011.

- The Internal Audit Standards Board has avoided the temptation to issue detailed, deep standards in every area of interest and has kept the *Standards* principles-based. The *Standards* remain at around 30 printed pages, including the Introduction and the Glossary. This makes the global use and recognition of the *Standards* easier.

Position Papers, Practice Advisories, and Practice Guides

Position Papers, Practice Advisories, and Practice Guides provide a great wealth of information and allow The IIA to provide information on leading practices to the profession that may be relevant to the more advanced internal audit groups without mandating the practices for every internal audit activity throughout the world, including those early on the internal audit maturity curve. Practice Guides in particular have proven to be a wonderful mechanism to deliver deeper guidance to practitioners seeking insights on leading practices.

The Top 10 Keys to Successful Implementation

Now that you have invested in increasing your understanding of the *Standards* and the IPPF, your charge is to apply them in the practice of internal auditing at your organization. What are key points on which you can focus? Here are 10 areas, with reference to the section of the *Standards* to which they relate.

1. **Align with key stakeholders.** Build strong relationships with the audit committee and key stakeholders. Ensure the internal audit charter and internal audit actions reflect their expectations for value. Build key relationships high in the organization to promote the stature of internal auditing and also promote objectivity. (1000, 1100)

2. **Get and develop the right resources.** Internal auditing is a people business, where individuals create the product coming out of internal auditing. It is critical to have the right resources linked to risk, and to attract and develop high-quality resources. Do not fear using sourcing as a source of strength to get the right resources as appropriate. (1200)

3. **Embrace quality and continuous improvement.** Have a proactive internal quality assessment and improvement program. Have notable continuous improvement coming from the internal quality effort. Fully embrace the spirit and the letter of the external quality standards. (1300, 2200, 2300)

4. **Continuously strive to deliver value.** Understand what value means to your key stakeholders, plan to deliver value in everyday internal audit operations, and measure the internal audit actions that result in value. Enable a client service culture. (1300)

5. **Manage internal auditing strategically.** Ensure that internal auditing is involved in key strategic initiatives and has a "seat at the table." Then see that internal auditing is addressing the organization's key strategic and emerging risks. Do not let major risks go undetected. (2000)

6. **Proactively assess your organization's governance and risk management processes.** Contribute to the organization developing more effective governance and risk management processes. Have a positive impact on the organization in these fast-evolving areas. (2100)

7. **Strive for excellence in internal audit execution.** Embrace innovation in the internal audit process and seek best practices that can benefit your organization. Embrace the power of technology and leverage knowledge management. (2200, 2300)

8. **Communicate with insight and impact.** The output of internal auditing is perceived by others through formal and informal written and oral communications. Develop an ongoing communications strategy to be relevant for management and the board. Develop systemic and trending information valuable for stakeholders. (2000, 2400)

9. **Get resolution.** Ensure that management is attentive to audit issues and that senior management and the audit committee are kept aware of management's corrective actions. Ensure through the follow-up process that issues are resolved and do not get caught in recycling past issues that are never adequately addressed. (2500)

10. **Tell it like it is**. When you believe the organization is facing unacceptable risk or certain actions are just not right — speak out. Use good judgment on what the real issues are, but make it clear that internal auditing has a voice and is willing to use it. (2600)

The Road Ahead

The profession of internal auditing is at its greatest stature ever. It is receiving more recognition by boards, audit committees, and management. More individuals are in the internal audit profession now than ever before. And with the global challenges at the end of this first decade of the new century, demands for internal audit effectiveness and efficiency are expected to grow. New issues in organizations around governance, risk management, and internal controls are emerging. The internal audit profession must step up to today's challenges and leverage the IPPF for success. The IPPF provides the vehicle to drive the profession forward, contributing to high-quality internal audit results and value in the eyes of key stakeholders.

References

[1] See Chapter 4 in *Common Body of Knowledge, 2006* (Altamonte Springs, FL: The Institute of Internal Auditors Research Foundation, 2007) and Chapter 7 in James A. Bailey, CBOK Report II: *Core Competencies for Today's Internal Auditor* (Altamonte Springs, FL: The Institute of Internal Auditors Research Foundation, 2010).

Appendix A

INTERNATIONAL STANDARDS FOR THE PROFESSIONAL PRACTICE OF INTERNAL AUDITING

Introduction to the International *Standards*

Internal auditing is conducted in diverse legal and cultural environments; within organizations that vary in purpose, size, complexity, and structure; and by persons within or outside the organization. While differences may affect the practice of internal auditing in each environment, conformance with The IIA's *International Standards for the Professional Practice of Internal Auditing* (*Standards*) is essential in meeting the responsibilities of internal auditors and the internal audit activity.

If internal auditors or the internal audit activity is prohibited by law or regulation from conformance with certain parts of the *Standards*, conformance with all other parts of the *Standards* and appropriate disclosures are needed.

If the *Standards* are used in conjunction with standards issued by other authoritative bodies, internal audit communications may also cite the use of other standards, as appropriate. In such a case, if inconsistencies exist between the *Standards* and other standards, internal auditors and the internal audit activity must conform with the *Standards*, and may conform with the other standards if they are more restrictive.

The purpose of the *Standards* is to:

1. Delineate basic principles that represent the practice of internal auditing.

2. Provide a framework for performing and promoting a broad range of value-added internal auditing.

3. Establish the basis for the evaluation of internal audit performance.

4. Foster improved organizational processes and operations.

The *Standards* are principles-focused, mandatory requirements consisting of:

*   Statements of basic requirements for the professional practice of internal auditing and for evaluating the effectiveness of performance, which are internationally applicable at organizational and individual levels.

*   Interpretations, which clarify terms or concepts within the Statements.

The *Standards* employ terms that have been given specific meanings that are included in the Glossary. Specifically, the *Standards* use the word "must" to specify an unconditional requirement and the word "should" where conformance is expected unless, when applying professional judgment, circumstances justify deviation.

It is necessary to consider the Statements and their Interpretations as well as the specific meanings from the Glossary to understand and apply the *Standards* correctly.

The structure of the *Standards* is divided between Attribute and Performance Standards. Attribute Standards address the attributes of organizations and individuals performing internal auditing. The Performance Standards describe the nature of internal auditing and provide quality criteria against which the performance of these services can be measured. The Attribute and Performance Standards are also provided to apply to all internal audit services.

Implementation Standards are also provided to expand upon the Attribute and Performance standards, by providing the requirements applicable to assurance (A) or consulting (C) activities.

Assurance services involve the internal auditor's objective assessment of evidence to provide an independent opinion or conclusions regarding an entity, operation, function, process, system, or other subject matter. The nature and scope of the assurance engagement are determined by the internal auditor. There are generally three parties involved in assurance services: (1) the person or group directly involved with the entity, operation, function, process, system, or other subject matter — the process owner, (2) the person or group making the assessment — the internal auditor, and (3) the person or group using the assessment — the user.

Consulting services are advisory in nature, and are generally performed at the specific request of an engagement client. The nature and scope of the consulting engagement are subject to agreement with the engagement client. Consulting services generally involve two parties: (1) the person or group offering the advice — the internal auditor, and (2) the person or group seeking and receiving the advice — the engagement client. When performing consulting services the internal auditor should maintain objectivity and not assume management responsibility.

The review and development of the *Standards* is an ongoing process. The Internal Audit Standards Board engages in extensive consultation and discussion prior to issuing the *Standards*. This includes worldwide solicitation for public comment through the exposure draft process. All exposure drafts are posted on The IIA's website as well as being distributed to all IIA institutes.

Suggestions and comments regarding the *Standards* can be sent to:

The Institute of Internal Auditors
Standards and Guidance
247 Maitland Avenue
Altamonte Springs, FL 32701-4201, USA
E-mail: guidance@theiia.org   Web: www.theiia.org

***

Attribute Standards

1000 – Purpose, Authority, and Responsibility

The purpose, authority, and responsibility of the internal audit activity must be formally defined in an internal audit charter, consistent with the Definition of Internal Auditing, the Code of Ethics, and the *Standards*. The chief audit executive must periodically review the internal audit charter and present it to senior management and the board for approval.

Interpretation:

The internal audit charter is a formal document that defines the internal audit activity's purpose, authority, and responsibility. The internal audit charter establishes the internal audit activity's position within the organization, including the nature of the chief audit executive's functional reporting relationship with the board; authorizes access to records, personnel, and physical properties relevant to the performance of engagements; and defines the scope of internal audit activities. Final approval of the internal audit charter resides with the board.

> **1000.A1** – The nature of assurance services provided to the organization must be defined in the internal audit charter. If assurances are to be provided to parties outside the organization, the nature of these assurances must also be defined in the internal audit charter.

> **1000.C1** – The nature of consulting services must be defined in the internal audit charter.

1010 – Recognition of the Definition of Internal Auditing, the Code of Ethics, and the *Standards* in the Internal Audit Charter

The mandatory nature of the Definition of Internal Auditing, the Code of Ethics, and the *Standards* must be recognized in the internal audit charter. The chief audit executive should discuss the Definition of Internal Auditing, the Code of Ethics, and the *Standards* with senior management and the board.

1100 – Independence and Objectivity

The internal audit activity must be independent, and internal auditors must be objective in performing their work.

Interpretation:

Independence is the freedom from conditions that threaten the ability of the internal audit activity to carry out internal audit responsibilities in an unbiased manner. To achieve the degree of independence necessary to effectively carry out the responsibilities of the internal audit activity, the chief audit executive has direct and unrestricted access to senior management and the board. This can be achieved through a dual-reporting relationship. Threats to independence must be managed at the individual auditor, engagement, functional, and organizational levels.

Objectivity is an unbiased mental attitude that allows internal auditors to perform engagements in such a manner that they believe in their work product and that no quality compromises are made. Objectivity requires that internal auditors do not subordinate their judgment on audit matters to others. Threats to objectivity must be managed at the individual auditor, engagement, functional, and organizational levels.

1110 – Organizational Independence

The chief audit executive must report to a level within the organization that allows the internal audit activity to fulfill its responsibilities. The chief audit executive must confirm to the board, at least annually, the organizational independence of the internal audit activity.

Interpretation:

Organizational independence is effectively achieved when the chief audit executive reports functionally to the board. Examples of functional reporting to the board involve the board:

- *Approving the internal audit charter;*

- *Approving the risk based internal audit plan;*

- *Receiving communications from the chief audit executive on the internal audit activity's performance relative to its plan and other matters;*

- *Approving decisions regarding the appointment and removal of the chief audit executive; and*

- *Making appropriate inquiries of management and the chief audit executive to determine whether there are inappropriate scope or resource limitations.*

1110.A1 – The internal audit activity must be free from interference in determining the scope of internal auditing, performing work, and communicating results.

1111 – Direct Interaction with the Board

The chief audit executive must communicate and interact directly with the board.

1120 – Individual Objectivity

Internal auditors must have an impartial, unbiased attitude and avoid any conflict of interest.

Interpretation:

Conflict of interest is a situation in which an internal auditor, who is in a position of trust, has a competing professional or personal interest. Such competing interests can make it difficult to fulfill his or her duties impartially. A conflict of interest exists even if no unethical or improper act results. A conflict of interest can create an appearance of impropriety that can undermine confidence in the internal auditor, the internal audit activity, and the profession. A conflict of interest could impair an individual's ability to perform his or her duties and responsibilities objectively.

1130 – Impairment to Independence or Objectivity

If independence or objectivity is impaired in fact or appearance, the details of the impairment must be disclosed to appropriate parties. The nature of the disclosure will depend upon the impairment.

Interpretation:

Impairment to organizational independence and individual objectivity may include, but is not limited to, personal conflict of interest, scope limitations, restrictions on access to records, personnel, and properties, and resource limitations, such as funding.

The determination of appropriate parties to which the details of an impairment to independence or objectivity must be disclosed is dependent upon the expectations of the internal audit activity's and the chief audit executive's responsibilities to senior management and the board as described in the internal audit charter, as well as the nature of the impairment.

1130.A1 – Internal auditors must refrain from assessing specific operations for which they were previously responsible. Objectivity is presumed to be impaired if an internal auditor provides assurance services for an activity for which the internal auditor had responsibility within the previous year.

1130.A2 – Assurance engagements for functions over which the chief audit executive has responsibility must be overseen by a party outside the internal audit activity.

1130.C1 – Internal auditors may provide consulting services relating to operations for which they had previous responsibilities.

1130.C2 – If internal auditors have potential impairments to independence or objectivity relating to proposed consulting services, disclosure must be made to the engagement client prior to accepting the engagement.

1200 – Proficiency and Due Professional Care
Engagements must be performed with proficiency and due professional care.

1210 – Proficiency
Internal auditors must possess the knowledge, skills, and other competencies needed to perform their individual responsibilities. The internal audit activity collectively must possess or obtain the knowledge, skills, and other competencies needed to perform its responsibilities.

Interpretation:
Knowledge, skills, and other competencies is a collective term that refers to the professional proficiency required of internal auditors to effectively carry out their professional responsibilities. Internal auditors are encouraged to demonstrate their proficiency by obtaining appropriate professional certifications and qualifications, such as the Certified Internal Auditor designation and other designations offered by The Institute of Internal Auditors and other appropriate professional organizations.

1210.A1 – The chief audit executive must obtain competent advice and assistance if the internal auditors lack the knowledge, skills, or other competencies needed to perform all or part of the engagement.

1210.A2 – Internal auditors must have sufficient knowledge to evaluate the risk of fraud and the manner in which it is managed by the organization, but are not expected to have the expertise of a person whose primary responsibility is detecting and investigating fraud.

1210.A3 – Internal auditors must have sufficient knowledge of key information technology risks and controls and available technology-based audit techniques to perform their assigned work. However, not all internal auditors are expected to have the expertise of an internal auditor whose primary responsibility is information technology auditing.

1210.C1 – The chief audit executive must decline the consulting engagement or obtain competent advice and assistance if the internal auditors lack the knowledge, skills, or other competencies needed to perform all or part of the engagement.

1220 – Due Professional Care

Internal auditors must apply the care and skill expected of a reasonably prudent and competent internal auditor. Due professional care does not imply infallibility.

1220.A1 – Internal auditors must exercise due professional care by considering the:

- Extent of work needed to achieve the engagement's objectives;

- Relative complexity, materiality, or significance of matters to which assurance procedures are applied;

- Adequacy and effectiveness of governance, risk management, and control processes;

- Probability of significant errors, fraud, or noncompliance; and

- Cost of assurance in relation to potential benefits.

1220.A2 – In exercising due professional care internal auditors must consider the use of technology-based audit and other data analysis techniques.

1220.A3 – Internal auditors must be alert to the significant risks that might affect objectives, operations, or resources. However, assurance procedures alone, even when performed with due professional care, do not guarantee that all significant risks will be identified.

1220.C1 – Internal auditors must exercise due professional care during a consulting engagement by considering the:

- Needs and expectations of clients, including the nature, timing, and communication of engagement results;

- Relative complexity and extent of work needed to achieve the engagement's objectives; and

- Cost of the consulting engagement in relation to potential benefits.

1230 – Continuing Professional Development

Internal auditors must enhance their knowledge, skills, and other competencies through continuing professional development.

1300 – Quality Assurance and Improvement Program

The chief audit executive must develop and maintain a quality assurance and improvement program that covers all aspects of the internal audit activity.

Interpretation:

A quality assurance and improvement program is designed to enable an evaluation of the internal audit activity's conformance with the Definition of Internal Auditing and the Standards *and an evaluation of whether internal auditors apply the Code of Ethics. The program also assesses the efficiency and effectiveness of the internal audit activity and identifies opportunities for improvement.*

1310 – Requirements of the Quality Assurance and Improvement Program
The quality assurance and improvement program must include both internal and external assessments.

1311 – Internal Assessments
Internal assessments must include:

- Ongoing monitoring of the performance of the internal audit activity; and

- Periodic reviews performed through self-assessment or by other persons within the organization with sufficient knowledge of internal audit practices.

Interpretation:
Ongoing monitoring is an integral part of the day-to-day supervision, review, and measurement of the internal audit activity. Ongoing monitoring is incorporated into the routine policies and practices used to manage the internal audit activity and uses processes, tools, and information considered necessary to evaluate conformance with the Definition of Internal Auditing, the Code of Ethics, and the Standards.

Periodic reviews are assessments conducted to evaluate conformance with the Definition of Internal Auditing, the Code of Ethics, and the Standards.

Sufficient knowledge of internal audit practices requires at least an understanding of all elements of the International Professional Practices Framework.

1312 – External Assessments
External assessments must be conducted at least once every five years by a qualified, independent reviewer or review team from outside the organization. The chief audit executive must discuss with the board:

- The need for more frequent external assessments; and

- The qualifications and independence of the external reviewer or review team, including any potential conflict of interest.

Interpretation:
A qualified reviewer or review team demonstrates competence in two areas: the professional practice of internal auditing and the external assessment process. Competence can be demonstrated through a mixture of experience and theoretical learning. Experience gained in organizations of similar size, complexity, sector or industry, and technical issues is more valuable than less relevant experience. In the case of a review team, not all members of the team need to have all the competencies; it is the team as a whole that is qualified. The chief audit executive uses professional judgment when assessing whether a reviewer or review team demonstrates sufficient competence to be qualified.

An independent reviewer or review team means not having either a real or an apparent conflict of interest and not being a part of, or under the control of, the organization to which the internal audit activity belongs.

1320 – Reporting on the Quality Assurance and Improvement Program

The chief audit executive must communicate the results of the quality assurance and improvement program to senior management and the board.

Interpretation:

The form, content, and frequency of communicating the results of the quality assurance and improvement program is established through discussions with senior management and the board and considers the responsibilities of the internal audit activity and chief audit executive as contained in the internal audit charter. To demonstrate conformance with the Definition of Internal Auditing, the Code of Ethics, and the Standards, the results of external and periodic internal assessments are communicated upon completion of such assessments and the results of ongoing monitoring are communicated at least annually. The results include the reviewer's or review team's assessment with respect to the degree of conformance.

1321 – Use of "Conforms with the *International Standards for the Professional Practice of Internal Auditing*"

The chief audit executive may state that the internal audit activity conforms with the *International Standards for the Professional Practice of Internal Auditing* only if the results of the quality assurance and improvement program support this statement.

Interpretation:

The internal audit activity conforms with the Standards *when it achieves the outcomes described in the Definition of Internal Auditing, Code of Ethics, and* Standards.

The results of the quality assurance and improvement program include the results of both internal and external assessments. All internal audit activities will have the results of internal assessments. Internal audit activities in existence for at least five years will also have the results of external assessments.

1322 – Disclosure of Nonconformance

When nonconformance with the Definition of Internal Auditing, the Code of Ethics, or the *Standards* impacts the overall scope or operation of the internal audit activity, the chief audit executive must disclose the nonconformance and the impact to senior management and the board.

Performance Standards

2000 – Managing the Internal Audit Activity
The chief audit executive must effectively manage the internal audit activity to ensure it adds value to the organization.

Interpretation:
The internal audit activity is effectively managed when:

- *The results of the internal audit activity's work achieve the purpose and responsibility included in the internal audit charter;*

- *The internal audit activity conforms with the Definition of Internal Auditing and the* Standards; *and*

- *The individuals who are part of the internal audit activity demonstrate conformance with the Code of Ethics and the* Standards.

The internal audit activity adds value to the organization (and its stakeholders) when it provides objective and relevant assurance, and contributes to the effectiveness and efficiency of governance, risk management, and control processes.

2010 – Planning
The chief audit executive must establish risk-based plans to determine the priorities of the internal audit activity, consistent with the organization's goals.

Interpretation:
The chief audit executive is responsible for developing a risk-based plan. The chief audit executive takes into account the organization's risk management framework, including using risk appetite levels set by management for the different activities or parts of the organization. If a framework does not exist, the chief audit executive uses his/her own judgment of risks after consultation with senior management and the board.

2010.A1 – The internal audit activity's plan of engagements must be based on a documented risk assessment, undertaken at least annually. The input of senior management and the board must be considered in this process.

2010.A2 – The chief audit executive must identify and consider the expectations of senior management, the board, and other stakeholders for internal audit opinions and other conclusions.

2010.C1 – The chief audit executive should consider accepting proposed consulting engagements based on the engagement's potential to improve management of risks, add value, and improve the organization's operations. Accepted engagements must be included in the plan.

2020 – Communication and Approval

The chief audit executive must communicate the internal audit activity's plans and resource requirements, including significant interim changes, to senior management and the board for review and approval. The chief audit executive must also communicate the impact of resource limitations.

2030 – Resource Management

The chief audit executive must ensure that internal audit resources are appropriate, sufficient, and effectively deployed to achieve the approved plan.

Interpretation:

Appropriate refers to the mix of knowledge, skills, and other competencies needed to perform the plan. Sufficient refers to the quantity of resources needed to accomplish the plan. Resources are effectively deployed when they are used in a way that optimizes the achievement of the approved plan.

2040 – Policies and Procedures

The chief audit executive must establish policies and procedures to guide the internal audit activity.

Interpretation:

The form and content of policies and procedures are dependent upon the size and structure of the internal audit activity and the complexity of its work.

2050 – Coordination

The chief audit executive should share information and coordinate activities with other internal and external providers of assurance and consulting services to ensure proper coverage and minimize duplication of efforts.

2060 – Reporting to Senior Management and the Board

The chief audit executive must report periodically to senior management and the board on the internal audit activity's purpose, authority, responsibility, and performance relative to its plan. Reporting must also include significant risk exposures and control issues, including fraud risks, governance issues, and other matters needed or requested by senior management and the board.

Interpretation:

The frequency and content of reporting are determined in discussion with senior management and the board and depend on the importance of the information to be communicated and the urgency of the related actions to be taken by senior management or the board.

2070 – External Service Provider and Organizational Responsibility for Internal Auditing

When an external service provider serves as the internal audit activity, the provider must make the organization aware that the organization has the responsibility for maintaining an effective internal audit activity.

Interpretation:

This responsibility is demonstrated through the quality assurance and improvement program which assesses conformance with the Definition of Internal Auditing, the Code of Ethics, and the Standards.

2100 – Nature of Work
The internal audit activity must evaluate and contribute to the improvement of governance, risk management, and control processes using a systematic and disciplined approach.

2110 – Governance
The internal audit activity must assess and make appropriate recommendations for improving the governance process in its accomplishment of the following objectives:

- Promoting appropriate ethics and values within the organization;

- Ensuring effective organizational performance management and accountability;

- Communicating risk and control information to appropriate areas of the organization; and

- Coordinating the activities of and communicating information among the board, external and internal auditors, and management.

  2110.A1 – The internal audit activity must evaluate the design, implementation, and effectiveness of the organization's ethics-related objectives, programs, and activities.

  2110.A2 – The internal audit activity must assess whether the information technology governance of the organization supports the organization's strategies and objectives.

2120 – Risk Management
The internal audit activity must evaluate the effectiveness and contribute to the improvement of risk management processes.

Interpretation:
Determining whether risk management processes are effective is a judgment resulting from the internal auditor's assessment that:

- *Organizational objectives support and align with the organization's mission;*

- *Significant risks are identified and assessed;*

- *Appropriate risk responses are selected that align risks with the organization's risk appetite; and*

- *Relevant risk information is captured and communicated in a timely manner across the organization, enabling staff, management, and the board to carry out their responsibilities.*

The internal audit activity may gather the information to support this assessment during multiple engagements. The results of these engagements, when viewed together, provide an understanding of the organization's risk management processes and their effectiveness.

Risk management processes are monitored through ongoing management activities, separate evaluations, or both.

2120.A1 – The internal audit activity must evaluate risk exposures relating to the organization's governance, operations, and information systems regarding the:

- Reliability and integrity of financial and operational information;

- Effectiveness and efficiency of operations and programs;

- Safeguarding of assets; and

- Compliance with laws, regulations, policies, procedures, and contracts.

2120.A2 – The internal audit activity must evaluate the potential for the occurrence of fraud and how the organization manages fraud risk.

2120.C1 – During consulting engagements, internal auditors must address risk consistent with the engagement's objectives and be alert to the existence of other significant risks.

2120.C2 – Internal auditors must incorporate knowledge of risks gained from consulting engagements into their evaluation of the organization's risk management processes.

2120.C3 – When assisting management in establishing or improving risk management processes, internal auditors must refrain from assuming any management responsibility by actually managing risks.

2130 – Control

The internal audit activity must assist the organization in maintaining effective controls by evaluating their effectiveness and efficiency and by promoting continuous improvement.

2130.A1 – The internal audit activity must evaluate the adequacy and effectiveness of controls in responding to risks within the organization's governance, operations, and information systems regarding the:

- Reliability and integrity of financial and operational information;

- Effectiveness and efficiency of operations and programs;

- Safeguarding of assets; and

- Compliance with laws, regulations, policies, procedures, and contracts.

2130.C1 – Internal auditors must incorporate knowledge of controls gained from consulting engagements into evaluation of the organization's control processes.

2200 – Engagement Planning

Internal auditors must develop and document a plan for each engagement, including the engagement's objectives, scope, timing, and resource allocations.

2201 – Planning Considerations

In planning the engagement, internal auditors must consider:

- The objectives of the activity being reviewed and the means by which the activity controls its performance;

- The significant risks to the activity, its objectives, resources, and operations and the means by which the potential impact of risk is kept to an acceptable level;

- The adequacy and effectiveness of the activity's risk management and control processes compared to a relevant control framework or model; and

- The opportunities for making significant improvements to the activity's risk management and control processes.

2201.A1 – When planning an engagement for parties outside the organization, internal auditors must establish a written understanding with them about objectives, scope, respective responsibilities, and other expectations, including restrictions on distribution of the results of the engagement and access to engagement records.

2201.C1 – Internal auditors must establish an understanding with consulting engagement clients about objectives, scope, respective responsibilities, and other client expectations. For significant engagements, this understanding must be documented.

2210 – Engagement Objectives
Objectives must be established for each engagement.

2210.A1 – Internal auditors must conduct a preliminary assessment of the risks relevant to the activity under review. Engagement objectives must reflect the results of this assessment.

2210.A2 – Internal auditors must consider the probability of significant errors, fraud, noncompliance, and other exposures when developing the engagement objectives.

2210.A3 – Adequate criteria are needed to evaluate controls. Internal auditors must ascertain the extent to which management has established adequate criteria to determine whether objectives and goals have been accomplished. If adequate, internal auditors must use such criteria in their evaluation. If inadequate, internal auditors must work with management to develop appropriate evaluation criteria.

2210.C1 – Consulting engagement objectives must address governance, risk management, and control processes to the extent agreed upon with the client.

2210.C2 – Consulting engagement objectives must be consistent with the organization's values, strategies, and objectives.

2220 – Engagement Scope
The established scope must be sufficient to satisfy the objectives of the engagement.

2220.A1 – The scope of the engagement must include consideration of relevant systems, records, personnel, and physical properties, including those under the control of third parties.

2220.A2 – If significant consulting opportunities arise during an assurance engagement, a specific written understanding as to the objectives, scope, respective responsibilities, and other expectations should be reached and the results of the consulting engagement communicated in accordance with consulting standards.

2220.C1 – In performing consulting engagements, internal auditors must ensure that the scope of the engagement is sufficient to address the agreed-upon objectives. If internal auditors develop reservations about the scope during the engagement, these reservations must be discussed with the client to determine whether to continue with the engagement.

2220.C2 – During consulting engagements, internal auditors must address controls consistent with the engagement's objectives and be alert to significant control issues.

2230 – Engagement Resource Allocation

Internal auditors must determine appropriate and sufficient resources to achieve engagement objectives based on an evaluation of the nature and complexity of each engagement, time constraints, and available resources.

2240 – Engagement Work Program

Internal auditors must develop and document work programs that achieve the engagement objectives.

2240.A1 – Work programs must include the procedures for identifying, analyzing, evaluating, and documenting information during the engagement. The work program must be approved prior to its implementation, and any adjustments approved promptly.

2240.C1 – Work programs for consulting engagements may vary in form and content depending upon the nature of the engagement.

2300 – Performing the Engagement

Internal auditors must identify, analyze, evaluate, and document sufficient information to achieve the engagement's objectives.

2310 – Identifying Information

Internal auditors must identify sufficient, reliable, relevant, and useful information to achieve the engagement's objectives.

Interpretation:

Sufficient information is factual, adequate, and convincing so that a prudent, informed person would reach the same conclusions as the auditor. Reliable information is the best attainable information through the use of appropriate engagement techniques. Relevant information supports engagement observations and recommendations and is consistent with the objectives for the engagement. Useful information helps the organization meet its goals.

2320 – Analysis and Evaluation

Internal auditors must base conclusions and engagement results on appropriate analyses and evaluations.

2330 – Documenting Information

Internal auditors must document relevant information to support the conclusions and engagement results.

2330.A1 – The chief audit executive must control access to engagement records. The chief audit executive must obtain the approval of senior management and/or legal counsel prior to releasing such records to external parties, as appropriate.

2330.A2 – The chief audit executive must develop retention requirements for engagement records, regardless of the medium in which each record is stored. These retention requirements must be consistent with the organization's guidelines and any pertinent regulatory or other requirements.

2330.C1 – The chief audit executive must develop policies governing the custody and retention of consulting engagement records, as well as their release to internal and external parties. These policies must be consistent with the organization's guidelines and any pertinent regulatory or other requirements.

2340 – Engagement Supervision

Engagements must be properly supervised to ensure objectives are achieved, quality is assured, and staff is developed.

Interpretation:
The extent of supervision required will depend on the proficiency and experience of internal auditors and the complexity of the engagement. The chief audit executive has overall responsibility for supervising the engagement, whether performed by or for the internal audit activity, but may designate appropriately experienced members of the internal audit activity to perform the review. Appropriate evidence of supervision is documented and retained.

2400 – Communicating Results

Internal auditors must communicate the results of engagements.

2410 – Criteria for Communicating

Communications must include the engagement's objectives and scope as well as applicable conclusions, recommendations, and action plans.

2410.A1 – Final communication of engagement results must, where appropriate, contain the internal auditors' opinion and/or conclusions. When issued, an opinion or conclusion must take account of the expectations of senior management, the board, and other stakeholders and must be supported by sufficient, reliable, relevant, and useful information.

Interpretation:
Opinions at the engagement level may be ratings, conclusions, or other descriptions of the results. Such an engagement may be in relation to controls around a specific process, risk, or business unit. The formulation of such opinions requires consideration of the engagement results and their significance.

2410.A2 – Internal auditors are encouraged to acknowledge satisfactory performance in engagement communications.

2410.A3 – When releasing engagement results to parties outside the organization, the communication must include limitations on distribution and use of the results.

2410.C1 – Communication of the progress and results of consulting engagements will vary in form and content depending upon the nature of the engagement and the needs of the client.

2420 – Quality of Communications
Communications must be accurate, objective, clear, concise, constructive, complete, and timely.

Interpretation:
Accurate communications are free from errors and distortions and are faithful to the underlying facts. Objective communications are fair, impartial, and unbiased and are the result of a fair-minded and balanced assessment of all relevant facts and circumstances. Clear communications are easily understood and logical, avoiding unnecessary technical language and providing all significant and relevant information. Concise communications are to the point and avoid unnecessary elaboration, superfluous detail, redundancy, and wordiness. Constructive communications are helpful to the engagement client and the organization and lead to improvements where needed. Complete communications lack nothing that is essential to the target audience and include all significant and relevant information and observations to support recommendations and conclusions. Timely communications are opportune and expedient, depending on the significance of the issue, allowing management to take appropriate corrective action.

2421 – Errors and Omissions
If a final communication contains a significant error or omission, the chief audit executive must communicate corrected information to all parties who received the original communication.

2430 – Use of "Conducted in Conformance with the *International Standards for the Professional Practice of Internal Auditing*"
Internal auditors may report that their engagements are "conducted in conformance with the *International Standards for the Professional Practice of Internal Auditing*" only if the results of the quality assurance and improvement program support the statement.

2431 – Engagement Disclosure of Nonconformance
When nonconformance with the Definition of Internal Auditing, the Code of Ethics or the *Standards* impacts a specific engagement, communication of the results must disclose the:

• Principle or rule of conduct of the Code of Ethics or Standard(s) with which full conformance was not achieved;

• Reason(s) for nonconformance; and

• Impact of nonconformance on the engagement and the communicated engagement results.

2440 – Disseminating Results
The chief audit executive must communicate results to the appropriate parties.

Interpretation:

The chief audit executive or designee reviews and approves the final engagement communication before issuance and decides to whom and how it will be disseminated.

2440.A1 – The chief audit executive is responsible for communicating the final results to parties who can ensure that the results are given due consideration.

2440.A2 – If not otherwise mandated by legal, statutory, or regulatory requirements, prior to releasing results to parties outside the organization the chief audit executive must:

- Assess the potential risk to the organization;
- Consult with senior management and/or legal counsel as appropriate; and
- Control dissemination by restricting the use of the results.

2440.C1 – The chief audit executive is responsible for communicating the final results of consulting engagements to clients.

2440.C2 – During consulting engagements, governance, risk management, and control issues may be identified. Whenever these issues are significant to the organization, they must be communicated to senior management and the board.

2450 – Overall Opinions

When an overall opinion is issued, it must take into account the expectations of senior management, the board, and other stakeholders and must be supported by sufficient, reliable, relevant, and useful information.

Interpretation:
The communication will identify:

- *The scope, including the time period to which the opinion pertains;*
- *Scope limitations;*
- *Consideration of all related projects including the reliance on other assurance providers;*
- *The risk or control framework or other criteria used as a basis for the overall opinion; and*
- *The overall opinion, judgment, or conclusion reached.*

The reasons for an unfavorable overall opinion must be stated.

2500 – Monitoring Progress

The chief audit executive must establish and maintain a system to monitor the disposition of results communicated to management.

2500.A1 – The chief audit executive must establish a follow-up process to monitor and ensure that management actions have been effectively implemented or that senior management has accepted the risk of not taking action.

2500.C1 – The internal audit activity must monitor the disposition of results of consulting engagements to the extent agreed upon with the client.

2600 – Resolution of Senior Management's Acceptance of Risks

When the chief audit executive believes that senior management has accepted a level of residual risk that may be unacceptable to the organization, the chief audit executive must discuss the matter with senior management. If the decision regarding residual risk is not resolved, the chief audit executive must report the matter to the board for resolution.

Glossary

Add Value

The internal audit activity adds value to the organization (and its stakeholders) when it provides objective and relevant assurance, and contributes to the effectiveness and efficiency of governance, risk management, and control processes.

Adequate Control

Present if management has planned and organized (designed) in a manner that provides reasonable assurance that the organization's risks have been managed effectively and that the organization's goals and objectives will be achieved efficiently and economically.

Assurance Services

An objective examination of evidence for the purpose of providing an independent assessment on governance, risk management, and control processes for the organization. Examples may include financial, performance, compliance, system security, and due diligence engagements.

Board

A board is an organization's governing body, such as a board of directors, supervisory board, head of an agency or legislative body, board of governors or trustees of a nonprofit organization, or any other designated body of the organization, including the audit committee to whom the chief audit executive may functionally report.

Charter

The internal audit charter is a formal document that defines the internal audit activity's purpose, authority, and responsibility. The internal audit charter establishes the internal audit activity's position within the organization; authorizes access to records, personnel, and physical properties relevant to the performance of engagements; and defines the scope of internal audit activities.

Chief Audit Executive

Chief audit executive describes a person in a senior position responsible for effectively managing the internal audit activity in accordance with the internal audit charter and the Definition of Internal Auditing, the Code of Ethics, and the *Standards*. The chief audit executive or others reporting to the chief audit executive will have appropriate professional certifications and qualifications. The specific job title of the chief audit executive may vary across organizations.

Code of Ethics

The Code of Ethics of The Institute of Internal Auditors (IIA) are Principles relevant to the profession and practice of internal auditing, and Rules of Conduct that describe behavior expected of internal auditors. The Code of Ethics applies to both parties and entities that provide internal audit services.

The purpose of the Code of Ethics is to promote an ethical culture in the global profession of internal auditing.

Compliance
Adherence to policies, plans, procedures, laws, regulations, contracts, or other requirements.

Conflict of Interest
Any relationship that is, or appears to be, not in the best interest of the organization. A conflict of interest would prejudice an individual's ability to perform his or her duties and responsibilities objectively.

Consulting Services
Advisory and related client service activities, the nature and scope of which are agreed with the client, are intended to add value and improve an organization's governance, risk management, and control processes without the internal auditor assuming management responsibility. Examples include counsel, advice, facilitation, and training.

Control
Any action taken by management, the board, and other parties to manage risk and increase the likelihood that established objectives and goals will be achieved. Management plans, organizes, and directs the performance of sufficient actions to provide reasonable assurance that objectives and goals will be achieved.

Control Environment
The attitude and actions of the board and management regarding the importance of control within the organization. The control environment provides the discipline and structure for the achievement of the primary objectives of the system of internal control. The control environment includes the following elements:

- Integrity and ethical values.
- Management's philosophy and operating style.
- Organizational structure.
- Assignment of authority and responsibility.
- Human resource policies and practices.
- Competence of personnel.

Control Processes
The policies, procedures, and activities that are part of a control framework, designed to ensure that risks are contained within the risk tolerances established by the risk management process.

Engagement
A specific internal audit assignment, task, or review activity, such as an internal audit, control self-assessment review, fraud examination, or consultancy. An engagement may include multiple tasks or activities designed to accomplish a specific set of related objectives.

Engagement Objectives
Broad statements developed by internal auditors that define intended engagement accomplishments.

Engagement Work Program

A document that lists the procedures to be followed during an engagement, designed to achieve the engagement plan.

External Service Provider

A person or firm outside of the organization that has special knowledge, skill, and experience in a particular discipline.

Fraud

Any illegal act characterized by deceit, concealment, or violation of trust. These acts are not dependent upon the threat of violence or physical force. Frauds are perpetrated by parties and organizations to obtain money, property, or services; to avoid payment or loss of services; or to secure personal or business advantage.

Governance

The combination of processes and structures implemented by the board to inform, direct, manage, and monitor the activities of the organization toward the achievement of its objectives.

Impairment

Impairment to organizational independence and individual objectivity may include personal conflict of interest, scope limitations, restrictions on access to records, personnel, and properties, and resource limitations (funding).

Independence

The freedom from conditions that threaten the ability of the internal audit activity to carry out internal audit responsibilities in an unbiased manner.

Information Technology Controls

Controls that support business management and governance as well as provide general and technical controls over information technology infrastructures such as applications, information, infrastructure, and people.

Information Technology Governance

Consists of the leadership, organizational structures, and processes that ensure that the enterprise's information technology supports the organization's strategies and objectives.

Internal Audit Activity

A department, division, team of consultants, or other practitioner(s) that provides independent, objective assurance and consulting services designed to add value and improve an organization's operations. The internal audit activity helps an organization accomplish its objectives by bringing a systematic, disciplined approach to evaluate and improve the effectiveness of governance, risk management and control processes.

International Professional Practices Framework

The conceptual framework that organizes the authoritative guidance promulgated by The IIA. Authoritative Guidance is comprised of two categories – (1) mandatory and (2) strongly recommended.

Must

The *Standards* use the word "must" to specify an unconditional requirement.

Objectivity

An unbiased mental attitude that allows internal auditors to perform engagements in such a manner that they believe in their work product and that no quality compromises are made. Objectivity requires that internal auditors do not subordinate their judgment on audit matters to others.

Residual Risk

The risk remaining after management takes action to reduce the impact and likelihood of an adverse event, including control activities in responding to a risk.

Risk

The possibility of an event occurring that will have an impact on the achievement of objectives. Risk is measured in terms of impact and likelihood.

Risk Appetite

The level of risk that an organization is willing to accept.

Risk Management

A process to identify, assess, manage, and control potential events or situations to provide reasonable assurance regarding the achievement of the organization's objectives.

Should

The *Standards* use the word "should" where conformance is expected unless, when applying professional judgment, circumstances justify deviation.

Significance

The relative importance of a matter within the context in which it is being considered, including quantitative and qualitative factors, such as magnitude, nature, effect, relevance, and impact. Professional judgment assists internal auditors when evaluating the significance of matters within the context of the relevant objectives.

Standard

A professional pronouncement promulgated by the Internal Audit Standards Board that delineates the requirements for performing a broad range of internal audit activities, and for evaluating internal audit performance.

Technology-based Audit Techniques

Any automated audit tool, such as generalized audit software, test data generators, computerized audit programs, specialized audit utilities, and computer-assisted audit techniques (CAATs).

Appendix B

THE INSTITUTE OF INTERNAL AUDITORS' CODE OF ETHICS

Introduction to the Code of Ethics

The purpose of The Institute's Code of Ethics is to promote an ethical culture in the profession of internal auditing.

> *Internal auditing is an independent, objective assurance and consulting activity designed to add value and improve an organization's operations. It helps an organization accomplish its objectives by bringing a systematic, disciplined approach to evaluate and improve the effectiveness of risk management, control, and governance processes.*

A code of ethics is necessary and appropriate for the profession of internal auditing, founded as it is on the trust placed in its objective assurance about governance, risk management, and control.

The Institute's Code of Ethics extends beyond the Definition of Internal Auditing to include two essential components:

1. Principles that are relevant to the profession and practice of internal auditing;

2. Rules of Conduct that describe behavior norms expected of internal auditors. These rules are an aid to interpreting the Principles into practical applications and are intended to guide the ethical conduct of internal auditors.

"Internal auditors" refers to Institute members, recipients of or candidates for IIA professional certifications, and those who perform internal audit services within the Definition of Internal Auditing.

Applicability and Enforcement

This Code of Ethics applies to both entities and individuals that perform internal audit services.

For IIA members and recipients of or candidates for IIA professional certifications, breaches of the Code of Ethics will be evaluated and administered according to The Institute's Bylaws and Administrative Guidelines. The fact that a particular conduct is not mentioned in the Rules of Conduct does not prevent it from being unacceptable or discreditable, and therefore, the member, certification holder, or candidate can be liable for disciplinary action.

Principles

Internal auditors are expected to apply and uphold the following principles:

1. Integrity

The integrity of internal auditors establishes trust and thus provides the basis for reliance on their judgment.

2. Objectivity

Internal auditors exhibit the highest level of professional objectivity in gathering, evaluating, and communicating information about the activity or process being examined. Internal auditors make a balanced assessment of all the relevant circumstances and are not unduly influenced by their own interests or by others in forming judgments.

3. Confidentiality

Internal auditors respect the value and ownership of information they receive and do not disclose information without appropriate authority unless there is a legal or professional obligation to do so.

4. Competency

Internal auditors apply the knowledge, skills, and experience needed in the performance of internal audit services.

Rules of Conduct

1. Integrity
Internal auditors:
1.1. Shall perform their work with honesty, diligence, and responsibility.
1.2. Shall observe the law and make disclosures expected by the law and the profession.
1.3. Shall not knowingly be a party to any illegal activity, or engage in acts that are discreditable to the profession of internal auditing or to the organization.
1.4. Shall respect and contribute to the legitimate and ethical objectives of the organization.

2. Objectivity
Internal auditors:
2.1. Shall not participate in any activity or relationship that may impair or be presumed to impair their unbiased assessment. This participation includes those activities or relationships that may be in conflict with the interests of the organization.
2.2 Shall not accept anything that may impair or be presumed to impair their professional judgment.
2.3 Shall disclose all material facts known to them that, if not disclosed, may distort the reporting of activities under review.

3. Confidentiality

Internal auditors:

3.1 Shall be prudent in the use and protection of information acquired in the course of their duties.

3.2 Shall not use information for any personal gain or in any manner that would be contrary to the law or detrimental to the legitimate and ethical objectives of the organization.

4. Competency

Internal auditors:

4.1. Shall engage only in those services for which they have the necessary knowledge, skills, and experience.

4.2 Shall perform internal auditing services in accordance with the *International Standards for the Professional Practice of Internal Auditing*.

4.3 Shall continually improve their proficiency and the effectiveness and quality of their services.

COMPLIANCE CHECKLIST

The following questions were derived from the *International Standards for the Professional Practice of Internal Auditing* (*Standards*), including the Glossary that accompanies the *Standards*.

The Charter

1. Do we have a written charter?

2. Has senior management and the board or other governing body approved the charter recently?

3. Does it clearly describe internal auditing's purpose, authority, and responsibility?

4. Does it describe internal auditing's role in governance, risk management, and control processes?

5. Does it include adding value and improving the organization's operations as part of the responsibility of the function?

6. Does it establish the internal audit function at a level within the organization that allows the internal audit activity to fulfill its responsibilities?

7. Does the charter recognize the nature of the chief audit executive's functional reporting relationship with the board, including the board's role in:

    - Approving the internal audit charter?
    - Approving the risk-based internal audit plan?
    - Receiving communications from the CAE on the internal audit activity's performance relative to its plan?
    - Approving decisions regarding the appointment and removal of the CAE?
    - Making appropriate inquiries of management and the CAE to determine whether there are inappropriate scope or resource limitations?

8. Does it authorize access to records, personnel, and physical properties relevant to the performance of engagements?

9. Does it clearly describe the scope of internal audit activities?

10. Does it define the nature of consulting and assurance services to be provided to the organization?

11. Does it define the nature of assurances that are to be provided to parties outside the organization?

12. Have we reviewed the elements of our charter and considered whether or not they are consistent with the definition and requirements of internal auditing as presented in the Definition of Internal Auditing, the Code of Ethics, and the *Standards*?

13. Does our charter recognize the mandatory nature of the Definition of Internal Auditing, the Code of Ethics, and the *Standards*?

Independence and Objectivity

14. Is our internal audit activity organizationally independent?

15. Does the CAE report to a level with sufficient status in the organization that allows us to fulfill our responsibility without interference?

16. When providing assurance to third parties, such as senior management or the board, are we able to determine the scope of internal auditing, perform our work, and communicate the results without interference?

17. Are our internal auditors objective?

18. Do we value and require individual auditor objectivity as essential to effective internal audit services?

19. Do we refuse to make quality compromises or subordinate our judgment on audit matters to others?

20. Do we have a policy and procedure for disclosing apparent or actual impairments to independence and objectivity?

21. Do we make every effort to keep internal auditors from assessing operations for which they were previously responsible if the engagement is designed to provide assurance?

22. Do we require auditors to wait at least one year before providing assurance in areas for which they were previously responsible or, if that is not the case, are these potential impairments disclosed before accepting engagements?

23. Do we employ someone outside the audit department (a manager from another organizational area or the person to whom the CAE reports, for example) to oversee assurance engagements for functions over which the CAE has responsibility?

Proficiency and Due Professional Care

24. Do we know what knowledge, skills, and other competencies are necessary to fulfill our responsibilities?

25. Do we ensure that our audit staff, as individuals and as a function, possess these capabilities?

26. Do we have a method for and successful history of acquiring the necessary capabilities that we may lack?

27. Have we made sure that our audit methods and procedures are in line with other professional internal auditors?

28. Do we make continuing professional development a priority?

29. When performing assurance services, do we obtain advice and assistance if needed to perform the audit through guest auditors, rotation programs, or cosourcing?

30. When performing assurance services, are we able to evaluate the risk of fraud and the manner in which fraud risks are managed by the organization?

31. When performing assurance services, do we have sufficient knowledge of key information technology risk and controls?

32. When performing assurance services, do we exercise due professional care by considering the:

    • Extent of the work needed to achieve the engagement's objectives?
    • Relative complexity, materiality, or significance of matters to which assurance procedures are applied?
    • Adequacy and effectiveness of governance, risk management, and control processes?
    • The probability of significant errors, fraud, or noncompliance?
    • The cost of assurance in relation to potential benefits?

33. When performing assurance services, are we alert to any significant risks that might affect objectives, operations, or resources?

34. When performing assurance services, have we adequately considered the use of technology-based tools and other data analysis techniques (such as data mining)?

35. Do we recognize that due care does not imply infallibility and that assurance procedures alone, even when performed with due professional care, do not guarantee that all significant risks will be identified?

36. If we lack the knowledge, skills, or other competencies needed to perform all or part of a proposed consulting engagement, do we either decline the engagement or obtain competent advice and assistance?

37. Do we exercise due professional care in consulting engagements by considering the:

    • Needs and expectations of clients, including the nature, timing, and communication of engagement results?
    • Relative complexity and extent of work needed to achieve the engagement's objectives?
    • Cost of the consulting engagement in relation to potential benefits?

Quality Assurance

38. Do we have a quality assurance and improvement program in place?

39. Does it address each of the various types of engagements we perform and cover all aspects of the internal audit activity?

40. Does our quality assurance program help us add value and improve the organization's operations?

41. Does it measure our conformance with the *Standards*?

42. Do we conduct adequate ongoing monitoring of our performance as part of our internal quality program, including supervision, review, and measurement of internal audit activities?

43. Do we conduct periodic reviews, including conformance with the *Standards*, through self-assessment or by others in the organization with sufficient knowledge of internal auditing and the *Standards* as part of our internal quality program?

44. Does the CAE communicate the results of the internal quality program periodically to senior management and the board?

45. Does a qualified, independent review team from outside the organization conduct an external assessment of our activity once every five years?

46. Prior to the external review does the CAE discuss with the board the qualifications and independence of the external reviewer or review team, including any potential conflict of interest?

47. Does the external quality assessment team we select demonstrate through their experience the appropriate knowledge of internal auditing and the external assessment process?

48. Is the external quality assessment team we select appropriate for our organization's size, nature, sector or industry, and technical issues?

49. Does the CAE discuss with the board the potential need for external assessments more frequent than every five years?

50. Does the CAE communicate the results of the external review to senior management and the board?

51. Is our use of the phrase "conforms with the *International Standards for the Professional Practice of Internal Auditing*" justified by the quality assurance program's confirmation of our conformance with the *Standards*?

52. If the internal quality program or the external review note incidences of nonconformance with the Definition of Internal Auditing, the Code of Ethics, or the *Standards* that affect the overall scope or operation of the internal audit activity, do we disclose that information to senior management and the board?

The Chief Audit Executive

53. Is there someone defined within the organization or within its internal audit external service provider who is ultimately responsible for internal audit activities and serves as CAE?

54. If internal auditing is fully outsourced, has the external service provider clearly communicated that the organization has the responsibility for internal auditing, as demonstrated by actions including the organization obtaining an external quality assessment of internal auditing?

55. Does the CAE report to a level in the organization that allows us to fulfill our responsibilities without interference?

56. Does the CAE communicate and interact directly with the board?

57. Does the CAE periodically discuss the Definition of Internal Auditing, the Code of Ethics, and the *Standards* with senior management and the board?

58. Does the CAE confirm to the board, at least annually, the organizational independence of the internal audit department?

59. Does the CAE manage the internal auditing department so that it adds value to the organization?

60. Does the CAE ensure that our resources are appropriate, sufficient, and effectively deployed to achieve the audit plan?

61. If we lack the knowledge, skills, or other competencies needed to perform all or part of an assurance engagement, does the CAE obtain competent advice and assistance?

62. If we lack the knowledge, skills, or other competencies needed to perform all or part of a proposed consulting engagement, does the CAE either decline the engagement or obtain competent advice and assistance through guest auditor, rotation, or cosourcing options?

63. Has the CAE established policies and procedures for the internal audit activity?

64. Does the CAE provide for the sharing of information and the coordination of activities with other internal and external providers of assurance and consulting services to ensure appropriate coverage and minimize duplication of efforts?

65. Has the CAE developed and does he or she continue to maintain a quality assurance and improvement program?

66. Does the CAE communicate the results of the internal quality program periodically to senior management and the board?

67. Does the CAE communicate the results of the external review to senior management and the board?

68. Are audit plans regarding assurance engagements based upon a documented annual risk assessment? Is that risk assessment based upon input from senior management and the board?

69. Does the CAE consider proposed consulting engagements based on the engagements' potential to improve management of risks, add value, and improve the organization's operations?

70. Are accepted consulting engagements included in the audit plan?

71. Does the CAE communicate our plans and resource requirements, including significant interim changes and the impact of resource limitations, to senior management and the board for review and approval?

72. Does the CAE report periodically to senior management and the board on our purpose, authority, responsibility, and performance relative to our plan? Do these reports also include significant risk exposures and control issues, including fraud risks, governance issues, and other matters needed or requested by senior management and the board?

73. Does the CAE disseminate audit engagement results to the appropriate individuals?

74. If a final communication contains a significant error or omission, does the CAE communicate corrected information to all individuals who received the original communication?

75. When disseminating the final results of an assurance engagement, does the CAE make sure he or she communicates those results to individuals who can ensure they are given due consideration?

76. Does the CAE communicate the final results of consulting engagements to the client?

77. If significant governance, risk management, and control issues are identified during a consulting engagement, does the CAE communicate them to senior management and the board?

78. In instances where the CAE believes that senior management has accepted a level of residual risk that is unacceptable to the organization, does the CAE discuss the matter with senior management? If the decision regarding residual risk is not resolved, does the CAE report the matter to the board for resolution?

79. Has the CAE established and does he or she continue to maintain a system to monitor the disposition of results communicated to management?

80. Has the CAE developed a follow-up process for assurance engagements that monitors and ensures that management actions have been effectively implemented or that senior management has accepted the risk of not taking action?

81. Has the CAE developed a follow-up process that allows the disposition of consulting engagement results to be monitored to the extent agreed upon with the client?

82. If the CAE has responsibility for an area that is the subject of an assurance engagement, is the engagement overseen by someone outside the internal audit activity?

83. Does the CAE control access to assurance engagement records? Does the CAE obtain the approval of senior management and/or legal counsel prior to releasing such records to external parties?

84. Has the CAE developed retention requirements for assurance engagement records? Are these requirements consistent with organizational guidelines and any pertinent regulatory or other requirements?

85. Has the CAE developed policies governing the custody and retention of consulting engagement records, as well as their release to internal and external parties? Are these policies consistent with the organization's guidelines and any pertinent regulatory or other requirements?

86. If internal auditing is fully outsourced and the CAE role is primarily being performed by the external service provider:

    - Has the provider clearly made the organization aware that the organization has the responsibility for maintaining an effective internal audit activity?
    - Has an internal audit quality assurance and improvement program, with both internal quality practices and periodic external quality assessments, been put in place to assess conformance with the Definition of Internal Auditing, the Code of Ethics, and the *Standards*?

Nature of Audit Work

87. Do we use a systematic and disciplined approach in all types of engagements?

88. Do we contribute to the organization's governance process by evaluating and improving the processes for:

    - Promoting appropriate ethics and values within the organization?
    - Ensuring effective organizational performance management and accountability?
    - Communicating risk and control information to appropriate areas of the organization?
    - Coordinating the activities of and communicating information among the board, external and internal auditors, and management?

89. As part of our effort to provide assurance to senior management and the board, do we evaluate the design, implementation, and effectiveness of the organization's ethics program?

90. Do we assess whether the information technology governance of the organization supports the organization's strategies and objectives?

91. Do we evaluate the effectiveness of the organization's risk management processes, whether through a specific engagement or through multiple engagements?

92. Do we contribute to the improvement of risk management processes?

93. Do we evaluate the adequacy and effectiveness of controls in responding to risks within the organization's governance, operations, and information systems, including risks to the reliability and integrity of financial and operational information; the effectiveness and efficiency of operations; the safeguarding of assets; and the compliance with laws, regulations, and contracts?

94. In consulting engagements, do we address risk consistent with the engagement's objectives? Are we also alert to the existence of significant control issues?

95. Do we incorporate knowledge of risks gained from consulting engagements into evaluation of the organization's control processes?

96. De we evaluate the potential for the occurrence of fraud and how the organization manages fraud risk? Do we explicitly perform a fraud risk assessment?

97. Do we help maintain effective controls by evaluating their effectiveness and efficiency in all types of engagements?

98. Do we promote continuous improvement of internal controls in all our engagements?

99. During consulting engagements, do we address controls consistent with the engagement's objectives? Are we also alert to significant control issues?

100. Do we incorporate knowledge of controls gained from consulting engagements evaluation of the organization's control processes?

101. Do we provide assurance to senior management and the board by evaluating the adequacy and effectiveness of controls encompassing the organization's governance, operations, and information systems?

102. Do our assurance engagements address whether controls ensure the reliability and integrity of financial and operational information; the effectiveness and efficiency of operations and programs; the safeguarding of assets; and compliance with laws, regulations, policies, procedures, and contracts?

Engagement Planning

103. Do we develop and document a plan for each engagement?

104. In developing our plans, do we consider:

- The objectives of the activity being reviewed?
- The means by which the activity controls its performance relative to meeting its objectives?
- The significant risks to the activity, its objectives, its resources, and its operations?
- The means by which the potential impact of risk is kept to an acceptable level?
- The adequacy and effectiveness of the activity's risk management and control processes compared to a relevant control framework or model?
- The opportunities for making significant improvements to the activity's risk management and control processes?

105. Do our engagement objectives address the governance, risk management, and control processes associated with the activities under review?

106. When planning an assurance engagement, do we perform a preliminary assessment of risks, identifying and assessing risks relevant to the activity to be reviewed?

107. Do our objectives for the assurance engagement reflect the results of this risk assessment?

108. When planning an assurance engagement for parties outside the organization, do we establish a written understanding with them related to the engagement?

109. When developing objectives for an assurance engagement, do we consider the probability of significant errors, fraud, noncompliance, and other exposures?

110. When planning a consulting engagement, do we establish an understanding with the client about objectives, scope, respective responsibilities, and other client expectations? If the engagement is a significant one, do we document this understanding?

111. If significant consulting opportunities arise during an assurance engagement, is a specific written understanding as to the objectives, scope, respective responsibilities reached and the results of the consulting engagement communicated in accordance with consulting standards?

112. Do the objectives of our consulting engagements address governance, risk management, and control processes to the extent agreed upon with the client?

113. Do we ensure that consulting engagement objectives are consistent with the organization's values, strategies, and objectives?

114. Are the scope statements of our engagements sufficient to satisfy the stated objectives?

115. Do we make sure that the scope of any assurance engagement includes consideration of relevant systems, records, personnel, and physical properties, including those under the control of third parties?

116. Do we ensure that the scope of our consulting engagements is sufficient to address the agreed-upon objectives?

117. If we develop reservations about the scope of a consulting engagement, do we discuss these reservations with the client to determine whether to continue with the engagement?

118. Do we determine appropriate and sufficient resources to achieve engagement objectives?

119. Is this determination based upon an evaluation of the nature and complexity of each engagement, the time constraints associated with the engagement, and the resources available at the time of the engagement?

120. Do we develop and document work programs that achieve the objectives of engagements?

121. Do our work programs for assurance engagements establish the procedures for identifying, analyzing, evaluating, and documenting information during the engagement?

122. Are our work programs for assurance engagements approved prior to the commencement of audit work, and are any adjustments approved promptly?

123. Do our work programs for consulting engagements vary in form and content depending upon the nature of the engagement?

Performing the Engagement

124. Do we identify, analyze, evaluate, and document sufficient information to achieve the engagement's objectives?

125. Is the information we identify sufficient, reliable, relevant, and useful to the achievement of the engagement's objectives?

126. Are conclusions and engagement results based on appropriate analyses and evaluations?

127. Do we document relevant information to support the conclusions and engagement results?

128. Is there proper supervision of each engagement so that objectives are achieved, quality is assured, and staff is developed?

Communicating Results

129. Do we communicate engagement results promptly?

130. Do our engagement communications include the engagement's objectives and scope, as well as applicable conclusions, recommendations, and action plans?

131. Does the level of assurance we provide on individual engagements (such as opinions, ratings, or conclusions) align with the form of communications key stakeholders expect?

132. In communications resulting from assurance engagements, do we include our opinion only when we have sufficient, reliable, relevant, and useful support?

133. Does our communication of the progress and results of consulting engagements vary in form and content depending upon the nature of the engagement and the needs of the client?

134. When communicating the results of assurance work, do we acknowledge satisfactory performance?

135. When communicating results to parties outside the organization, does the communication include limitations on distributions and use of the results?

136. When communicating results to parties outside the organization, have we assessed the potential risk of such communications to the organization and consulted with management and legal counsel?

137. Do we provide our customers with quality communications, meaning that the communication of engagement results is:

- Accurate?
- Objective?
- Clear?
- Concise?
- Constructive?
- Complete?
- Timely?

138. When we are unable to conform fully with the Definition of Internal Auditing, the Code of Ethics, or the *Standards,* and the nonconformance impacts a specific engagement, do we disclose the:

- Principle or rule of conduct in the Code of Ethics or Standard(s) with which full conformance was not achieved;
- The reasons for nonconformance; and
- The impact of nonconformance on the engagement and the communicated engagement results?

139. If an overall opinion is issued:

- Does it consider key stakeholder expectations on form of reporting?
- Is it supported by sufficient information needed to express such an opinion?
- Is it supported by reliable, relevant, and useful information?

140. If an overall opinion is issued, does the communication include:

- The scope, including the time period?
- Scope limitations?
- Consideration of all related projects, including reliance on other assurance providers?
- The risk or control framework or other criteria used as a basis for the overall opinion?
- The overall opinion, judgment, or conclusion?
- The reasons for any unfavorable overall opinion?

Appendix D

TOPICAL INDEX TO THE POSITION PAPERS, PRACTICE ADVISORIES, AND PRACTICE GUIDES

The following is a categorized list of Position Papers, Practice Advisories (PAs), and Practice Guides (PGs) developed as of publication date. IIA members may access this guidance by visiting The IIA's web site at www.theiia.org.

Assumption of Nonaudit Duties
PA 1130.A1-1: Assessing Operations for Which Internal Auditors Were Previously Responsible
PA 1130.A2-1: Internal Audit's Responsibility for Other (Non-audit) Functions

Audit Charter
PA 1000-1: Internal Audit Charter
PA 1130.A2-1: Internal Audit's Responsibility for Other (Non-audit) Functions
PA 1310-1: Requirements of the Quality Assurance and Improvement Program
PA 2500.A1-1: Follow-up Process
PG: CAEs — Appointment, Performance Evaluation, and Termination

Board & Senior Management Reporting
PA 1000-1: Internal Audit Charter
PA 1111-1: Board Interaction
PA 1130-1: Impairment to Independence or Objectivity
PA 1311-1: Internal Assessments
PA 1312-1: External Assessments
PA 1312-2: External Assessments-Self-assessment with Independent Validation
PA 2020-1: Communication and Approval
PA 2050-1: Coordination
PA 2060-1: Reporting to Senior Management and the Board
PA 2130-1: Assessing the Adequacy of Control Processes
PA 2440.A2-1: Communications Outside the Organization
PG: Formulating and Expressing Internal Audit Opinions
PG: CAEs — Appointment, Performance Evaluation, and Termination

CAE Responsibilities
PA 1000-1: Internal Audit Charter
PA 1110-1: Organizational Independence
PA 1111-1: Board Interaction
PA 2040-1: Policies and Procedures
PA 2050-1: Coordination

PA 2050-2: Assurance Maps
PA 2050-3: Relying on the Work of Other Assurance Providers
PA 2060-1: Reporting to Senior Management and the Board
PA 2120-2: Managing the Risk of the Internal Audit Activity
PA 2200-1: Engagement Planning
PA 2330-1: Documenting Information
PA 2330.A1-1: Control of Engagement Records
PA 2330.A2-1: Retention of Records
PA 2340-1: Engagement Supervision
PA 2410-1: Communication Criteria
PA 2440-1: Disseminating Results
PA 2440.A2-1: Communications Outside the Organization
PA 2500-1: Monitoring Progress
PA 2500.A1-1: Follow-up Process
PG: Measuring Internal Audit Effectiveness and Efficiency
PG: CAEs — Appointment, Performance Evaluation, and Termination

Compliance with the *Standards*

PA 1311-1: Internal Assessments
PA 1312-1: External Assessments
PA 1312-2: External Assessments: Self-assessment With Independent Validation
PA 1321-1: Use of "Conforms with the *International Standards for the Professional Practice of Internal Auditing*"
PA 2120-2: Managing the Risk of the Internal Audit Activity

Disclosures

PA 1130-1: Impairment to Independence or Objectivity
PA 1130.A1-1: Assessing Operations for Which Internal Auditors Were Previously Responsible
PA 1130.A2-1: Internal Audit's Responsibility for Other (Non-audit) Functions

Engagement Communications

PA 1130.A1-1: Assessing Operations for Which Internal Auditors Were Previously Responsible
PA 1130.A2-1: Internal Audit's Responsibility for Other (Non-audit) Functions
PA 1210.A1-1: Obtaining External Service Providers to Support or Complement the Internal Audit Activity
PA 2050-1: Coordination
PA 2340-1: Engagement Supervision
PA 2400-1: Legal Considerations in Communicating Results
PA 2410-1: Communication Criteria
PA 2420-1: Quality of Communications
PA 2440-1: Disseminating Results
PA 2440-2: Communicating Sensitive Information Within and Outside the Chain of Command
PA 2440.A2-1: Communications Outside the Organization
PG: Formulating and Expressing Internal Audit Opinions

Engagement Performance

PA 1220-1: Due Professional Care
PA 2300-1: Use of Personal Information in Conducting Engagements
PA 2320-1: Analytical Procedures
PA 2330-1: Documenting Information
PA 2340-1: Engagement Supervision
PG: Auditing Executive Compensation and Benefits
PG: Evaluating Corporate Social Responsibility/Sustainable Development

Engagement Planning & Scope

PA 1130-1: Impairment to Independence or Objectivity
PA 2200-1: Engagement Planning
PA 2200-2: Using a Top-down, Risk-based Approach to Identify the Controls to be Assessed in an Internal Audit Engagement
PA 2210-1: Engagement Objectives
PA 2210.A1-1: Risk Assessment in Engagement Planning
PA 2230-1: Engagement Resource Allocation
PA 2240-1: Engagement Work Program
PA 2320-1: Analytical Procedures
PA 2340-1: Engagement Supervision
PG: Formulating and Expressing Internal Audit Opinions
PG: Auditing Executive Compensation and Benefits
PG: Evaluating Corporate Social Responsibility/Sustainable Development

Engagement Workpapers

PA 2300-1: Use of Personal Information in Conducting Engagements
PA 2330-1: Documenting Information
PA 2330.A1-1: Control of Engagement Records
PA 2330.A1-2: Granting Access to Engagement Records
PA 2330.A2-1: Retention of Records
PA 2340-1: Engagement Supervision

Fraud

PA 1210-1: Proficiency
PA 2400-1: Legal Considerations in Communicating Results
PA 2440-2: Communicating Sensitive Information Within and Outside the Chain of Command
PG: Internal Auditing and Fraud
PG:*GTAG 13: Fraud Prevention and Detection in an Automated World*

Governance

PA 2110-1: Governance: Definition
PA 2110-2: Governance: Relationship With Risk and Control
PA 2110-3: Governance: Assessments
PG: *GTAG 15: Information Security Governance*

Independence & Objectivity

PA 1110-1: Organizational Independence

PA 1111-1: Board Interaction

PA 1120-1: Individual Objectivity

PA 1130-1: Impairment to Independence or Objectivity

PA 1130.A1-1: Assessing Operations for Which Internal Auditors Were Previously Responsible

PA 1130.A2-1: Internal Audit's Responsibility for Other (Non-audit) Functions

PA 1210.A1-1: Obtaining External Service Providers to Support or Complement the Internal Audit Activity

Information Technology

PA 2130.A1-1: Information Reliability and Integrity

PA 2130.A1-2: Evaluating an Organization's Privacy Framework

PG: Global Technology Audit Guides (GTAG):

- *GTAG 1: Information Technology Controls*
- *GTAG 2: Change and Patch Management Controls: Critical for Organizational Success*
- *GTAG 3: Continuous Auditing: Implications for Assurance, Monitoring, and Risk Management*
- *GTAG 4: Management of IT Auditing*
- *GTAG 5: Managing and Auditing Privacy Risks*
- *GTAG 6: Managing and Auditing IT Vulnerabilities*
- *GTAG 7: Information Technology Outsourcing*
- *GTAG 8: Auditing Application Controls*
- *GTAG 9: Identity and Access Management*
- *GTAG 10: Business Continuity Management*
- *GTAG 11: Developing the IT Audit Plan*
- *GTAG 12: Auditing IT Projects*
- *GTAG 13: Fraud Prevention and Detection in an Automated World*
- *GTAG 14: Auditing User-developed Applications*
- *GTAG 15: Information Security Governance*

PG: Guide to the Assessment of IT Risk (GAIT):

- The GAIT Methodology
- GAIT for IT General Control Deficiency Assessment
- GAIT for Business and IT Risk (GAIT-R)
- Case Studies Using GAIT-R to Scope PCI Compliance

Internal Control

PA 2110-2: Governance: Relationship With Risk and Control

PA 2130-1: Assessing the Adequacy of Control Processes

PA 2130.A1-1: Information Reliability and Integrity

PA 2130.A1-2: Evaluating an Organization's Privacy Framework

Outsourcing or Cosourcing

Position Paper: The Role of Internal Auditing in Resourcing the Internal Audit Activity

PA 1130.A2-1: Internal Audit's Responsibility for Other (Non-audit) Functions
PA 1210.A1-1: Obtaining External Service Providers to Support or Complement the Internal Audit Activity
PA 2050-3: Relying on the Work of Other Assurance Providers

Proficiency and Due Care

PA 1200-1: Proficiency and Due Professional Care
PA 1210-1: Proficiency
PA 1210.A1-1: Obtaining External Service Providers to Support or Complement the Internal Audit Activity
PA 1220-1: Due Professional Care
PA 1230-1: Continuing Professional Development
PA 2050-3: Relying on the Work of Other Assurance Providers
PA 2300-1: Use of Personal Information in Conducting Engagements
PA 2340-1: Engagement Supervision

Quality Assurance and Improvement Program

PA 1300-1: Quality Assurance and Improvement Program
PA 1310-1: Requirements of the Quality Assurance and Improvement Program
PA 1311-1: Internal Assessments
PA 1312-1: External Assessments
PA 1312-2: External Assessments: Self-assessment With Independent Validation
PA 1321-1: Use of "Conforms with the *International Standards for the Professional Practice of Internal Auditing*"
PA 2050-3: Relying on the Work of Other Assurance Providers
PA 2120-2: Managing the Risk of the Internal Audit Activity
PG: Measuring Internal Audit Effectiveness and Efficiency

Resource Management

Position Paper: The Role of Internal Auditing in Resourcing the Internal Audit Activity
PA 1130.A1-1: Assessing Operations for Which Internal Auditors Were Previously Responsible
PA 1210.A1-1: Obtaining External Service Providers to Support or Complement the Internal Audit Activity
PA 2030-1: Resource Management
PA 2050-2: Assurance Maps
PA 2050-3: Relying on the Work of Other Assurance Providers
PA 2230-1: Engagement Resource Allocation

Risk-based Planning

PA 2010-1: Linking the Audit Plan to Risk and Exposures

PA 2020-1: Communication and Approval

PA 2200-2: Using a Top-down, Risk-based Approach to Identify the Controls to be Assessed in an Internal Audit Engagement

PA 2210.A1-1: Risk Assessment in Engagement Planning

Risk Management & Assessment

Position Paper: The Role of Internal Auditing in Enterprise Risk Management

PA 2010-1: Linking the Audit Plan to Risk and Exposure

PA 2050-2: Assurance Maps

PA 2110-2: Governance: Relationship With Risk and Control

PA 2120-1: Assessing the Adequacy of Risk Management Processes

PA 2120-2: Managing the Risk of the Internal Audit Activity

PA 2210.A1-1: Risk Assessment in Engagement Planning

PG: Assessing the Adequacy of Risk Management

Appendix E

SUGGESTED READINGS/ADDITIONAL RESOURCES

The Professional Practices Framework (the Definition and *Standards*)

O'Regan, David, "Standards for the Small Shop," *Internal Auditor* (February 2011), pp. 21–23.

Cain, Jackie, "Developing the Standards," *Internal Auditing (UK)* (June 2008), pp. 38-41.

A Vision for the Future: Guiding the Internal Audit Profession to Excellence – Report from The IIA's Vision for the Future Task Force by The Institute of Internal Auditors (Altamonte Springs, FL: The Institute of Internal Auditors, 2007).

Fraser, Bruce W., "Roland DeMeulder: Setting the Standard," *Internal Auditor* (April 2005), pp. 40–43.

Rittenberg, Larry E., "A Guide for the Future," *Internal Auditor* (June 2001), pp. 63–67.

A Vision for the Future: Professional Practices Framework for Internal Auditing (Altamonte Springs, FL: The Institute of Internal Auditors, 1999).

Assurance

Parkinson, Michael, "A Strategy for Providing Assurance," *Internal Auditor* (December 2004), pp. 63–68.

Anderson, Urton, "Assurance and Consulting Services," *Research Opportunities in Internal Auditing* (Altamonte Springs, FL: The Institute of Internal Auditors Research Foundation, 2003), pp. 97–129.

Atwater, Geoffrey, "Culture of Assurance," *Internal Auditor* (June 2001), pp. 56–61.

Gray, Glen L., and Maryann Jacobi Gray, *Assurance Services within the Audit Profession* (Altamonte Springs, FL: The Institute of Internal Auditors Research Foundation, 2000).

Leech, Tim, "The Next Wave in Assurance Thinking," *Internal Auditor* (August 2000), pp. 66–71.

Consulting

Head, Michael J., Kurt F. Reding, and Cris Riddle, "Blended Engagements," *Internal Auditor* (October 2010), pp. 40–44.

White, S., "The Auditor as Internal Consultant," *Internal Auditor* (February 2007), pp. 60–64.

Reding, Kurt F., Paul J. Sobel, Urton L. Anderson, Michael J. Head, Sridhar Ramamoorti, Mark Salamasick, and Chris Riddle, *Internal Auditing: Assurance and Consulting Services, 2nd Edition* (Altamonte Springs, FL: The Institute of Internal Auditors Research Foundation, 2009), Chapter 15.

Berk, Jeffrey A., "Change Champions," *Internal Auditor* (April 2006), pp. 64–68.

Anderson, Urton, "Assurance and Consulting Services," *Research Opportunities in Internal Auditing* (Altamonte Springs, FL: The Institute of Internal Auditors Research Foundation, 2003), pp. 97–129.

Roth, James, *Adding Value: Seven Roads to Success* (Altamonte Springs, FL: The Institute of Internal Auditors Research Foundation, 2002).

"Partnership Auditing: A Fine Line," published in *Audit Wire*, January 1999.

Frigo, Mark L., *Providing Benchmarking Services for Internal Auditing Clients* (Altamonte Springs, FL: The Institute of Internal Auditors Research Foundation, 1997).

Independence and Objectivity

Internal Audit Reporting Relationships: Serving Two Masters (Altamonte Springs, FL: The Institute of Internal Auditors Research Foundation, 2003).

Mutchler, Jane, *Independence and Objectivity: A Framework for Internal Auditors* (Altamonte Springs, FL: The Institute of Internal Auditors Research Foundation, 2001).

"Preserving Objectivity," published in *Audit Wire*, July 2000.

Proficiency and Professionalism

Bailey, James A., CBOK Report II: *Core Competencies for Today's Internal Auditor* (Altamonte Springs, FL: The Institute of Internal Auditors Research Foundation, 2010).

A Global Summary of the Common Body of Knowledge (CBOK) (Altamonte Springs, FL: The Institute of Internal Auditors Research Foundation, 2007).

Applegate, Dennis, "Training New Auditors," *Internal Auditor* (April 2004), pp. 55–73.

Reding, Kurt F., et al., "Benchmarking Against CFIA," *Internal Auditor* (August 2000), pp. 41–46.

Proficiency Requirements for Comprehensive Auditing — A Guide for Practitioners (Ottawa: Canadian Comprehensive Auditing Foundation, 1998).

The Competency Framework for Internal Auditing (Altamonte Springs, FL: The Institute of Internal Auditors Research Foundation, 1998).

Quality Assurance and Effectiveness

Maximizing Internal Audit: A Ten Step Imperative for Thriving in a Challenging Economy (PricewaterhouseCoopers, 2010).

MacRae, Elizabeth, "A Framework for Audit Evolution," *Internal Auditor* (February 2010), pp. 68–69.

The Quality Assessment Manual, 6th Edition (Altamonte Springs, FL: The Institute of Internal Auditors Research Foundation, 2009).

Fraser, John, and Hugh Lindsay, "20 Questions Directors Should Ask About Internal Audit" (The Canadian Institute of Chartered Accountants, August 2004).

Marks, Norman, "How Much Is Enough?" *Internal Auditor* (February 2000), pp. 28–34.

Ziegenfuss, Douglas E., "Measuring Performance," *Internal Auditor* (February 2000), pp. 36–40.

Salierno, David, "The Right Measures," *Internal Auditor* (February 2000), pp. 41–44.

The CAE

Chambers, Richard F., Charles B. Eldridge, and Paula Park, *Licensed to Lead: Seven Personal Attributes that Maximize the Impact of the Most Successful Chief Audit Executives* (Korn Ferry Institute and The Institute of Internal Auditors, 2010).

Reding, Kurt F., Paul J. Sobel, Urton L. Anderson, Michael J. Head, Sridhar Ramamoorti, Mark Salamasick, and Cris Riddle, *Internal Auditing: Assurance and Consulting Services, 2ⁿᵈ Edition* (Altamonte Springs, FL: The Institute of Internal Auditors Research Foundation, 2009), Chapter 9.

Thomas, Archie, Essentials: Internal Auditing Operations Manual (Altamonte Springs, FL: The Institute of Internal Auditors Research Foundation, 2007).

Cangemi, Michael P., and Tommie Singleton, *Managing the Audit Function: A Corporate Audit Department Procedures Guide, 3rd Edition* (Hoboken, NJ: John Wiley and Sons, Inc., 2003).

CAE's Role In:

Adding Value

MacRae, Elizabeth, "A Framework for Audit Evolution," *Internal Auditor* (February 2010), pp. 68–69.

Business Upheaval: Internal Audit Weighs Its Role Amid the Recession and Evolving Enterprise Risks, State of the Internal Audit Profession Study (PricewaterhouseCoopers LLP, 2009).

Internal Audit 2012: A Study Examining the Future of Internal Auditing and the Potential Decline of a Controls-centric Approach (PricewaterhouseCoopers LLP, 2007).

Best Practices in Audit Committee Oversight of Internal Audit (Moody's Investor Services, October 2006).

Roth, James, *Adding Value: Seven Roads to Success* (Altamonte Springs, FL: The Institute of Internal Auditors Research Foundation, 2002).

Roth, James, *Best Practices: Value-added Approaches of Four Innovative Auditing Departments* (Altamonte Springs, FL: The Institute of Internal Auditors, June 2000).

Resource Management and Outsourcing

Anderson, Urton, Margaret Christ, Karla Johnstone, and Larry Rittenberg, *Effective Sizing of Internal Audit Departments* (Altamonte Springs, FL: The Institute of Internal Auditors Research Foundation, 2010).

Figg, Jonathan, "Outsourcing — A Runaway Train," *Internal Auditor* (June 2000), pp. 48–55.

Rittenberg, Larry, et al., "The Outsourcing Phenomenon," *Internal Auditor* (April 1999), pp. 42–46.

Widener, S., and F. Selto, "Management Control Systems and Boundaries of the Firm: Why do Firms Outsource Internal Auditing Activities?" *Journal of Management Accounting Research* (Vol. XI, 1999), pp. 45–73.

Rittenberg, Larry, *The Outsourcing Dilemma: What's Best for Internal Auditing* (Altamonte Springs, FL: The Institute of Internal Auditors Research Foundation, 1997).

Communication with the Board and Senior Management

Bromilow, Catherine L., Barbara L. Berlin, and Richard J. Anderson, "Stepping Up," *Internal Auditor* (December 2005), pp. 52–57.

Jackson, Russell A., "Roger Raber: In Praise of Independent Insiders," *Internal Auditor* (June 2005), pp. 68–71.

"Audit Committee Briefing . . . Internal Audit Standards: Why They Matter" (Altamonte Springs, FL: The Institute of Internal Auditors, 2005).

Ridley, Anthony J., "An Audit Committee Event Matrix," *Internal Auditor* (April 2000), pp. 52–56.

Governance

http://www.ecgi.org/codes/all_codes.php. Website providing a comprehensive listing of, and links to, sites containing corporate governance codes, principles of corporate governance, and corporate governance reforms.

www.calpers-governance.org. Site for viewing the governance principles promulgated by The California Public Employees' Retirement System, which has long been a leader in the corporate governance movement.

Report of the NACD Blue Ribbon Commission on The Audit Committee (Washington, D.C.: National Association of Corporate Directors, 2010).

Principles for Enhancing Corporate Governance, Basel Committee on Banking Supervision (Bank for International Settlements, October 2010).

Preparation, Perseverance, Payoff: Implementing a Combined Assurance Approach in the Era of King III (PricewaterhouseCoopers, 2010).

UK Corporate Governance Code (Financial Reporting Council, 2010).

Third King Report on Governance for South Africa – 2009 (Johannesburg: Institute of Directors in South Africa, 2009).

Risk Governance: Balancing Risk and Reward (Report of the NACD Blue Ribbon Commission, 2009).

Reding, Kurt F., Paul J. Sobel, Urton L. Anderson, Michael J. Head, Sridhar Ramamoorti, Mark Salamasick, and Cris Riddle, *Internal Auditing: Assurance and Consulting Services, 2nd Edition* (Altamonte Springs, FL: The Institute of Internal Auditors Research Foundation, 2009), Chapter 3.

Cutler, Sally, *Audit Committee Reporting: A Guide for Internal Auditing Success* (Altamonte Springs, FL: The Institute of Internal Auditors Research Foundation, 2009).

Code of Professional Ethics for Compliance and Ethics Professionals (The Society of Corporate Compliance and Ethics, 2007).

Corporate Governance Handbook 2005: Developments in Best Practices, Compliance, and Legal Standards (The Conference Board, 2005). www.conference-board.org.

http://www.tiaa-cref.org/pubs/pdf/governance_policy.pdf. The TIAA-CREF Policy Statement on Corporate Governance, 2004.

The Role of Internal Audit in Corporate Governance and Management (RMIT University, The Institute of Internal Auditors Research Foundation, and The Institute of Internal Auditors Australia, 2003).

Risk Management

ISO 31000, Risk Management: Principles and Guidelines, International Organization for Standardization, 2009.

AS/NZS ISO 31000:2009, Standards Australia, 2009.

Frigo, Mark, and Dick Anderson, *Embracing Enterprise Risk Management: Practical Approaches for Getting Started* (Committee of Sponsoring Organizations of the Treadway Commission [COSO]), 2010.

Risk Management Lessons from the Global Financial Crisis of 2008 (Senior Supervisors Group, October 2009).

Clayton, Daniel, "A Risk-centric Approach that Works," *Internal Auditor* (February 2009), pp. 35–39.

Reding, Kurt F., Paul J. Sobel, Urton L. Anderson, Michael J. Head, Sridhar Ramamoorti, Mark Salamasick, and Cris Riddle, *Internal Auditing: Assurance and Consulting Services, 2nd Edition* (Altamonte Springs, FL: The Institute of Internal Auditors Research Foundation, 2009), Chapters 4 and 5.

Sobel, Paul, *Auditor's Risk Management Guide: Integrating Auditing and ERM* (Chicago, IL: CCH Inc., 2007).

Chambers, R., and R. Jacobs, "Assessing Political Risk," *Internal Auditor* (August 2007), pp. 58–64.

Sobel, Paul, "Building on Section 404," *Internal Auditor* (April 2006), pp. 38–44.

Australian-New Zealand Standard HB 158-2006. Delivering Assurance Based on AS/NZS 4360:2004 Risk Management, 2006, www.standards.org.au.

Beumer, Hans, "A Risk Oriented Approach," *Internal Auditor* (February 2006), pp. 72–76.

Gramling, Audrey A., and Patricia M. Meyers, "Internal Auditing's Role in ERM," *Internal Auditor* (April 2006), pp. 52–58.

Beasley, Mark S., Richard Clune, and Dana R. Hermanson, "ERM: A Status Report," *Internal Auditor* (February 2005), pp. 67–72.

Enterprise Risk Management – Integrated Framework, COSO and PricewaterhouseCoopers LLP, September 2004.

"The Role of Internal Auditing in Enterprise-wide Risk Management" (The Institute of Internal Auditors UK and Ireland, September 2004).

"Recognize and Manage Risk," by The Group of 100, Melbourne Australia, 2003, www.group100.com.au.

Miccolis, Jerry A., Kevin Hively, and Brian W. Merkley, *Enterprise Risk Management — Trends and Emerging Practices* (Altamonte Springs, FL: The Institute of Internal Auditors Research Foundation, 2001).

Aerts, Luc, "A Framework for Managing Operational Risk," *Internal Auditor* (August 2001), pp. 53–59.

Understanding Enterprise Risk Management (KPMG, LLP, 2001).

Lemant, Olivier, "Risk as a Tripod," *Internal Auditor* (June 2001), pp. 39–43.

McNamee, David, "Targeting Business Risk," *Internal Auditor* (October 2000), pp. 46–51.

DeLoach, James, *Enterprise-wide Risk Management: Strategies for Linking Risk and Opportunity* (London: Financial Times/Prentice Hall, 2000).

McNamee, David, "Risk-Based Auditing," *Internal Auditor* (August 1997), pp. 22–27.

Control

Guidance on Monitoring Internal Control Systems, COSO, 2009.

Reding, Kurt F., Paul J. Sobel, Urton L. Anderson, Michael J. Head, Sridhar Ramamoorti, Mark Salamasick, and Chris Riddle, *Internal Auditing: Assurance and Consulting Services, 2ⁿᵈ Edition* (Altamonte Springs, FL: The Institute of Internal Auditors Research Foundation, 2009), Chapter 6 and for entity-level control assessment – Supplemental Case 1.

Internal Control over Financial Reporting — Guidance for Smaller Public Companies, COSO, 2006.

Rittenberg, Larry, "There Is No Shortcut to Good Controls," *Internal Auditor* (August 2005), pp. 62–67.

Perry, William E., and H.C. "Pete" Warner, "A Quantitative Assessment of Internal Controls," *Internal Auditor* (April 2005), pp. 51–55.

Brune, Christina, "Embracing Internal Control," *Internal Auditor* (June 2004), pp. 75–81.

Tritter, Richard P., *Control Self-Assessment: A Guide to Facilitation-based Consulting* (New York: John Wiley & Sons, 2000).

Hubbard, Larry, *Control Self-assessment: A Practical Guide* (Altamonte Springs, FL: The Institute of Internal Auditors, 2000).

Crawford, D., "Levels of Control," *Internal Auditor* (October 2000), pp. 42–45.

Tritter, Richard P., *Control Self-Assessment: A Guide to Facilitation-based Consulting* (New York: John Wiley & Sons, 2000).

Hubbard, Larry, *Control Self-assessment: A Practical Guide* (Altamonte Springs, FL: The Institute of Internal Auditors, 2000).

Wade, Keith, and Andy Wynne, editors, *Control Self-Assessment: For Risk Management and Other Practical Applications* (West Sussex, England: John Wiley & Sons, 1999).

Roth, James, *Control Model Implementation* (Altamonte Springs, FL: The Institute of Internal Auditors Research Foundation, 1997).

Internal Control – Integrated Framework, Committee of Sponsoring Organizations of the Treadway Commission, 1992.

Ethics and Fraud

Roth, James, *Best Practices: Evaluating the Corporate Culture* (Altamonte Springs, FL: The Institute of Internal Auditors Research Foundation, 2011).

Fraudulent Financial Reporting 1998-2007: An Analysis of US Public Companies, Committee of Sponsoring Organizations of the Treadway Commission, 2010.

The Global Economic Crime Survey: Fraud in a Downturn, PricewaterhouseCoopers, November 2009.

Reding, Kurt F., Paul J. Sobel, Urton L. Anderson, Michael J. Head, Sridhar Ramamoorti, Mark Salamasick, and Cris Riddle, *Internal Auditing: Assurance and Consulting Services, 2nd Edition* (Altamonte Springs, FL: The Institute of Internal Auditors Research Foundation, 2009), For fraud, Chapter 8, and for Ethics and Compliance, Supplemental Case 2.

Managing the Business Risk of Fraud: A Practical Guide (The Institute of Internal Auditors, the American Institute of Certified Public Accountants, and the Association of Certified Fraud Examiners, 2008).

Burch, S., "Auditing for Compliance," *Internal Auditor* (December 2008), pp. 53–59.

Baker, N., "See No Evil, Hear No Evil, Speak No Evil," *Internal Auditor* (April 2008), pp. 38–43.

Vona, Leonard W., *Fraud Risk Assessment: Building a Fraud Audit Program* (Hoboken, NJ: John Wiley and Sons, 2008).

Brazel, Joseph F., Keith Jones, and Mark F. Zimbelman, *Using Nonfinancial Measures to Assess Fraud Risk* (Altamonte Springs, FL: The Institute of Internal Auditors Research Foundation, 2008).

Biegelman, Martin T., and Daniel R. Biegelman, *Building a World-Class Compliance Program: Best Practices and Strategies for Success* (Hoboken, NJ: John Wiley and Sons, 2008).

Biegelman, Martin T., and Joel T. Bartow, *Executive Roadmap to Fraud Prevention and Internal Control; Creating a Culture of Compliance* (Hoboken, NJ: John Wiley and Sons, 2006).

Salierno, David, "The Fight Against Fraud," *Internal Auditor* (February 2005), pp. 62–66.

Zwim, Ed, "Joseph T. Wells: Sound Skepticism," *Internal Auditor* (February 2005), pp. 73–77.

Moyes, Glen D., Ping Lin, and Raymond M. Landry Jr., "Raise the Red Flag," *Internal Auditor* (October 2005), pp. 47–51.

Frank, Jonny, "Fraud Risk Assessments," *Internal Auditing* (April 2004), pp. 40–47.

Johnson, Carol B., and Charlotte J. Wright, "Make It Easy, They Will Come," *Internal Auditor* (February 2004), pp. 69–73.

Kreuze, Jerry G., et al., "Shades of Gray," *Internal Auditor* (April 2001), pp. 48–53.

Anderson, Urton, "Effective Compliance Programs," *Internal Auditor* (Spring 1994), pp. 46–50.

Assessing the Board

Audit Committee Effectiveness — What Works Best, 3rd Edition, sponsored by The Institute of Internal Auditors Research Foundation and prepared by PricewaterhouseCoopers (Altamonte Springs, FL: The Institute of Internal Auditors Research Foundation, 2005).

Corporate Governance and the Board — What Works Best, sponsored by The Institute of Internal Auditors Research Foundation and prepared by PricewaterhouseCoopers (Altamonte Springs, FL: The Institute of Internal Auditors Research Foundation, 2000).

Horton, Thomas R., "Assisting the Board," *Internal Auditor* (October 2000), pp. 53–57.

Steinberg, Richard M., and Deborah Pojunis, "Corporate Governance: The New Frontier," *Internal Auditor* (December 2000), pp. 34–39.

Effective Governance (The Institute of Internal Auditors-UK, 1999).

Planning and Performing the Engagement

Reding, Kurt F., Paul J. Sobel, Urton L. Anderson, Michael J. Head, Sridhar Ramamoorti, Mark Salamasick, and Cris Riddle, *Internal Auditing: Assurance and Consulting Services, 2nd Edition* (Altamonte Springs, FL: The Institute of Internal Auditors Research Foundation, 2009), Chapters 12 and 13.

Coderre, David, *Internal Audit: Efficiency Through Automation* (Hoboken, NJ: John Wiley and Sons, 2008).

Cangemi, Michael P., and Tommie Singleton, *Managing the Audit Function: A Corporate Audit Department Procedures Guide, 3rd Edition* (Hoboken, NJ: John Wiley and Sons, Inc., 2003).

Communicating Engagement Results

HM Treasury, *Good Practice Guide: Reporting* (London: HM Treasury, 2010).

Reding, Kurt F., Paul J. Sobel, Urton L. Anderson, Michael J. Head, Sridhar Ramamoorti, Mark Salamasick, and Cris Riddle, *Internal Auditing: Assurance and Consulting Services, 2nd Edition* (Altamonte Springs, FL: The Institute of Internal Auditors Research Foundation, 2009), Chapter 14.

Feierman, Joanne, "Write it Right the First Time," *Internal Auditor* (February 2006), pp. 27–32.

Maniak, Angela, *Writing High-Impact Reports: Proven Practices for Auditors and Accountants* (Skill-Builders Press, 2005).

Bossle, Francis X., "The Single Page Audit Report," *Internal Auditor* (April 1997), pp. 37–41.

Didis, Stephen, "Communicating Audit Results," *Internal Auditor* (October 1997), pp. 36–38.